I0819120

"Culinarily speaking, I would follow Ham to the ends of the earth. His approach to food is right up my alley: delicious staples with a twist, executed with the highest levels of research and expertise. That's why this cookbook is a game changer. He's sharing his wisdom in such an easy and approachable way that it actually makes me want to cook. And for anyone who knows me, that's saying A LOT. Buy this book if you know what's good for you!"
—**Dan Levy,** actor

"Ham strikes a wonderful balance between the practical and the whimsical as he guides us through the foods that bring him, and subsequently all of us, lots of joy. This book is for the curious, the adventurous, and anyone who appreciates really good food with diverse flavors. I want to cook and eat it all."
—**Noor Murad,** chef and cookbook author

"As someone who turns religiously to the Do Better with Ham episode about fond every time I need to make a pan sauce, *Hello, Home Cooking* is a welcome wealth of riches for my kitchen. These recipes are heartfelt, illuminating, and delectable, covering the perfect range from low to highbrow fun."
—**Michelle Zauner,** author of *Crying in H Mart*

"This book has it all: expert instruction from years of fine-dining experience, extraordinarily exciting and original recipes, and a style of storytelling that just makes you love Ham. *Hello, Home Cooking* strikes such a great balance between being fun and authoritative, and it will truly inspire you to become a better cook. I can't wait to bring Ham's energy and flavor into my kitchen. I'll be starting with the overnight oats with rose, cherries, and pistachios!"
—**Molly Yeh,** cookbook author

Hello,
Home
Cooking

Hello, Home Cooking

Do-Able Dishes for Every Day

HISHAM "HAM" EL-WAYLLY

Photographs by Laura Murray

Clarkson Potter/Publishers

New York

Contents

Contents

3. Vegetables 100

4. Rice, Grains & Pasta 160

5. Meat, Poultry & Seafood *196*

6. Desserts *248*

Introduction

For the longest time, I considered myself strictly a fine dining chef. I was in the phase many young cooks go through when first getting into fine dining: There is so much more to food! It must be innovative. It must be beautiful. It must be... art—that phase.

I never cooked at home during this phase. Why would I? I had already spent up to eighteen hours a day standing over something hot, standing next to something hot, or accidentally bumping into something hot. On the rare occasion that my wife, Sohla, an equally strained chef, and I would have the same day off, we would order in or eat out. On the even rarer occasion when we were game for a home-cooked meal, it was always an event: a 3-inch dry-aged rib eye, basted in as much butter as most people eat in two weeks; a salt-baked potato, piled high with crème fraîche; and a crisp wedge salad, smothered in creamy blue cheese dressing. During this phase, a part of me even looked down on home cooking. If it wasn't plated with tweezers, I didn't want it. (If I made something as "simple" as a hot dog at home, you best believe that frank was brought to temperature using the thermal immersion circulator we got as a wedding gift.)

Then the pandemic hit and brought the restaurant industry to an immediate halt. The indestructible New York City restaurant group I worked at closed all fifteen-ish of their stores. It was time for me to get reacquainted with home cooking.

Transitioning from restaurant chef to home cook came with some unexpected struggles. I was incapable of making food for fewer than ten people. Many people struggle with guessing the right portion of pasta to cook, but I'm not talking about that. I'm talking about double-digit egg omelets for the two of us and enough lentil soup for the entire building. I would baste everything in butter—not just steaks. And not just a little bit of butter—my wife was horrified when she caught me basting four asparagus spears with a quarter pound of the stuff. Those buttery fun times lasted about four months, before we started getting tired of spending every second of every day coexisting in a cramped studio apartment and cooking like the apocalypse was just around the corner.

It took me a long time to turn to the foods I grew up eating. I had turned off that part of my brain; I wanted to be a newer, better Ham with a blank slate ready to absorb all the culinary techniques coming my way. It was almost as if I felt like I had to replace what I knew about food with a new, modern style to be successful. I grew up in a diverse international community, experiencing comforting home cooking from all over the world. My dad left his village on the outskirts of Cairo to study at Howard University. My mom left tropical Santa Cruz de la Sierra in Bolivia to work on her English at the same school. They married in DC and moved to Doha, Qatar, where I was born and raised.

I moved to the United States, by myself, when I was nineteen. At the end of the first year my mom and sister came to visit me. When I welcomed them at my front door my mom was wheezing and clearly struggling to breathe. I took her to the emergency room and she was admitted into intensive care immediately. She passed less than two weeks later. Dealing with the grief of her sudden passing was something that I struggled with, and was probably the main reason I locked away the memories of her home cooking. Reliving the times we spent crimping empanadas or layering lasagna was simply too painful, and it was easier to just bury it deep. My dad had all our things shipped from Doha to a storage unit in Cairo after he and my sister moved to America—everything except one thing, my mom's Madonna notebook, which I found hidden in a pile of my dad's things in his attic. That tattered notebook, with its spine held together with black electrical tape, had one of the most nostalgic images on it: bleached-blonde-era Madonna in red lingerie holding a microphone. This book held a collection of all my mother's favorite recipes. I carried that notebook with me, from apartment to apartment, without looking at it, hiding it away like my most prized treasure.

The need for comfort during the uncertainty of the pandemic caused me to dig deep and finally unlock those memories and recipes of my Mom's home cooking. I found cooking those recipes to be the most fun and impactful time in the kitchen since I had first learned how to use a Thermomix at Wd~50. As I started cooking at home instead of in a restaurant, I started thinking thriftier, more streamlined, and in terms of how many pots will this dirty. I stopped cooking thinly sliced onions in barely bubbling butter before blending and passing them through a fine-mesh strainer to make the soubise to accompany sous vide chicken breast; instead, I started roasting a whole chicken over a bed of peeled whole shallots and butter. The results were more straightforward, often tastier, and more comforting. Combining vital home cooking skills with basic professional knowledge like how to season properly (it's often more than you think), precise protein cookery, and exposure to a wide array of flavor combinations has made me the best version of myself as a cook.

Eventually, I developed versions of all kinds of fondly remembered dishes, using ingredients I could easily find and employing some tips and tricks I had learned along the way. These form most of the recipes in this book. You'll find recipes for most any occasion, from an easy morning smoothie to a show-stopping turkey replacement for Thanksgiving. There are recipes for when you're feeling lazy or when you're looking to sink yourself into a project after a long week at work. More importantly, these are recipes for when you need the incomparable comfort of a home-cooked meal.

The Obligatory "Basics" Section

What Have You Gotten Yourself Into?

READ THE ENTIRE RECIPE

Few things annoy me more than sitting at a restaurant and having somebody explain to me how a menu works, especially when they kneel, so they are at eye level, and rest their arms on the table. Look, I get it. Every menu works the same way: You order food off it, and then the food comes.

So, please excuse me for including this section, which "explains" how to read a recipe. Before you try to tip me 13 percent, let me explain why I think this is a worthwhile exercise: Sometimes you just need a reminder.

Although every recipe developer likes to write their recipes differently, there are some basics that apply to all of us, and if you follow them, they will improve your success rate.

- Before doing anything, make sure you read the entire recipe. You want a good idea of what you will be doing, and many recipes sneak in a measurement of water or salt instead of including it in the ingredient list. You want to be fully prepared for what's to come.
- Check the complete ingredient list and make sure you have everything. Then make a list of any ingredients you may need to get from the store.
- You'll notice no total cook times under any of the recipes. Recipe timings can vary wildly, depending on how experienced a cook you are or how fast you are with the prep. Read through the steps in the recipe and estimate how long it will take you to perform each step. Add that time up along with the cooking times, and you will have a much more accurate preparation time specific to you.
- When you are about to start, pull out everything you need, including equipment and measuring tools, and read through the recipe one last time, visualizing each step. You're getting ready for the big game. Visualizing the process will familiarize you with it and ensure success. Take note of all the cues the recipe provides and make sure you understand them. The sound a pan makes can sometimes tell you more than a visual description.

CLEAN AS YOU GO

I am the type of person who can't start eating until the kitchen is clean. Yes, my food is often at room temperature, but I'll take that over a sink full of crusty dishes. You don't need to be as extreme as I am, but a lot of cleaning can be done as you cook to save you time in the long run.

Before cooking, ensure your dishwasher and kitchen sink are empty, clean, and ready.

Have two kitchen towels ready, a dry one to lift and move hot things and a wet one to wipe down messes and sweep away crumbs.

Always have a "trash container" to use for any scraps or trash. It can be anything from a plastic quart container to a metal bowl. The more you can do without moving around, the cleaner and more efficient you will work.

Do all your chopping and cutting first, allowing you to clean your cutting board and knife immediately. Measure out any other ingredients that you can, too. This will make the cooking process more fun and streamlined.

As you finish using vessels, empty them and pop them right in the dishwasher. If you don't have a dishwasher, wash them as you finish each step. If you spill something or make a mess, clean it up immediately.

You should never be standing around watching something cook. If you have time to lean, you have time to clean. Your future self will thank you for your contributions.

If you've done your cleaning right, by the time you are ready to serve, the only things you'll have left to clean are the serving vessels and the plates you eat on.

DON'T BE AFRAID TO MAKE MISTAKES

I was a terrible cook for a long time: too slow, too nervous. I had trouble understanding basic steps. But I kept making mistakes and learning from them instead of using them as a reason to stop. Eventually, I made all the mistakes you could make and built a comprehensive list of what not to do to base all my cooking. You can do the same. Mistakes are the most significant part of cooking, so don't let them slow you down.

Use every mistake as a learning opportunity. Whenever I taste a bite I don't like, for example, I treat it as a puzzle. Why don't I like this?

There are six basic principles that I go through when tasting something I don't like:

1. Sad basic seasoning (needs more or less salt/sugar/acid)
2. Needs more complex seasoning (savoriness/bitterness/heat)
3. Overcooked or undercooked
4. Bad flavor combination
5. Textural problem (needs a hard sear, served at the wrong temp, missing a crunchy garnish, etc.)
6. Fuck, I guess those chunks meant it DID go bad

Taste your failures and use them to do better.

Tasting is the best way to improve your cooking. Taste everything and taste often. Tasting isn't always for seasoning; sometimes, it's to taste how flavors develop. You're creating a subconscious database of flavors and how they work together; the more you have in it, the better equipped you are.

THE BEST KNIFE IS A SHARP KNIFE

I only ever use one knife at a time. Right now, it's the Nenox G-type. It's been my go-to knife for over seven years. I cook a lot and don't want to sharpen more than one knife. I don't even use a petty knife. Instead, I have a cheap, plastic-handled tourne or bird's-beak knife for fine detail work like peeling sticky fresh garlic cloves. I prefer it because once it's too dull to do the job, I get a new one. There's no need to bother sharpening; I only need to replace it once every year.

Nenox is a Japanese knife brand from Sakai, Japan, a region revered for its knife craftsmanship. I like the weight of the handle and the thinness of the blade. But I can't tell you which knife to buy. You need to decide on your own. If you are somebody who enjoys cooking and likes to invest in kitchen equipment, then you might want to consider getting a fancier knife. They last a lifetime and can take your knife work to the next level. Like a perfect pair of shoes, a blade must fit your hand just right. Don't order one online. Find a knife store in your area and feel out a few of their knives before committing. As the owner of a fancy knife, you will need to get accustomed to a whetstone, which can grind your knife's edge to the sharpness of a razor's edge. It takes a while to master, but the payoff is outrageous.

If cooking is something you do just to get by, whatever knife you have around is fine, but be sure to sharpen it regularly using whichever method you find most comfortable. The cheapest sharp knife is better than the fanciest dull knife.

Here are some tips to get the most out of your knives:

- Always use a cutting board (ideally wooden or soft Japanese rubber). Cutting on hard surfaces like a counter will dull your knife quickly.

- Never wash anything sharp in the dishwasher; hand-wash with a sponge and dish soap. This doesn't just apply to knives, but to Microplanes, graters, and blender tops, too. The heat of the dishwasher ruins sharp edges.

- Store your knives properly. Store them dry and sheathed to protect the blades.

- Sharpen your knives when needed and hone them often. Affordable honing steels are easy to come by these days, and while they don't technically sharpen your knife (which is the act of grinding off a little bit of the metal so the edge thins out), they hone the blade by realigning tiny metal fibers along the edge that get knocked out of place through use, and make a straighter blade that cuts better.

PREHEAT YOUR PAN PROPERLY

First things first. Get out of the toxic relationship you have with your nonstick. The easiest way to immediately upgrade your cooking is to stop using a nonstick pan almost entirely. You can't get them hot enough to do any searing without transferring toxic PFAs or PTFE (aka Teflon) to your food. They don't retain heat well and need to be replaced often. A well-seasoned cast-iron skillet can flip your omelets and last an eternity, so it will double as a family heirloom. You may keep your nonstick for egg cookery and egg cookery alone.

Stainless steel pans

Stainless steel pans are a solid option for your kitchen. They are durable and versatile—they can work within various temperatures and pH levels (aka you can cook high-acid food in them). They are fantastic conductors of heat: They heat up quickly and evenly. Stainless steel pans can also get a slick surface with the proper preheat. Remember, unless you are rendering something with a lot of fat, like duck breasts, bacon, or chicken thighs, never start with a cold stainless steel pan.

Preheating stainless steel pans

- Heat your pan over medium heat until it feels hot when you hold your hand (palm-side down) an inch from its surface.

- If you sprinkle droplets of water on the surface of the pan and they form dancing beads, your pan is hot.

- Now that your pan is preheated, adjust the heat to the desired level. Make sure to give your pan time to adjust after changing the temperature.

Cast-iron pans

Cast-iron skillets are my go-to pans. They are unmatched in their heat retention and durability. They're practically indestructible so long as you keep them seasoned.

As with a stainless steel pan, make sure your cast-iron pan is properly preheated before cooking with it.

Preheating cast-iron pans

- Heat cast iron over medium-low heat until the handle feels warm.

- Now that your pan is preheated, adjust the heat to the desired level. Make sure to give your pan time to adjust after changing the temperature.

KNEADING DOUGHS

1. Rub your hands and your (clean, obviously) work surface with a neutral oil. (I prefer oil to flour, since adding flour to prevent sticking can mess with the hydration of your dough.)

2. Place the dough in front of you and fold the dough on top of itself.

3. Using the heel of your hand, push the dough away from you.

4. Fold the stretched part of the dough back toward you and turn the dough 90 degrees.

5. Repeat the process of pushing the dough with the heel of your hand and folding and turning until the dough is smooth, elastic, and not as sticky.

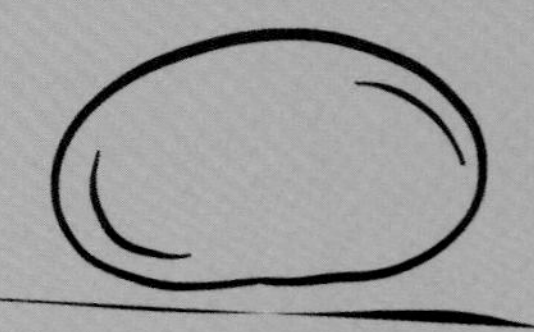

A BONEHEAD'S GUIDE TO BONE BROTH

1. In a large pot, cover bones with cold water. Bring to a boil and cook for five minutes.

2. Dump out the water, cover the bones with cold water again, and return to medium-high heat.

3. Add a sprinkle of your favorite vinegar and gently simmer the bones for six hours, topping off with more water if the level gets too low.

4. Add your desired aromatics (onion, garlic, bay leaf, etc.) and simmer for as long as you can, for at least two hours and up to six hours, topping off with more water if the level gets too low.

5. Strain the broth through a sieve into a container and discard the solids. After cooling, tightly cover the container and store it in the fridge for one week or in the freezer for up to six months.

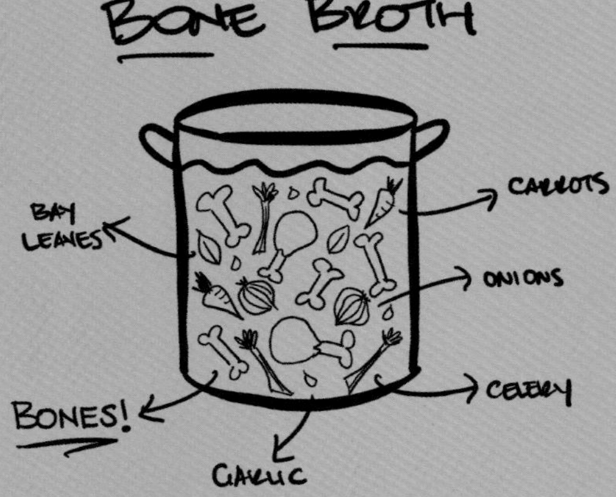

THINGS TO HAVE IN YOUR KITCHEN AND PANTRY

Some of these things are edible, and some I really don't recommend eating.

TOOLS

Immersion blender

I end up using my Vitamix immersion blender more often than the larger blender that sits on my countertop. It can blend soups and purees in the same pot that they're cooked in, saving you scary transfers. The immersion blender is also great for making emulsions like mayonnaise and hollandaise. Most of the brands I've used are feeble and can buckle under the pressure of pureeing boiled peas, but the Vitamix immersion blender, much like its countertop version, is best in class. (If I want something super smooth or I'm blending something frozen, I make sure to turn to my larger countertop Vitamix blender, which has more power.)

Fish spatula

A fish spatula is long, thin, and slightly flexible, with slots to allow fat to drip through. It is designed to flip delicate pieces of fish, but I like to use it as my main metal spatula. Its tapered edge makes it perfect for sliding under a pancake or for lightly scraping food off the bottom of a pan. You can't go wrong with either a Winco or Wüsthof, depending on your budget.

Chef press

A chef press is simply a weight that applies even pressure to a food as it cooks. It's ideal to use for crispy-skin fish, evenly seared broccoli, and golden-brown quesadillas. Bricks of varying sizes wrapped in aluminum foil can do the same thing, but chef press weights are much easier to clean.

Vollrath silicone spatula

This is my most used kitchen utensil. I reach for it when I'm making delicate things like a soft scrambled egg or when stirring the heartiest of chilis. It can fold egg whites into a soufflé or stir spaghetti into Bolognese. It's heat resistant up to 500°F, so it will withstand almost anything. I have multiples of these spatulas in different sizes.

Kunz spoon

These are the cooking spoons that many fine dining kitchens use. I always have a few in my spoon rest whenever I cook. They fit perfectly in my hand and hold an ideal amount in the bowl of the spoon. To many, the Kunz may just look like a spoon, but to me, it carries memories of working in Michelin-starred kitchens. Just holding one in my hand makes me feel like a fancy boy. They come in various sizes and in perforated versions. You can't go wrong having one of each type. The larger ones are great for basting a steak or as a utility serving spoon; the perforated ones are great for removing eggs, or really anything, from poaching liquid; and the small ones are better than any other spoon you own. There should be a Kunz spoon in every kitchen where food is made, whether that's at home or in a professional kitchen.

Kitchen scale

You need a scale to weigh ingredients accurately and consistently, especially for pastry. OXO makes a quality one.

PANTRY

Eggs

For all my recipes, use large eggs (and organic if your budget allows).

Buttermilk

Use more buttermilk. I always have it in my fridge to use in marinades. I use buttermilk instead of milk in my cereal. I drink it as a quick snack whenever I'm feeling a little hungry. It lasts for a long time—two weeks opened in the fridge, or months in the freezer—and is the key to many recipes in this book.

Labneh

Labneh is, simply, yogurt hung until the excess moisture drips out. Turkish-style labneh tends to lean more toward cream cheese, while Lebanese varieties tend to be tangier. If you can't find any in a store, you can easily make it yourself:

1. Lightly season plain Skyr or Greek yogurt with salt.

2. Lay out a double layer of cheesecloth or a kitchen towel. Place the yogurt in the middle.

3. Bring all the corners to the middle and twist until the cloth turns the yogurt into a tautly wrapped ball.

4. Place the towel-wrapped ball in a fine-mesh sieve set on top of a bowl and place a weight on top (the weight can be a couple of cans). Let the bowl sit in the fridge overnight.

5. Unwrap your labneh and discard the whey.

Chocolate

I don't use chocolate often, but when I do, I want it to be impactful. The secret to chocolate desserts in proper restaurants is simple: They use Valrhona chocolate. Order some online and keep it in your pantry for whenever you want that special hit. Valrhona Jivara will be the best milk chocolate you've ever had.

Kosher salt

I live in a Diamond Crystal household. I season by pinches, and the flakes of Diamond Crystal are easier to hold and distribute. Morton is twice as salty as Diamond Crystal by volume, so I also find that Diamond Crystal allows me to season more precisely. The recipes in this book were tested with Diamond Crystal; if you have Morton, either add salt to taste or use about half the amount of salt listed.

Flaky salt

Flaky salt is pricey and often unnecessary, but it adds a final bit of luxurious salty crunch. My flake of choice comes from Jacobsen Salt Co. or Maldon.

Fish sauce

A salty and savory condiment made from fermenting fish in large barrels. Red Boat or Megachef are my go-to brands.

Neutral oil

Neutral oil is an oil without any discernible flavor; it has a high smoke point. You can use avocado, peanut, canola, etc. I buy my neutral oil online from Zero Acre Farms. Their oil is derived from fermented sugarcane juice, using science I do not understand. I even use it at my restaurant. It is pricier than other neutral oils, but it imparts no flavor or greasiness even when frying. Fried items come out crispier than any other oil that I've fried in.

Extra-virgin olive oil

Treat yourself to one high-quality finishing olive oil. These oils shouldn't be cooked with high heat, which kills their subtle aromas and flavors. Use them to finish pasta, use on salads (see page 108), or mix with za'atar. I spoil myself with a bottle from Grove and Vine. Store it in a dark, cool place.

Spices

I should use whole spices, lightly toasted, then grind them all myself. That would result in undeniably tastier food. But I'm lazy, and for most applications, preground is fine—except for black pepper; black pepper should always be freshly ground. Store-bought spices are okay, but I get my spices online from Burlap & Barrel. They source all their spices responsibly, and their spices are significantly fresher than anything you will find at a supermarket.

Tahini

This is sesame seed paste. Look for a Lebanese brand like Beirut or Al Kanater.

Za'atar

Some brands of za'atar sold at supermarkets are old, dry, and flavorless. Look for a blend that comes from Palestine or Lebanon. The za'atar should lightly clump together when pressed in your palm. Look at the ingredient list—it should have za'atar or wild thyme as the first ingredient. Za'atar is both the name of a plant (wild thyme) and the spice blend.

Instant yeast

I use Saf-instant Red yeast. Unlike active dry yeast, it can be mixed directly into dry ingredients without having to dissolve it first. (I like avoiding extra work.) Store the yeast in the freezer.

Knorr bouillon powder

Think of it as MSG with personality. It is my favorite seasoning to use when dry-brining meat. The tomato version is great for seasoning raw tomatoes to give them extra oomph.

Short grain rice

Tamaki Gold is my go-to rice. If you are feeling like a splurge, check out Yamagata Tsuyahime; a rice grown in the nutrient-rich Shonai Plain in the city of Tsuruoka.

CHAPTER 1

Breakfast

More than just eggs

DATE AND BANANA SMOOTHIE
p. 56

BARLEY AND YOGURT
p. 48

BUÑUELOS
p. 61

HASH BROWNS
p. 34

BLUEBERRY MUFFINS IN-SPIRED BY COSTCO
p. 58

BODEGA CHILAQUILES WITH CHARRED TOMATO SALSA
p. 44

SAUSAGE, EGG, AND CHEESE
p. 40

POMEGRANATE MOLASSES AND TAHINI FRENCH TOAST
p. 51

REFRIED BUTTER BEAN TACOS
p. 43

MAPLE-GLAZED BASTURMA BACON
p. 30

CARDAMOM PANCAKES
p. 36

EVERYTHING PITA
p. 47

MASA WAFFLES (AKA MASAFFLES)
p. 39

CINNAMON PITA CRUNCH
p. 52

OVERNIGHT OATS WITH ROSE, CHERRIES, AND PISTACHIOS p. 55

IN HIGH SCHOOL in Doha, the cool kids would take advantage of a gap in the security system by hopping over one specific concrete wall to smoke hash. I hopped over that concrete wall at least once a week, but not because I was a cool kid. My drug of choice was not hash but the breakfast spread at Johnny Rockets. To get there, I would trek in the blazing sun through the barren lot at my school to the highway, which was a mile away. Then I would flag down a decrepit orange-and-white cab.

My excitement swelled when the cab creaked up to that golden-and-red neon Johnny Rockets sign. I slowly walked through the restaurant to soak everything up before sitting down in the back. I loved the classic black-and-white tile and red pleather stools; they plopped me into my favorite scenes from *A Goofy Movie* and *Pulp Fiction*. Johnny Rockets was the closest thing I had to a diner in Doha. I always ordered the same thing and played the same Frankie Lymon song (you know the one) on the jukebox while I waited. I was there for the classic American breakfast.

That breakfast was a category of food that, for as long as I could remember, my parents had reminisced about fondly. And at Johnny Rockets, it could be mine: a cheese omelet with country potatoes, a side of bacon (turkey bacon because it was halal country), and a short stack drowned in that cloyingly sweet fake maple syrup.

My parents met at Howard University in Washington, DC. I don't know much about their time in the United States; it's just random anecdotes. It seemed like every story I did hear centered around food. For example: My dad first ran into my mom as she was picketing outside her classroom for not being allowed in due to her perpetual tardiness. He convinced her to abandon her cause, and they had their first date at a local Chinese restaurant, where they bonded over crab and corn egg drop soup and kung pao chicken. The anecdote they used to tell the most was about how they used to spend Sundays at diners with a spread consisting of black coffee, pancakes, eggs, and hash browns. Even after they moved to Doha and had me and my sister, they kept that ritual of American breakfasts alive. (Only our Sundays were Fridays, because Sundays in America are Fridays in Qatar; I like to keep you on your toes.) So, every Friday my dad would wake up early, bust out a box of Bisquick, cut potatoes, and fry some eggs.

These days my breakfasts are an eclectic mishmash of all the different types of breakfasts I grew up eating. Some things, like the Barley and Yogurt (page 48), I turn to when it's brick and I want something to warm up my soul. Other recipes, like the SEC (Sausage, Egg, and Cheese, page 40), are the perfect balance of convenience and flavor. Obviously, there is also the spin on the classic American breakfast that I find on my table most Sundays.

Egg Virtuosos Only

Even when I moved into fine dining restaurants, breakfast foods were always close at hand. When I got promoted to sous chef at the first New York restaurant I worked at, brunches were my primary responsibility. I had to help develop the brunch menu, order all the ingredients, staff and train the cooks, and call tickets. It was a gentle way to get used to the longer, more demanding dinner services, and it made me feel like I was running my own little restaurant. I had to deal with fun things like balancing reprimanding rambunctious line cooks, and washing dishes whenever the dishwasher would call out, or figuring out how to expedite to the line while cooking four orders of over-easy eggs, three French omelets, and a couple of poached eggs because the egg cook called out.

It was also where I mastered the art of cooking eggs. Eggs in all ways. Chefs, traditional and modern, place a lot of importance on a cook's ability to master eggs. It's an especially revealing aspect of the line; there's no frilly greenery or glossy sauce to hide behind. A cook's proficiency in egg cookery shows whether they can handle the most delicate of proteins and have a mastery of the stove that takes experience to achieve. That's what cooking eggs is all about, experience and a mastery of the flame. Luckily, with the right guidance, all it takes to become an egg virtuoso is some practice. And once you nail the techniques, you can bust them out on Sundays, Fridays, or the next time you skip class.

SOFT-BOILED EGG

A soft-boiled egg is one of my favorite styles of eggs. It's perfect to dip a heavily buttered piece of toast into or for topping a simple bowl of steamed rice, pickles, and a generous shake of furikake for a luxuriously easy dinner. It's also very simple to prepare.

Bring a pot of water to a gentle boil over medium-high heat. More water is always better, since it helps avoid a big temperature drop when you pop your cold egg in, ensuring a more consistent product.

Use a utensil to gently lower the egg into the simmering bath. Lawlessly plopping it in from the top of the water can result in cracked shells and muddy water. We don't want that; we're egg virtuosos, remember? Remember?

Once the egg has been added to the water, set your timer for six minutes. When it goes off, immediately go to the sink, dump out the hot water, and replace it with cold water from the tap. Leave the pot under running cold water. Pull out the egg and tap the top and bottom against the counter hard enough to crack both sides. Return to the cold water, turn off the faucet, and let it sit for a few minutes. The water will seep into the cracks, separating that pesky membrane that makes eggs impossible to peel. Peel the egg and eat it or pop it into a container with a tight-fitting lid and keep it in the fridge for up to two days.

Bonus tip: If you want an egg that is too soft-boiled to peel but perfect for slicing the top off and dipping into, European-breakfast style, follow the same instructions as above but simmer for about five minutes, give or take thirty seconds, depending on how loose you want your whites and yolks.

JAMMY EGG

The cool egg that all cool people eat. This is the ultimate utility egg. It's great for making egg salads, popping on top of things, or eating with a sprinkle of salt like the ripest of hand fruit.

To prepare, follow the same procedure as for a soft-boiled egg but cook for seven minutes in gently boiling water.

HARD-BOILED EGG

I'm not a fan of the hard-boiled egg, but if you enjoy doing that to yourself, follow the same procedure as for soft-boiled eggs but cook for eleven minutes in gently boiling water.

SUNNY-SIDE-UP EGG

A telltale sign of an inexperienced cook is that they always try to cook things on high heat. The truth is, if you aren't bringing water to a boil, there are few things that require high heat. The key to the perfect sunny-side up egg (a fully set, tender white without any color, and a flowing yolk) is to make sure your pan is on low heat.

To prepare, crack your egg into a small bowl. (Always crack into a vessel in case the yolk breaks. Those dramatic shots you see on TV of people cracking eggs directly into their pan with one hand are for insecure show-offs. You are an egg virtuoso.)

Preheat your nonstick pan over low heat for two to three minutes. When you float your hand an inch away from the pan, it should feel warm but not so hot that you need to move your hand away. Toss in a bit of butter. It should melt and slowly begin to gently foam. Pop in the egg and cook until the bottom of the egg is set; there should still be a layer of uncooked white on the top. Cover the pan with a lid and cook until the rest of the white is fully set and not see-through. Place the back of a finger on the top of the yolk; it should feel warm and liquidy. Slide the egg around in the pan to make sure it is slick enough for a smooth dismount. If it seems caught on one side, gently scrape it free with a silicone spatula. Slide your sunny-side up egg onto a plate, season with salt and freshly cracked black pepper, and you have arrived.

OVER-EASY EGG

This egg is the bane of many a brunch cook's existence. You're one sloppy flip and a burst yolk away from having to start all over again. But you always become what you hate, and so naturally, this has become my favorite egg to order out. I like the guarantee that there will be no snotty white on my eggs, and using this method is the best way to ensure that.

Start with the same process as for a sunny-side up egg. Get to the point where the bottom of the egg is fully set but there is still a thin layer of uncooked white on top. Instead of putting a lid on this time, swirl the pan around. The egg should slide around effortlessly and in one even disk. (If it doesn't, use a silicone spatula to gently dislodge any sticking bits.) With confidence, jerk the pan forward and tilt the front of the pan upward. The egg should uniformly flip over. (This takes practice, so don't be discouraged by a few stray yolk grenades.) Let the egg cook on the yolk side for five to ten seconds, then repeat the motion to flip again. Slide the egg onto a plate, season, and serve.

CRISPY FRIED EGG

The crispy fried egg is a textural marvel. Wispy, crispy, browned edges of white encase a flowing yolk. This was the first egg I ever learned to cook. It was my grandfather's go-to egg; he would serve it on top of rice with some fried plantains and an acidic tomato salad. This is my favorite egg to eat with any kind of rice.

Do not make a crispy fried egg in a nonstick pan. A well-seasoned cast-iron pan or even a stainless steel pan is ideal. You will need to heat up the pan to unsafe temperatures for a nonstick (or temperatures that would ruin the coating on one of those new-age "microplastic-free" nonsticks).

To prepare, heat your skillet over medium heat until wisps of smoke just start to appear. Add a glug of a neutral oil, enough to coat the bottom of the pan, and swirl. Immediately dump your egg into the hot fat (precracked into a vessel because you are an egg… virtuoso!). It should immediately start to sputter violently. Cook until the edges of the white are a light golden brown. Tilt the pan toward you so the oil pools, then, using a spoon, scoop some of the hot fat and pour it anywhere you see uncooked white. Repeat until the egg is devoid of snotty patches. Using a slotted spatula, gently scoop the egg from the pan and transfer it to a serving vessel. Season and consume immediately.

CLASSIC SCRAMBLED EGG

This is the egg I want alongside waffles, bacon, or any other traditional American breakfast dish. The curds are larger than those of a soft scramble, but they are still buttery and tender. Place a nonstick skillet over medium-low heat to warm through. Crack the eggs into a medium bowl and whisk vigorously with a splash of milk or cream and a small pinch of salt per egg, until the contents are completely homogeneous. That means no stray bits of white; it takes longer than you think. (But you know what you are.) When you're certain that you've whisked enough and couldn't possibly whisk any more, whisk for another thirty seconds. Place a generous pat of butter in the pan and swirl until the butter is melted. It should be hot enough for the butter to get foamy, but not enough for it to start turning brown. If the butter starts to brown, dump it out, lower the heat, and start over with a fresh pat of butter.

Pour the eggs into the buttered pan and use a silicone spatula to slowly stir the eggs. You are looking for a skin to form at the bottom. Then, you'll use the spatula to move that skin so that fresh uncooked eggs come in contact with the warm pan. Keep repeating the process until no loose eggs remain. Transfer to a plate and eat immediately.

SOFT-SCRAMBLED EGG

This is the luxury egg. The one that chefs like Gordon, Thomas, and Heston tell you to master. The signature of the dish is small curds suspended in custardy, creamy eggs. Make this when you want to treat yourself or somebody that you don't hate. (Who am I kidding; egg virtuosi don't have enemies.)

Crack the eggs into a bowl, add a small pinch of salt per egg and a splash of milk or cream, and whisk until completely homogeneous; no stray whites allowed.

Place a saucepan, ideally with sloped edges, over medium-low heat to heat up. Add a pat of butter and swirl to melt. It should foam but not brown. If it browns, start over.

Add the eggs all at once and start whisking the eggs as they cook. If you find the eggs are sticking to the sides of the pan, switch to a silicone spatula to scrape them down, then continue whisking. Don't stop whisking until the eggs start to thicken and small curds form. The eggs should be loose but the consistency of a thick custard. Kill the heat, add a spoonful of butter, crème fraîche, or sour cream, and whisk to incorporate. Transfer to a serving bowl right away. Garnish with some finely chopped chives—if you can find chives that aren't wilted, yellow, and sad at the grocery store—and a sprinkle of flaky salt. I enjoy these topped with a dollop of caviar or smoked trout roe, and served with some buttered toast on the side.

YANKEE OMELET

This omelet is significantly easier to master than the French one and can be loaded with fillings. You can use any filling you want; just make sure that it is fully cooked or ready to eat. Omelet fillings are always just warmed through; they don't get hot enough to cook in the omelet.

Start by setting a nonstick pan over medium heat. Whisk four eggs in a bowl with a small pinch of salt per egg and a splash of milk or cream. Make sure there are no loose whites. Add a pat of butter to the pan and swirl to melt. It should be foamy but not brown. If it browns, throw in another pat of cold butter to lower the temperature of the pan; color on the eggs is not an issue here, so no need to waste that browned butter. Add the eggs all at once and stir with a rubber

HARD-BOILED EGG
p. 22

JAMMY EGG
p. 22

SOUS VIDE
p. 27

YANKEE OMELET
p. 25

CRISPY FRIED EGG
p. 24

FRITTATA
p. 27

SOFT-SCRAMBLED EGG
p. 25

FRENCH OMELET
YouTube it.

OVER-EASY EGG
p. 24

POACHED EGG
p. 27

CLASSIC SCRAMBLED EGG
p. 24

SOFT-BOILED EGG
p. 21

spatula until curds begin to form and the eggs start to thicken. Add your desired toppings on half of the omelet and fold the other half over. Cook until one side is lightly browned, then flip and cook on the other side until lightly browned as well. Slide onto a plate and serve immediately.

POACHED EGG

The poached egg really puts the dramatics of a molten yolk center stage. It's all about that puncture shot when the egg pops like a water balloon and the yolk flows freely.

Bring a pot of water to a gentle simmer over medium heat, meaning that the water is steaming hot but only an occasional bubble breaks the surface. Crack an egg into a fine-mesh strainer and let any watery egg white drain away, then transfer the remaining egg to a small bowl. Using a slotted spoon, swirl the gently simmering water until a vortex forms. Carefully lower the egg into the middle of the vortex. Repeat until all the eggs are in the water. Using the slotted spoon, very gently lift the eggs if they start to sink to the bottom. Cook until the whites feel set when poked, but the yolks still feel molten. Transfer to a paper towel to blot, season with salt and pepper, and serve immediately.

SOUS VIDE

I have an immersion circulator at home, and I use it only for eggs. This is the best example of a poached egg because the white is set but still tender, and the yolk is molten but slightly thickened. Use it anywhere you would use a poached egg. It's perfect for benedicts and for topping pasta.

Set your circulator to 63.5°C and drop your large eggs in. Set a timer for twenty-five minutes. After twenty-five minutes have elapsed, raise the temperature to 65°C and cook for ten more minutes. Remove the eggs from the water bath. (You can also make a large batch of these before you need them and hold them at 55°C for a couple of hours.) Using the side of a spoon, crack each one right in its middle and open up the shell to reveal a perfectly poached egg. (You want to crack it over wherever you want it to land, because this egg is too delicate to move around willy-nilly.) Season and serve.

FRITTATA

A frittata is a great way to use up things in the fridge that you don't really want to eat on their own or that you say are "past their prime," but your wife swears are still good. The fillings in a frittata follow the same rules as an omelet: Everything should be ready to eat because you are just warming things through. Make sure everything is bite-size or sliced very thinly so they warm through quickly as the frittata cooks.

Preheat the oven to 325°F. Set an appropriately sized skillet over medium-low heat to warm up. (Based on the number of eggs you are using, you can change the size of the pan to get a different effect. A larger pan can yield a thinner frittata, while a smaller pan can yield a thicker frittata that has more of a custardy interior.)

Whisk your eggs in a bowl with a small pinch of salt per egg and a splash of milk or cream. Make sure there are no errant whites. Add your desired mix-ins and stir to combine. Add a pat of butter to your pan and swirl to melt and coat. It should foam but not brown. If it browns, add another pat of cold butter to lower the temperature of the pan. Add your eggs and let them cook until a very thin layer of cooked egg appears around the perimeter of the pan. Use a spatula to pry the egg from the pan; it should move cleanly and in one piece. Transfer the pan to the oven and cook until the frittata is fully set. You can pierce the center of the frittata with a knife to make sure the eggs are fully cooked.

When cooked, place a plate that is slightly larger than the pan on top of the pan and firmly place your hand on top. With confidence, flip the pan onto the plate and remove the pan. The frittata should now be on the plate. Serve hot, at room temperature, or cold.

CHAWANMUSHI (JAPANESE STEAMED EGG CUSTARD)

Chawanmushi isn't served exclusively for breakfast. It is just my favorite time to eat it. I like dressing it with a little maple and soy sauce and having it with a side of steamed rice. The best part is that the mix is better when made the night before, to make sure any air bubbles you whisked in have time to dissipate. Then in the morning, all you need to do is steam (or microwave!) your way to silky, custardy breakfast bliss.

In a bowl, whisk three eggs and two cups of broth or dashi (this can be any broth you want; the better the broth, the better the "mushi," as I always say/try to print on T-shirts that I fail to convince my friends to buy) until fully combined. Season with a pinch of kosher salt. Transfer to a container with a tight-fitting lid and let it sit overnight in the fridge.

Set up a steamer: Divide the egg mixture between two heatproof bowls and tightly wrap with plastic wrap. Cook in the steamer until the custard is set (about fifteen to twenty minutes depending on how well your cooking vessel conducts heat) but still jiggly when jostled. Serve right away.

Alternatively, you can also cook in a microwave on low for 45 seconds, then in 30-second bursts until the custard sets. It won't be as perfect as in the steamer, but for an easy breakfast, it'll do just fine.

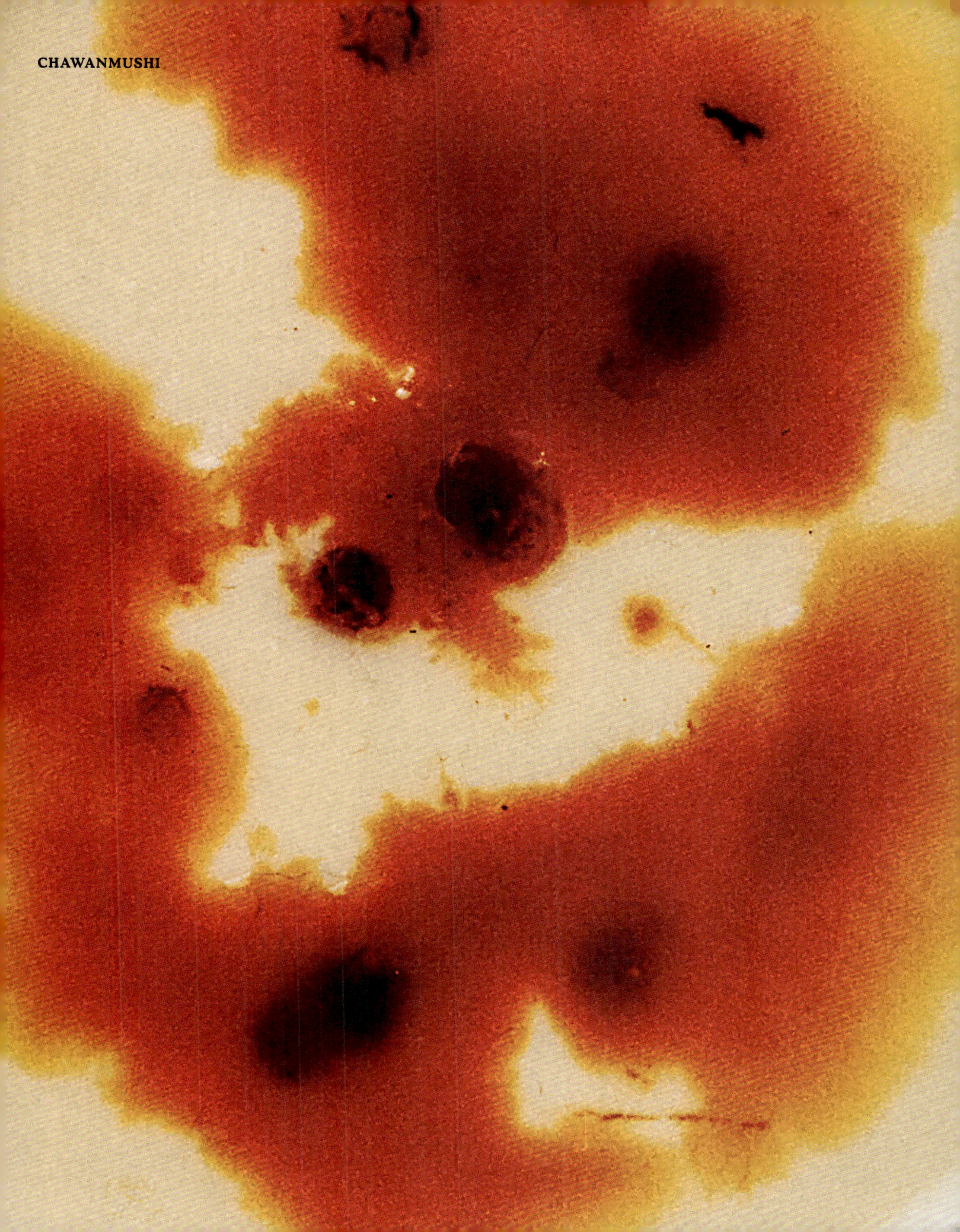

Maple-Glazed Basturma Bacon

Who knew bacon needed more seasoning?

SERVES 3 TO 6
(depending on what kind of a bacon monster you are)

My dad would only take a few weeks off to join us on our summer break in Cairo every other year. It was the closest thing to a vacation I ever saw him take, even though he spent most of it red-faced, irately yelling into his cell phone. I am convinced that his craving for basturma was the reason why. He refused to have any basturma outside Egypt, deeming it subpar and an insult to the revered pepper-coated, air-dried beef. On the first day of each vacation, he would wake up with the sun to book it to the local Metro Market, where he would stock up on sharp Roumy cheese and thinly sliced, peppery basturma. We would roll out of bed to find a spread of crisp veggies, hard-boiled eggs, warm and pillowy baladi bread, chunks of cheese, vats of thick labneh, smashed fava beans, and stacks of basturma on the two large cardboard boxes we used as a dining table at our sparsely furnished Cairo apartment. The basturma was always the first thing to get eaten, with its piquant, peppery notes complementing everything on the (cardboard) table.

I haven't been back to Egypt since I was a teen, so I developed this seasoning to bring back a hint of those Cairo summers. Maple-glazed bacon is the perfect foil for the aggressive spice blend, elevating this humble breakfast meat into something greater than it ever thought it could be. You can also use this spice blend to "basturma" anything, from chicken thighs to salmon fillets to carrots; just add some salt as well.

INGREDIENTS:

- **1 tablespoon coriander seeds**
- **2 teaspoons black peppercorns**
- **1 teaspoon cumin seeds**
- **1 teaspoon garlic powder**
- **1 teaspoon hot paprika**
- **8 ounces thick-cut bacon**
- **¼ cup maple syrup or honey**

1. Arrange a rack in the center of the oven. Preheat the oven to 350°F. Line a sheet pan with aluminum foil.

2. Place the **coriander seeds, peppercorns, cumin seeds, garlic powder,** and **paprika** in a spice grinder and pulse until the coriander seeds and peppercorns are all cracked. Check it after every couple of pulses. You aren't looking for a refined, snortable powder; you should still be able to see distinct chunks of coriander seeds and peppercorns. Set aside.

3. Lay the **bacon** on top of the prepared pan in a single layer without letting the slices overlap. Pin the slices in place by setting an upside-down wire baking rack on top of the bacon so the rack's feet face upward in the air. (This keeps them flat as they cook.) Pop the pan into the oven.

4. Bake until some of the fat renders and the bacon starts to brown around the edges, 25 to 30 minutes, flipping the bacon halfway through. Move the pan to the sink when flipping so it can catch any stray drips.

5. Remove the pan from the oven and adjust the temperature to 400°F. Remove the baking rack and brush the bacon with the **maple syrup** and sprinkle the reserved seasoning over each slice. Return the pan to the oven and bake until it's as crisp as you want. I go for 5 minutes because I like it crispy, but you may like it flaccid and floppy. It's your bacon; do whatever you want. Bacon crispiness levels are personal.

Hash Browns

Or how I tricked myself into liking sweet potatoes

SERVES 4

Hash browns are a crucial component of my full Sunday breakfast. A spread of eggs, sausage, and pancakes doesn't feel right without them. One fateful Sunday, though, I didn't have enough russets for a batch, but I did have an extra sweet potato. The gods smiled on me that day. A little hint of sweet potato adds sweetness and brings pockets of extra caramelization. Never again have I made a hash brown devoid of sweet potato.

These hash browns are easy to make, but technique is essential. Make sure to squeeze as much liquid out of the potatoes as possible; the excess liquid makes them go soggy instead of crisp. Use all your strength; if you need to split it into smaller batches to wring it out properly, do so. The grated potatoes should look dry after squeezing. The other vital step is pressing the hash browns as thinly as possible while keeping them in one solid sheet; you want to maximize your crunch ratio. If the hash browns seem dry, drizzle in more oil, ensuring they get crisp and brown instead of drying out and scorching.

INGREDIENTS:

- **2 large russet potatoes (about 2 pounds)**
- **1 medium sweet potato**
- **1 small yellow onion**
- **1 tablespoon Diamond Crystal kosher salt, plus more to taste** **(see page 16)**
- **2 teaspoons garlic powder**
- **2 teaspoons dried parsley**
- **1 teaspoon onion powder**
- **1 teaspoon hot paprika**
- **4 tablespoons neutral oil, plus more as needed**
- **Freshly cracked black pepper**

1. In a large bowl, use the large holes of a box grater to grate the **potatoes, sweet potato,** and **onion.** You want to be zippy with this process; dillydallying will leave you with oxidized potatoes. Toss with the **salt** and let sit for 5 minutes.

2. Transfer the potato mixture to the center of a kitchen towel you don't care about ruining (pouring away any expelled liquid and wiping out the bowl). Bring the corners to the center and twist it over a sink to wring out as much liquid as possible.

3. Transfer the potato mixture to the bowl and toss with the **garlic powder, parsley, onion powder, paprika,** and 2 tablespoons of the **oil.**

4. Place a large skillet or griddle over medium-high heat until lightly smoking. Add 1 tablespoon of the oil to the pan and swirl to coat. Add half of the potato mixture and, using a spatula, flatten until it is no thicker than ½ inch. Add the remaining 1 tablespoon oil around the perimeter of the pan. Cook until one side is golden-brown, 3 to 4 minutes, then flip to brown the other side, another 3 to 4 minutes. If you must split the hash brown in half to flip, do so. Transfer to a wire rack and season with salt and black pepper. Repeat with the remaining potato mixture, adding fresh oil to every batch.

Cardamom Pancakes

Fluffy pancakes with a dash of Sweden

MAKES 6 PANCAKES

While I liked the peppery, floral, almost citrusy cardamom flavor as a kid, I would navigate dishes containing its pods with anxious hesitation. Biting into a cardamom pod would cause it to detonate in my mouth, and I would taste only cardamom for the rest of the day. When La Cabra, a Scandinavian bakery, opened in my neighborhood, serving glistening, buttery cardamom buns, the valiant crew of bakers gave cardamom its redemptive arc. It turned out that the key to my allowing cardamom into my heart was grinding the pods after toasting them and running the ground bits through a sieve for maximum flavor distribution and exactly zero mouth grenades. Before those buns, I'd always known cardamom as a chaotic team player, a spice to mingle and coexist with others, but never the main event. Those buttery cardamom buns turned me into a cardamom-as-a-main-character believer. And, reformed as I am, I feel a duty to spread the word. These pancakes put cardamom front and center and pair wonderfully with a butter-slick and a generous (I mean generous*) pour of real maple syrup.*

INGREDIENTS:

- **Scant 1 cup / 125g all-purpose flour**
- **1 teaspoon baking powder**
- **1 teaspoon Diamond Crystal kosher salt (see page 16)**
- **¼ teaspoon baking soda**
- **¾ cup buttermilk**
- **1 large egg**
- **2 tablespoons (packed) dark brown sugar**
- **2 tablespoons neutral oil, plus more for cooking**
- **2 teaspoons vanilla extract**
- **1½ teaspoons ground cardamom**
- **½ teaspoon ground black pepper**
- **Room-temperature butter, for serving**
- **Maple syrup (a ridiculous amount), for serving**

1. In a medium bowl, combine the **flour, baking powder, salt,** and **baking soda** Whisk for about a minute (it's hard to tell what's going on visually and you want everything evenly distributed). Create a well in the center.

2. In a blender, add the **buttermilk, egg, sugar, oil, vanilla, cardamom,** and **black pepper** and blend on high for 1 full minute. (If you don't want to bust out the blender, you can also whisk this mixture vigorously in a large bowl for a couple of minutes.) Pour into the well of the dry ingredients and gently whisk together until combined and there are no patches of dry flour; some lumps are fine. Let the batter rest for 5 minutes.

3. Place a large skillet or griddle over medium heat until lightly smoking. Add 1 tablespoon oil to the pan and swirl to coat. Add ¼ cup of the batter and cook until bubbles appear along the sides of the pancake, 2 to 3 minutes. Flip and cook until the other side is golden-brown and the batter is cooked through, another 2 to 3 minutes. Set the pancake aside and repeat the process with the rest of the batter, adding more oil as needed. Serve the pancakes immediately with **room-temperature butter** and **unlimited maple syrup.**

PS:
To make a "treat yourself" pancake, cook a larger pancake (½ cup of batter) in a medium skillet over medium heat with ¼ cup clarified butter or ghee. This will give you a pancake with crisp edges and a deep buttery flavor. Be sure to heat the butter in the pan before pouring in the batter.

Masa Waffles (aka Masaffles)

SO LIGHT AND FLUFFY with corny undertones

MAKES 6 TO 8 WAFFLES

I am fully on Team Waffle. Pancakes and waffles are just conduits for maple syrup, and waffles make a much better vessel with natural syrup containers built in. Another advantage of the waffle's shape is the variety of textures it allows, as the maple syrup slowly seeps into the crisp peaks and then the ragged pockets.

These waffles are much lighter and crispier than ones made entirely with all-purpose flour. Using masa harina—the corn "flour" used to make tortillas—gives them that light crispiness, with corny undertones, making it easy to turn them savory or sweet. This base is also very receptive to mix-ins. Add a cup of blueberries for a waffle that traps summer in a crunch or shredded Cheddar (and some roasted and chopped jalapeños!) for more of a cheesy cornbread vibe. Don't jump the gun and make these the same day; the overnight rest is the secret. The flavor development and texture of the waffle suffer if you use the batter the same day.

INGREDIENTS:

- 1¾ **cups / 430g whole milk**
- 1 **cup / 135g all-purpose flour**
- 1 **cup / 117g masa harina**
- ¼ **cup / 63g neutral oil**
- 3 **tablespoons / 52g honey**
- 2 **large eggs**
- 2 **teaspoons vanilla paste or extract**
- 1½ **teaspoons Diamond Crystal kosher salt** **(see page 16)**
- 1½ **teaspoons instant yeast**

Toppings of Your Choice

- **Room-temperature butter**
- **Maple syrup**
- **Honey**
- **Whipped cream**
- **Canned peaches**
- **Candied nuts**
- **Grated chocolate**
- **Your favorite jam**
- **OR if you go savory, dare I say chicken liver mousse?**

1. In a medium pot over medium heat, warm the **milk** until it reaches body temperature.

2. Turn off the heat and add the **flour, masa, oil, honey, eggs, vanilla, salt,** and **yeast** to the same pot. Whisk until the batter is smooth.

3. Transfer the waffle batter to a container or bowl that will allow it to poof to twice its size.

4. Let the batter sit at room temperature until bubbles form, about 1 hour. Cover with a lid or dish towel and transfer to the fridge to chill overnight.

5. The next day, mix the batter with a spatula to knock the air out.

6. Preheat your waffle maker. In my Breville, I use the fourth level.

7. Cook the batter according to machine instructions or the way you usually make waffles. Be sure to let your machine heat up again in between each waffle.

8. As the waffles finish cooking, set them on a wire rack and tent with aluminum foil to keep them crisp. It's best not to wait too long; I serve them as they come out of the waffle iron.

9. Serve with your ideal waffle accoutrements.

Sausage, Egg, and Cheese

Skip the bodega trip.

MAKES 8 SANDWICHES

Please don't make a big thing about it, but I am team SEC over BEC. I like the sausage's texture and built-in spice on an egg sandwich. If you plan it out, you can have a breakfast sandwich in your hands faster than a trip to the corner convenience store.

This is a fresh sausage recipe disguised as an SEC. There are three main takeaways to making fresh sausage: Make sure you use enough salt, work the mixture well, and, for best results, let it sit for at least six hours.

I use English muffins as my vehicle because they are the fastest bread that can go from frozen to toasted, and on team SEC, we prioritize efficiency. We also prioritize ideal bite construction, so I portion my sausage into 2-ounce patties, also known to fellow SEC team members as "the perfect size for an English muffin." I freeze the preportioned sausage patties on a tray, then transfer them to resealable plastic bags. Once I have all the pieces in place, each SEC comes together in under ten minutes and only dirties one pan. Which, if you squint, is a particular sort of breakfast magic. You can make all eight sandwiches at once or keep the pieces ready for an order on the fly. Okay, fine, you can make a big thing about it.

INGREDIENTS:

For the Sausage

- **2 teaspoons Diamond Crystal kosher salt (see page 16)**
- **1 teaspoon dried oregano**
- **1 teaspoon garlic powder**
- **1 teaspoon paprika (smoked, hot, or sweet; I like hot, but you do you)**
- **1 teaspoon black peppercorns**
- **½ teaspoon cumin**
- **A few grates of nutmeg**
- **1 pound ground lamb or pork**

For the Sandwiches

- **8 English muffins**
- **1 tablespoon neutral oil**
- **8 large eggs**
- **8 cheese slices (I like American, but again, YDY)**
- **One or 15 condiments (such as some combination of ketchup; mayonnaise; hot sauce; mustard, if you are a savage; chili crisp; BBQ sauce; honey mustard; tears of your rivals; relish; pesto; blackberry jam; maple syrup . . .)**

1. ***To make the sausage:*** Combine the **salt** and all the **sausage spices** in a spice grinder and process until finely ground.

2. In a large bowl, combine the spice mix and **lamb.** Knead as though you were working some bread dough until it is uniform and feels a little springy, about 3 minutes. Ideally, let this sit in the fridge for 6 hours to let the seasoning fully penetrate and improve the texture. Portion into 2-ounce patties about ¼ inch thick, and if you're not making the sandwiches immediately, place the patties on a sheet pan in the freezer until fully frozen. Transfer to a freezer-safe bag and store frozen until the need for sausage strikes. (Frozen patties will last up to 6 months in the freezer.)

3. ***To prepare the sandwiches:*** Pry open an **English muffin** by sticking a fork along the sides. Pop it in your toaster, but don't start toasting quite yet. (Also, don't forget that it's already chilling in your toaster because that's how you go down an exhausting internet wormhole about whether you're losing your mind.)

4. Place a medium skillet over medium heat until lightly smoking, then turn down the heat to low until it stops smoking. Then—and this will sound crazy but trust me—return to medium heat.

5. Add the **oil** to the pan, then swirl the pan to coat. Add the sausage patty to one side of the pan. Cook until deeply brown, pressing it down with a spatula to ensure even cooking, about 2 minutes,

Note:
The seasoning blend in this recipe reminds me of the chorizo I used to eat in Santa Cruz, Bolivia. You can also make a batch to use in recipes that call for chorizo or for any other uncased sausage.

then flip over. Wait for the other side to get some color, about 1 minute, before getting your English muffin going in the toaster. Once the muffin starts toasting, crack your **egg** into the other side of the pan. When the white has almost entirely set, after about 2 minutes, place the **cheese slice** on top of the sausage, turn down the heat to low, and cover the pan with a lid.

6. Once the cheese has melted and your egg is cooked, build your sandwich: sauce on the bottom of the muffin, followed by the sausage patty, the egg, and the top bun (with more sauce if you wish; generally, I wish). Repeat for any additional sandwiches. Eat immediately. And please, let me be the first to welcome you to the team.

Refried Butter Bean Tacos

Ful medames in the style of refried beans

SERVES 3 TO 4

Ful medames, aka fava beans cooked with olive oil, spices, and aromatics until they burst into a chunky puree, always remind me of my dad. He used to regale us with tales of how he would live off cans of ful to fuel his youth, asserting this was the reason for his unrivaled strength. (He would always demonstrate said strength by lifting a makeshift barbell he had made by filling two large soda bottles with cement and attaching them to the opposite ends of an old broom handle.) He was Popeye, and cans of ful were his spinach. If he oversaw dinner, he would crack open a can of ful, season it meticulously, and serve it with loaves of pillowy, sour baladi bread from an Egyptian bakery in our neighborhood. Baladi bread is hard to come by in New York City, but tortillas are not. I like flour tortillas here, but feel free to use corn. I also switch up the fava beans with butter beans, since they are easier to find. I like their silken texture, but you can really use any bean here. Take a page from my dad's book and assemble a spread of cilantro, jalapeño slices, thinly sliced onions, radishes, and jammy eggs to serve with this recipe for a make-your-own breakfast taco situation.

INGREDIENTS:

- **1 (15.5-ounce) can beans of your choice**
- **3 tablespoons extra-virgin olive oil**
- **3 garlic cloves, thinly sliced**
- **1 small onion, diced**
- **1 teaspoon hot paprika**
- **1 teaspoon ground cumin**
- **1 teaspoon ground coriander**
- **Kosher salt**
- **2 tablespoons tahini**
- **¼ cup parsley leaves, coarsely chopped**
- **1 small tomato, diced**
- **Juice of 1 freshly squeezed lemon**
- **6 flour or corn tortillas**
- **4 ounces sharp Cheddar cheese, shredded**
- **Jalapeño or serrano chile slices, to taste**

1. Drain your beans, reserving ¼ cup of the liquid.

2. Place a medium skillet over medium heat until blurry heat waves radiate above the pan. Add the **oil, garlic,** and **onion.** Sauté, stirring often, until the onion has softened and become translucent, 4 to 6 minutes.

3. Add the **paprika, cumin,** and **coriander** and cook until fragrant, about 1 minute.

4. Add the **beans** and reserved liquid and lightly mash with a spoon, potato masher, or spatula. You aren't looking for a smooth puree; let it be chunky. Cook until the beans are hot and season with a big pinch of salt.

5. Add the **tahini** and stir until fully incorporated and no streaks are left. Taste and add more salt as needed.

6. Turn off the heat. Add the **parsley, tomato,** and **lemon juice** and gently stir to combine. Set aside while you heat the tortillas.

7. In a dry pan over low heat, warm the **flour tortillas** one at a time, flipping them every 10 seconds. If you're using corn tortillas, I like to heat them by wrapping them in a lightly moistened kitchen towel and sending them for 15-second bursts in the microwave. This keeps them supple and tender. You can also go tradish and heat the tortillas directly over a gas flame on medium, flipping them every 5 seconds until they are charred in spots and hot all the way through.

8. To serve, load up a tortilla with a generous scoop of beans and a hearty helping of **Cheddar.** Add chile slices to taste.

PS:
To level up these beans, replace the oil with ⅓ cup of finely diced bacon. Cook over low heat until the fat renders and the bacon is golden-brown before proceeding with the recipe.

Bodega Chilaquiles with Charred Tomato Salsa

Fritos can be breakfast, too.

SERVES 2

Chilaquiles was the first breakfast I ever made for my wife, Sohla. Chilaquiles is a Mexican breakfast/hangover cure of tortilla chips simmered in salsa and topped with an array of garnishes. I had never made it before that morning, but we had just started dating, and I wanted to impress her with my improvisational cooking. We didn't have the energy (or money) to leave our five-square-foot sublet to find sustenance after a long night of "unwinding." I had to base my version on a description she mumbled while half asleep. I knew I had nailed it when she mumble-asked for chilaquiles again the next day. (Hungover was a regular state in our early courtship.)

I've learned that chilaquiles can be as fancy or as simple as you like. I worked at a fine dining Mexican spot where we cut stale corn tortillas into identical ⅛-inch squares before frying them into shatteringly crisp chips. We would toss them in a bright tomatillo salsa before finishing them with butter, garnishing with seasonal vegetables, and topping with an egg, slow poached at precisely 63.5°C (you know you're working at a fancy place when temperatures are in Celsius). The simultaneous crunching of the little chips was texturally amazing, but I don't hate myself enough to spend that much time cutting tiny brunoise tortilla chips anymore. A bag of Takis from my corner bodega works just as well, or whatever kind of crunchy corn-based snack you desire. I don't even simmer my chilaquiles in the salsa. Just make sure the salsa is delicious and load up the toppings.

INGREDIENTS:

For the Salsa

- **1 large tomato, halved**
- **4 large garlic cloves**
- **1 small onion, root removed and halved**
- **1 jalapeño, stemmed and halved**
- **1 tablespoon neutral oil**
- **Kosher salt**
- **2 (3.5-ounce-ish) bags of corn-based crunchy snacks (such as Doritos, Fritos, Takis, or any tortilla chip)**

For the Garnish (use as many or as few as you like)

- **Egg cooked however you want it**
- **Shredded iceberg lettuce**
- **Thinly sliced radishes**
- **Yellow or red onion, minced**
- **Avocado, diced**
- **Cilantro leaves and tender stems, coarsely chopped**
- **Shredded cheese**
- **Cooked beans, warm (without liquid)**
- **Limes, cut into wedges**
- **Sour cream**
- **Hot sauce, preferably Valentina**

1. ***To make the salsa:*** Preheat the broiler. In a medium bowl, toss the **tomato, garlic, onion,** and **jalapeño** with the **oil** and season with a few pinches of **salt.** Place on an unlined sheet pan, cut-sides down, and put under the broiler. Broil until the tomato halves have softened and everything else has a nice layer of char, about 15 minutes.

2. Transfer the tomato mixture to a blender and blend on high until smooth. Taste and adjust the seasoning with more salt as needed.

3. ***To assemble the chilaquiles:*** You can spoon the salsa and garnishes into open bags of chips, hold them shut, shake them up, and eat one like a monster. Or, split the bag open, top the snacks with the salsa, then layer on the garnishes. Do whatever you want. I don't care, as long as you don't ask me to come over to cut stale tortillas into ⅛-inch squares.

Note:
This is a great base salsa for anything from huevos rancheros to braising meat for tacos. To make this a green salsa, swap the large tomato for 6 peeled tomatillos and blend it with a handful of fresh cilantro after broiling. Boom. Your red salsa just became green salsa.

Junior Mints
Junior Mints
Junior Mints
Junior Mints

Everything Pita

Yes, it's better than a bagel.

MAKES 4 PITAS

Seinfeld *taught me to love New York City. When I was growing up in Doha, I would watch the same episodes on repeat and fantasize about mundane experiences, like ordering Chinese food for delivery, biting into a stale black-and-white cookie, or picking up a chocolate babka. To a young Ham, there seemed no experience more New York City than getting an everything bagel with scallion cream cheese. Instead of convincing someone to buy me a plane ticket, I made my "bagels" by punching out the center of a pita with a ring cutter and schmearing it with cream cheese. I walked around my room with an empty mug and bagel, waving hello to my (completely imaginary) local dry cleaner.*

Even though I live in NYC now, and my completely real dry cleaner, May, yells at me for all my crusty food stains, I still prefer the pita bagels of my youth to the city's classic. I like the ratio of filling to bread that a bageled-up pita allows. This seasoning is good on… everything, too. Make a big batch, keep it in a tightly sealed container (with a silicone moisture-absorption packet from another snack if you have one), and sprinkle it on salads, eggs, or truly whatever you like. You'll never need to slum it with the Trader Joe's version again.

INGREDIENTS:

- **2 medium shallots**
- **Cloves from 1 large head garlic**
- **½ cup neutral oil**
- **Kosher salt**
- **1 teaspoon onion powder**
- **1 teaspoon garlic powder**
- **2 tablespoons sesame seeds**
- **1 tablespoon poppy seeds**
- **½ teaspoon flaky salt**
- **1 egg white, lightly whisked**
- **4 pita (preferably the thick and fluffy kind, not the thin kind)**

1. Line a plate with paper towels.

2. Thinly slice the **shallots** and **garlic** using a mandoline or sharp knife. You want the slices to be as thin as possible while maintaining their shape.

3. In a small skillet over medium heat, combine the **oil** and shallots. Using chopsticks or a fork, stir the shallots until they turn golden-brown, 6 to 7 minutes. Transfer the shallots to the prepared plate and season with salt.

4. Add the garlic to the oil and keep stirring with chopsticks until the garlic is a light golden brown, 3 to 4 minutes. Transfer the garlic to the same paper towel–lined plate and season with salt. Cool and save the shallot- and garlic-infused oil for future cooking or to make a salad dressing.

5. In a medium bowl, add the fried shallots, garlic, **onion powder, garlic powder, sesame seeds, poppy seeds,** and **flaky salt.** Stir to combine and lightly crush with your hands so the shallot and garlic pieces aren't so large.

6. Arrange a rack in the center of the oven. Preheat the oven to 350°F.

7. Brush a layer of the egg white on top of the pitas with a pastry brush or spoon and press them into the bagel seasoning. Lightly tap the pitas against the interior edge of the bowl, with the seasoning pointing down, to remove any excess. Sprinkle more seasoning on top of any naked spots. Save any leftover seasoning in the fridge for later use.

8. Lay the pitas, topping-sides up, on a rack inside a large sheet pan and bake until the toppings set, 5 to 8 minutes.

9. Slice the pitas in half and fill the pockets with the fillings of your choice—remember, anything a bagel can do, a pita can do better. My favorite filling is labneh mixed with chives, lightly salted cucumbers, and a jammy egg.

Barley and Yogurt

A porridge that food critic Goldilocks would love

SERVES 4

Doha is a desert. Our summers were unbearably hot, and winters gave us the occasional cool breeze, but even then, it was barely hoodie weather. My mom had no tolerance for even a little chill; she would walk around shivering and hunched over, draped in the thick alpaca wool blanket she had brought back from Bolivia (the ones used to combat subzero Andean temperatures) with long wool socks pulled up to her knees. On those mornings, my mom would make this yogurt and barley porridge to warm us up. It was always one of my favorite savory breakfasts. It was easy on the stomach and kept me warm enough to wear a T-shirt on the ride to school. The barley maintains its chew, so you don't feel like Oliver Twist eating mushy gruel, and the yogurt brings a creamy richness and bright acidity to keep the porridge from feeling stodgy.

This process works for any grain. Just toast it until fragrant, add liquid, and cook it until tender, then finish with a hefty dollop of yogurt or any other creamy sour dairy product (I like to use sour cream when I'm feeling lush). You can adjust the consistency to match whatever you're vibing with; it can be a loose, brothy soup with grains floating in it or a tight porridge that clings to your spoon. For something brothier, keep adding liquid until you're happy. The proportions in this recipe yield my ideal, almost risotto-like, tight porridge. If you increase the broth, be sure to adjust the seasoning accordingly.

INGREDIENTS:

- **1 cup pearl barley**
- **2 tablespoons unsalted butter**
- **30 ounces (about 4 cups) bone broth, buy it or make it (see page 14)**
- **Kosher salt**
- **½ cup Greek yogurt**
- **Paprika, for garnish**

1. In a small bowl, rinse the **pearl barley** under cold running water for 30 seconds while swirling it around with your hand. Drain well.

2. In a medium pot over medium heat, melt the **butter.** Add the barley and toast, stirring frequently, until lightly golden brown and giving off a nutty aroma, about 5 minutes.

3. Add the **broth** and a large pinch of **salt** and bring to a simmer. Turn down the heat to medium-low, maintaining a gentle simmer, and cook until the grains are tender, about 30 minutes. If the grains are still tough but all the liquid is gone, add water in ½-cup increments until the grains are fully cooked. Once the grains are tender, keep simmering until you get your desired porridge consistency or add water to loosen. Taste and adjust the seasoning with more salt if needed.

4. Kill the heat and stir in the **yogurt** until it is evenly incorporated. Taste again and adjust the seasoning as needed. Divide among four bowls, garnish with a couple of dashes of **paprika,** and devour immediately, ideally draped in your plushest blanket.

Pomegranate Molasses and Tahini French Toast

French toast with PB&J energy

MAKES 4 SLICES

I am very picky when it comes to French toast. I want it to be so custardy that it has the texture of bread soaked in melted ice cream. The following custard-to-carb ratio gets me there.

If you don't feel like assembling all these spices, this French toast is just as delicious with vanilla and cinnamon. And I don't want to hear any whining about the egg yolk. Keep the extra white in the freezer or make the Everything Pita (page 47). Or keep it in the fridge and add it to the mix next time you make a scramble. Or throw it away and lie to everybody.

The other star of this recipe is the topping. It tastes like a cross between condensed milk and tahini. It will change your life. Use it on ice cream. Use it in your coffee. Drizzle it on top of pies and cakes. Use it as a sensual massage oil, a mask for your skincare routine, or on that weird rash on your foot. No matter what it is used for, it will leave you grinning like Guy Fieri after a detour into Flavortown.

INGREDIENTS:

- ½ **cup whole milk**
- ½ **cup heavy cream**
- 1 **large egg**
- 1 **large egg yolk**
- 2 **tablespoons maple syrup**
- 1 **teaspoon vanilla extract**
- ½ **teaspoon Diamond Crystal kosher salt (see page 16)**
- ½ **teaspoon ground cinnamon**
- ¼ **teaspoon ground ginger**
- ¼ **teaspoon ground cardamom**
- ¼ **teaspoon ground black pepper**
- 4 **slices of bread (about 1½ inches thick)**
- **Neutral oil or ghee**

For the Topping

- ½ **cup tahini, plus more as needed**
- ½ **cup maple syrup**
- ¼ **cup whole milk, plus more as needed**
- ½ **teaspoon Diamond Crystal kosher salt**
- ⅓ **cup pomegranate molasses**

1. Arrange a rack in the center of the oven. Preheat the oven to 325°F.

2. In a medium bowl, whisk together the **milk, cream, egg, yolk, maple syrup, vanilla, salt, cinnamon, ginger, cardamom,** and **black pepper** until homogeneous and no streaks of egg remain.

3. Transfer the custard to a casserole-type dish and arrange the **bread** in one layer. Press the bread firmly into the custard to absorb for 5 minutes, then flip over and repeat. (You can let the bread soak up the custard overnight. Cover and transfer to the fridge if you are soaking the bread overnight or for over 30 minutes. Obviously.)

4. In a large oven-safe skillet over medium heat, add enough oil to coat the bottom of the pan. Add the bread and cook on both sides until golden-brown, 2 to 3 minutes per side. Transfer the skillet to the oven and bake until cooked through, about 10 minutes. (If your pan doesn't fit all your bread, do it in waves.) Check by making a shallow incision in the toast's center and making sure it doesn't look wet. It's hard to overcook the French toast at such a low temperature, so don't worry about ensuring they all go in simultaneously. Relax—it's just freedom toast.

5. ***To make the topping:*** While the bread bakes, in a medium bowl, combine the **tahini, maple syrup, milk,** and **salt** and whisk until homogeneous. If it feels too thick, add small splashes of milk until you are happy. If it's too thin, thicken it with little dabs of tahini. Set aside.

6. Transfer the French toast to a plate, smother it with tahini sauce, and drizzle with **pomegranate molasses.** Eat immediately.

Cinnamon Pita Crunch

Anything can be breakfast cereal with enough cinnamon sugar.

MAKES 8 CUPS

My mom had some strange rules. We couldn't have any "fun" cereals… during the school year. No Lucky Charms, no Cocoa Krispies, no Cap'n Crunch. It was all Special K and Raisin Bran. Come summertime, I guess she stopped caring about feeding our brains, because my sister and I would go nuts on Cookie Crisp and, my favorite, Cinnamon Toast Crunch. But I found a loophole during the other months of the year, being the cheeky brat that I was. I learned to make my own CTC by toasting chopped pita in butter and then tossing them in cinnamon sugar. They would tide me over until summer. The older I got, the more I craved my CPC more than the OG stuff. I've since perfected the recipe, borrowing a technique from saltine bark. And like true CTC, CPC is just as delicious dry as it is in some milk. Store it in a resealable plastic bag in the freezer for maximum freshness.

INGREDIENTS:

6 pita (ideally the thin ones) cut into ½-inch squares

For the Cinnamon Glaze

- **¾ cup unsalted butter**
- **¾ cup (packed) brown sugar**
- **2 teaspoons ground cinnamon**
- **1 teaspoon vanilla extract**
- **Kosher salt**

For the Cinnamon Sugar

- **¼ cup granulated sugar**
- **1 teaspoon ground cinnamon**

1. Preheat the oven to 325°F.

2. Spread the **pita** pieces in one even layer on a large sheet pan and bake until fully dry but not deeply browned, about 30 minutes. Remove the pan from the oven and set aside. Increase the oven temperature to 400°F.

3. While the pita bakes, in a medium saucepan over medium heat, combine the **butter** and **brown sugar** and cook until the sugar melts and bubbles vigorously. Kill the heat and add the **cinnamon, vanilla,** and a large pinch of **salt.** Whisk to combine.

4. In a large bowl, combine the baked pita with the glaze and toss to combine. Return the pita pieces to the sheet pan and spread them out in one even layer. Bake until the sugar bubbles on the edges and the pitas are a deep golden brown, about 6 minutes. Remove the pan from the oven and let sit for 10 minutes to cool slightly.

5. While the pita cools, whisk the **granulated sugar** and **cinnamon** in a small bowl until evenly combined.

6. Sprinkle the cinnamon sugar on top of the warm pita pieces to taste. Once fully cool, eat immediately or transfer to a resealable plastic bag and store in the freezer for up to 3 months.

PS: Any leftover cinnamon sugar can be used to season the milk you have with your CPC.

Overnight Oats with Rose, Cherries, and Pistachios

Ali's mom has got it going on.

MAKES 2 CUPS

In Arabic, Umm Ali (Ali's mom) is a ubiquitous Egyptian dessert found at chaotic and often volatile iftar buffets throughout the Middle East. (Chaotic as in, I once saw a grown man threaten an eight-year-old's life for taking the last scoop of Umm Ali, even though another tray was already en route.) It's made by baking thin, dried crepes in rose-scented sweetened milk and cream studded with nuts and raisins.

These overnight oats take Umm Ali as inspiration but lighten what can be a stodgy dessert while keeping its soul-warming essence intact. Use this easy nut-candying method for any nut. Change the seasoning to adapt it for other applications; candy some pecans and season with your favorite chili flakes to top salads. For this recipe, toasting the oats is critical. There is no reason to have untoasted oats around—every oat recipe you've ever made will benefit from it. Pretoasting the oats and keeping them in your freezer make this recipe easy to assemble, ensuring your breakfasts are threat-free.

INGREDIENTS:

For the Overnight Oats

- 1 **cup rolled or stone-cut oats**
- 1 **cup whole milk**
- ½ **cup buttermilk**
- ⅓ **cup dried cherries**
- 1 **tablespoon rose or orange blossom water**
- 1 **teaspoon vanilla extract**
- ¼ **teaspoon Diamond Crystal kosher salt (see page 16)**

For the Candied Pistachios

- 2 **tablespoons unsalted butter**
- 2 **tablespoons sugar**
- 1 **cup whole, shelled, unsalted pistachios**
- ½ **teaspoon fennel seeds**
- ½ **teaspoon ground ginger**
- ½ **teaspoon Diamond Crystal kosher salt**

Honey or maple syrup, for serving (optional)

Rose or orange blossom water, for serving (optional)

1. Preheat the oven to 325°F.

2. ***To prepare the oats:*** Spread out your oats on a sheet pan and bake until they smell nutty and are light golden brown, occasionally tossing to toast evenly, about 30 minutes.

3. In a large container, mix the **toasted oats, milk, buttermilk, dried cherries, orange blossom water, vanilla,** and **salt.** Cover with a lid or plastic wrap and place in the fridge for at least 12 hours.

4. Prepare a landing station for the candied nuts (aka line a sheet pan with parchment paper).

5. ***To candy the pistachios:*** In a medium skillet over medium heat, melt the **butter.** Add the **sugar** and stir until it dissolves. Add the **pistachios** and toss to coat. Cook until the mixture simmers, tossing to coat the entire time. Keep cooking until the pistachios are evenly caramelized and the foaming settles, 3 to 5 minutes. Kill the heat, add the **fennel seeds, ginger,** and **salt,** and toss to coat. Transfer the mixture to your prepared pan and spread out thinly to cool. While the nuts are still warm, separate them so they don't clump as they cool. When cool, transfer to a container with a tight-fitting lid and store at room temperature.

6. To serve, scoop some of the soaked oats into a bowl and top with the candied pistachios. If you want it to be sweeter, top with **honey** to taste or, if you're feeling it, add a dash more **rose water.**

PS:
I love this ratio of milk and buttermilk for overnight oats. You can change the fruit or seasonings, but the buttermilk is the key. It adds a beautiful tang and results in a much better texture than yogurt provides.

Date and Banana Smoothie

A twist on Persian majoon and the shake I used to get at the burger restaurant that fed me vegetables

MAKES 1 SMOOTHIE

Brooks Headley's Superiority Burger was my only means of eating quality vegetables for years. I was working long hours and didn't have the time to get seasonal produce to eat at home. When this New York institution closed and reopened in a space down the street, I was invited to their opening party and the Date Shake was the first thing I tried. I would have slept in their kitchen if they had let me so I could wake up to drink that shake and not have to put on pants.

What made it especially memorable were the larger chunks of partially frozen dates that were too big to fit through the straw, leaving me no choice but to dig them out with a spoon. They had the texture of the most fabulous soft and chewy caramel candy.

The restaurant is fiercely seasonal, so I was forced to create my own smoothie variant when they rotated the Date Shake off the menu, despite my impassioned pleas. I mimic the SB Date Shake effect by holding back a few dates to lightly blend at the end, so they stay chunky. I season this smoothie with cardamom, cinnamon, and orange blossom water just like the classic Persian majoon, a traditional date and banana shake. (Don't fear the orange blossom water. It plays off the other flavors and adds a mirage of sweetness without the need for any added sugar. If you don't have any, you can leave it out.) This is the perfect way to kick off the morning when you have a sweet tooth and don't feel like tackling the stove. For maximum freshness, always store your dates in the freezer. As a bonus, frozen dates make a great treat when you've got a serious case of the munchies and want something sweet without any effort, especially if you split them and fill them with a bit of smooth peanut butter. If smoothies are your go-to breakfast, you can streamline the prep by keeping an airtight bag of peeled bananas in your freezer.

INGREDIENTS:

- 1 **banana, peeled and frozen**
- ⅓ **cup pitted, chopped, and frozen Medjool dates, plus 2 more, pitted and frozen**
- ½ **cup milk of your choice**
- ½ **cup ice (roughly 4 to 6 standard-sized cubes)**
- ¼ **cup roasted or raw salted cashews**
- ½ **teaspoon ground cardamom**
- ½ **teaspoon ground cinnamon**
- ¼ **teaspoon orange blossom water**

1. This is the easiest recipe in this book. Put everything in your blender, except the two extra dates, and let it rip. Blend until smooth.

2. Toss in the reserved dates and pulse a couple of times just to break up the dates into large chunks. Serve in a tall glass with a wide straw and a spoon.

PS:
Boost the nutrition in this smoothie with protein powder, chia seeds, or flax seeds; adjust the consistency with more milk as needed. If you want a lighter version, this shake works great with coconut water instead of milk, but if you're feeling extra saucy, replace the ice with vanilla ice cream for a fantastic shake.

Blueberry Muffins Inspired by Costco

Reverse cream FTW

MAKES 24 MUFFINS

I'm not going to lie. These are cakes disguised as muffins. But they're cake-muffins with a sweet backstory, so you can feel good about eating them for breakfast. I moved to the United States by myself when I was nineteen. I knew nothing about my surroundings, had no access to public transportation, and didn't have my driver's license yet. A sympathetic older lady in my building would drive me to Costco once a month for provisions. I would awkwardly sit in the car as she snarled in agreement every time Sean Hannity talked about the ongoing immigrant infestation on the radio. That was my first experience with grocery store shopping in the United States.

I assumed all grocery stores in the United States were warehouses stocked with pallets of Kirkland mixed nuts. I didn't know how special Costco was until I gained access to other grocery stores. On each monthly visit, I would try different things I couldn't access in Doha: mini beef sticks, Cheez-Its, and all the different kinds of pretzels. There was always one constant, though: the Costco blueberry muffins. I would get a tray of twenty-four and keep them in my freezer. I'd let them thaw and eat them as they were, slice them in half and toast them in butter, slice them into rings and fill them with scoops of vanilla ice cream for muffin ice cream sandwiches. I loved them. Living in Manhattan now means that I have let Costco go—but not those muffins. I use the reverse-creaming method to mimic a Costco muffin's moist, delicate crumb. That's a cheffy way of saying you add the fat after the dry ingredients instead of the other way around, so fat coats the flour to inhibit gluten development, resulting in a more tender and fluffy cake. I mean… muffin. Please follow the recipe when it asks for room-temperature ingredients. I promise it's worth it; it's the other key to getting the right amount of lift in the muffins. (And okay, fine: This batter also works as an incredible sheet cake in a greased 9 × 13-inch pan.) Under no circumstances should you serve them while listening to Sean Hannity.

INGREDIENTS:

- **2 cups / 400g sugar**
- **3¼ cups / 400g cake flour**
- **1 tablespoon baking powder**
- **1 teaspoon Diamond Crystal kosher salt (see page 16)**
- **½ teaspoon baking soda**
- **½ cup / 110g unsalted butter, room temperature**
- **⅓ cup / 70g neutral oil**
- **¾ cup / 160g sour cream, room temperature**
- **¾ cup / 170g whole milk, room temperature**
- **2 teaspoons imitation (or real, if that's all you've got) vanilla extract**
- **½ teaspoon almond extract**
- **4 large eggs, room temperature**
- **10 ounces / 280g frozen wild blueberries**

1. Arrange one rack in the top third and another in the bottom third of the oven. Preheat the oven to 400°F. Line two 12-cup muffin tins with liners.

2. In the bowl of a stand mixer fitted with the paddle attachment, add the **sugar, flour, baking powder, salt,** and **baking soda.** Mix on low until everything is well incorporated, about 1 minute.

3. Add the **butter** and **oil** and mix on low for 2 minutes, until the mixture resembles wet sand.

4. In a small bowl, whisk together the **sour cream, milk, vanilla,** and **almond extract** until combined and no lumps of sour cream remain. Pour into the mixer bowl and beat on low for 30 seconds, then on medium for 30 seconds.

5. Add one **egg** at a time, mixing on medium for 30 seconds and pausing to scrape down the bowl and paddle with a spatula before adding the next egg.

6. At this stage you can either bake the batter immediately or, for the best result, let it rest, covered, overnight, in the refrigerator for up to 12 hours before scooping and baking. When ready to bake, fold the **blueberries** into the batter with a spatula until they are evenly distributed. Using a ¼-cup / 2-ounce scoop, fill the liners up to the top.

7. Bake until evenly browned, 14 to 15 minutes, and then turn down the temperature to 325°F. Continue to bake until a wooden skewer inserted into the middle of a muffin comes out clean, 10 to 12 more minutes. This is tough, but you must wait and let them cool before eating so the structure sets and you don't end up with a mouthful of mush.

Buñuelos

Go from 0 to fried dough in a snap.

MAKES 18 BUÑUELOS

This may be controversial, but I do not like donuts. They are only good right out of the fryer, and you can rarely find one that fresh unless you are frying them yourself. I don't even like them enough to wait the hours it takes to make a properly proofed yeasted donut (don't you dare mention cake donuts to me; they are a blemish on civilization).

Buñuelos, on the other hand, are much faster to make and are as light and fluffy as any yeasted donut. Buñuelos are found throughout Central and South America in many different variations. This recipe combines the best parts of a donut (the cloudlike interior), a Mexican buñuelo (the cinnamon-sugar coating), and a Bolivian buñuelo (the fennel seeds). If you want to lean harder into a Bolivian vibe, omit the cinnamon sugar and drizzle some molasses on top instead. The deep, almost savory notes play off the licorice flavor of the fennel well and pair swimmingly with a hot chocolate sidecar, which is how I used to have them at Christmastime.

INGREDIENTS:

- 2½ **cups / 300g all-purpose flour, plus a little more for the rolling pin**
- 2 **tablespoons sugar**
- 1 **teaspoon Diamond Crystal kosher salt (see page 16)**
- 2 **teaspoons fennel seeds**
- ½ **teaspoon baking powder**
- ¼ **teaspoon baking soda**
- ¼ **cup / 50g lard or room temperature butter**
- ½ **cup / 120g whole milk**
- 1 **large egg**
- **Neutral oil, for frying**

For the Topping

- ½ **cup / 100g sugar**
- 1 **tablespoon ground cinnamon**
- ¼ **teaspoon Diamond Crystal kosher salt**

1. In a medium bowl, combine the **flour, sugar, salt, fennel seeds, baking powder,** and **baking soda** and whisk for a minute until evenly distributed. Rub the **lard** into the dry ingredients with your fingers until evenly coated with fat and the mixture looks like lightly moistened sand on the beach.

2. In a small bowl, whisk together the **milk** and the **egg** until there are no unincorporated bits of egg.

3. Add the milk mixture to the flour-lard mixture and, using stiff, rigid fingers, "whisk" until there are no pockets of lard and flour.

4. Transfer the dough to a clean surface and knead until a smooth dough forms, 3 to 5 minutes. Cover the dough with a kitchen towel and let it rest for at least 20 minutes and up to 1 hour.

5. Divide the dough into eighteen portions, about 1 ounce / 30g each, and roll each portion into a ball. Keep all the dough covered under a kitchen towel while you aren't using it. Take one ball and flatten it into a disk about 3 inches wide, using a floured rolling pin. Repeat with the remaining dough balls. Keep the rolled-out disks under the kitchen towel until all the balls have been rolled out.

6. Fill a large pot with an inch of **oil** and heat over medium heat until the oil registers between 325°F and 350°F on an instant-read thermometer.

7. ***To mix the topping:*** In a medium bowl, whisk together the **sugar, cinnamon,** and **salt.**

8. In small batches, fry each disk in the oil until one side is browned and puffed, about 3 minutes, then flip and fry on the other side until browned as well, another 3 minutes. Adjust the stove temperature as needed while frying.

9. Remove the cooked buñuelos from the oil with tongs, carefully shaking off any excess fat, and transfer to the bowl with the topping mixture. Toss to coat, then transfer to a large plate. Repeat until all the dough has been fried. Serve warm.

CHAPTER 2

Dips &

TAHINI AND SILKEN TOFU DIP
p. 74

ZA'ATAR AND LABNEH CRESCENT ROLLS
p. 92

REALLY FRESH RICOTTA AND ZA'ATAR
p. 73

FOCACCIA BALADI
p. 83

BETTER THAN BOURSIN
p. 80

SHRIMP TOAST
p. 90

Blueberry Muffins Inspired by Costco

Reverse cream FTW

MAKES 24 MUFFINS

I'm not going to lie. These are cakes disguised as muffins. But they're cake-muffins with a sweet backstory, so you can feel good about eating them for breakfast. I moved to the United States by myself when I was nineteen. I knew nothing about my surroundings, had no access to public transportation, and didn't have my driver's license yet. A sympathetic older lady in my building would drive me to Costco once a month for provisions. I would awkwardly sit in the car as she snarled in agreement every time Sean Hannity talked about the ongoing immigrant infestation on the radio. That was my first experience with grocery store shopping in the United States.

I assumed all grocery stores in the United States were warehouses stocked with pallets of Kirkland mixed nuts. I didn't know how special Costco was until I gained access to other grocery stores. On each monthly visit, I would try different things I couldn't access in Doha: mini beef sticks, Cheez-Its, and all the different kinds of pretzels. There was always one constant, though: the Costco blueberry muffins. I would get a tray of twenty-four and keep them in my freezer. I'd let them thaw and eat them as they were, slice them in half and toast them in butter, slice them into rings and fill them with scoops of vanilla ice cream for muffin ice cream sandwiches. I loved them. Living in Manhattan now means that I have let Costco go—but not those muffins. I use the reverse-creaming method to mimic a Costco muffin's moist, delicate crumb. That's a cheffy way of saying you add the fat after the dry ingredients instead of the other way around, so fat coats the flour to inhibit gluten development, resulting in a more tender and fluffy cake. I mean… muffin. Please follow the recipe when it asks for room-temperature ingredients. I promise it's worth it; it's the other key to getting the right amount of lift in the muffins. (And okay, fine: This batter also works as an incredible sheet cake in a greased 9 × 13-inch pan.) Under no circumstances should you serve them while listening to Sean Hannity.

INGREDIENTS:

- **2 cups / 400g sugar**
- **3¼ cups / 400g cake flour**
- **1 tablespoon baking powder**
- **1 teaspoon Diamond Crystal kosher salt (see page 16)**
- **½ teaspoon baking soda**
- **½ cup / 110g unsalted butter, room temperature**
- **⅓ cup / 70g neutral oil**
- **¾ cup / 160g sour cream, room temperature**
- **¾ cup / 170g whole milk, room temperature**
- **2 teaspoons imitation (or real, if that's all you've got) vanilla extract**
- **½ teaspoon almond extract**
- **4 large eggs, room temperature**
- **10 ounces / 280g frozen wild blueberries**

1. Arrange one rack in the top third and another in the bottom third of the oven. Preheat the oven to 400°F. Line two 12-cup muffin tins with liners.

2. In the bowl of a stand mixer fitted with the paddle attachment, add the **sugar, flour, baking powder, salt,** and **baking soda.** Mix on low until everything is well incorporated, about 1 minute.

3. Add the **butter** and **oil** and mix on low for 2 minutes, until the mixture resembles wet sand.

4. In a small bowl, whisk together the **sour cream, milk, vanilla,** and **almond extract** until combined and no lumps of sour cream remain. Pour into the mixer bowl and beat on low for 30 seconds, then on medium for 30 seconds.

5. Add one **egg** at a time, mixing on medium for 30 seconds and pausing to scrape down the bowl and paddle with a spatula before adding the next egg.

Buñuelos

Go from 0 to fried dough in a snap.

MAKES 18 BUÑUELOS

This may be controversial, but I do not like donuts. They are only good right out of the fryer, and you can rarely find one that fresh unless you are frying them yourself. I don't even like them enough to wait the hours it takes to make a properly proofed yeasted donut (don't you dare mention cake donuts to me; they are a blemish on civilization).

Buñuelos, on the other hand, are much faster to make and are as light and fluffy as any yeasted donut. Buñuelos are found throughout Central and South America in many different variations. This recipe combines the best parts of a donut (the cloudlike interior), a Mexican buñuelo (the cinnamon-sugar coating), and a Bolivian buñuelo (the fennel seeds). If you want to lean harder into a Bolivian vibe, omit the cinnamon sugar and drizzle some molasses on top instead. The deep, almost savory notes play off the licorice flavor of the fennel well and pair swimmingly with a hot chocolate sidecar, which is how I used to have them at Christmastime.

INGREDIENTS:

- **2½ cups / 300g all-purpose flour, plus a little more for the rolling pin**
- **2 tablespoons sugar**
- **1 teaspoon Diamond Crystal kosher salt (see page 16)**
- **2 teaspoons fennel seeds**
- **½ teaspoon baking powder**
- **¼ teaspoon baking soda**
- **¼ cup / 50g lard or room temperature butter**
- **½ cup / 120g whole milk**
- **1 large egg**
- **Neutral oil, for frying**

For the Topping

- **½ cup / 100g sugar**
- **1 tablespoon ground cinnamon**
- **¼ teaspoon Diamond Crystal kosher salt**

1. In a medium bowl, combine the **flour, sugar, salt, fennel seeds, baking powder,** and **baking soda** and whisk for a minute until evenly distributed. Rub the **lard** into the dry ingredients with your fingers until evenly coated with fat and the mixture looks like lightly moistened sand on the beach.

2. In a small bowl, whisk together the **milk** and the **egg** until there are no unincorporated bits of egg.

3. Add the milk mixture to the flour-lard mixture and, using stiff, rigid fingers, "whisk" until there are no pockets of lard and flour.

4. Transfer the dough to a clean surface and knead until a smooth dough forms, 3 to 5 minutes. Cover the dough with a kitchen towel and let it rest for at least 20 minutes and up to 1 hour.

5. Divide the dough into eighteen portions, about 1 ounce / 30g each, and roll each portion into a ball. Keep all the dough covered under a kitchen towel while you aren't using it. Take one ball and flatten it into a disk about 3 inches wide, using a floured rolling pin. Repeat with the remaining dough balls. Keep the rolled-out disks under the kitchen towel until all the balls have been rolled out.

6. Fill a large pot with an inch of **oil** and heat over medium heat until the oil registers between 325°F and 350°F on an instant-read thermometer.

7. ***To mix the topping:*** In a medium bowl, whisk together the **sugar, cinnamon,** and **salt.**

8. In small batches, fry each disk in the oil until one side is browned and puffed, about 3 minutes, then flip and fry on the other side until browned as well, another 3 minutes. Adjust the stove temperature as needed while frying.

9. Remove the cooked buñuelos from the oil with tongs, carefully shaking off any excess fat, and transfer to the bowl with the topping mixture. Toss to coat, then transfer to a large plate. Repeat until all the dough has been fried. Serve warm.

CHAPTER 2

Dips &

TAHINI AND SILKEN TOFU DIP
p. 74

ZA'ATAR AND LABNEH CRESCENT ROLLS
p. 92

REALLY FRESH RICOTTA AND ZA'ATAR
p. 73

FOCACCIA BALADI
p. 83

BETTER THAN BOURSIN
p. 80

SHRIMP TOAST
p. 90

Snacks

Dip me baby one more time

CRUNCHY GREENY-BEANY FRITTERS
p. 87

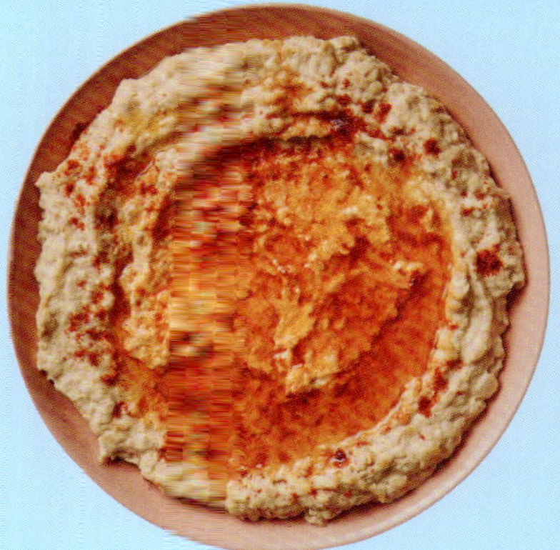

LAZY HUMMUS
p. 84

GARLIC BREAD CHEWY BUNS
p. 98

SHISHITO-PISTACHIO DIP
p. 79

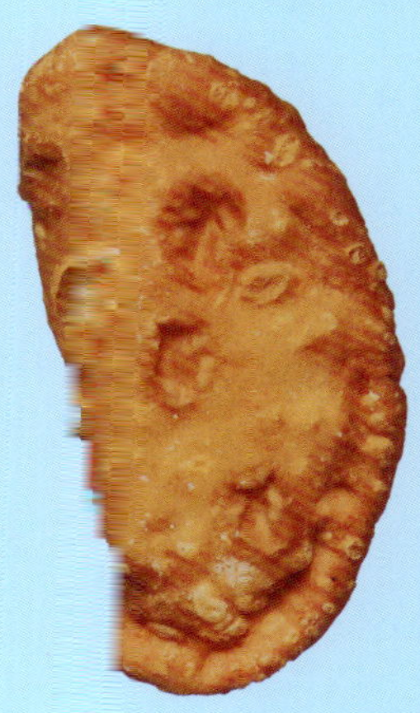

CHEESE EMPANADAS
p. 95

EDAMAME DIP WITH CRISPY ONIONS
p. 77

F*INAL FANTASY 7*, which came out in 1997, was the game that brought role-playing games out of Japan and into the American mainstream. A trademark feature of most role-playing games is how many hoops the player needs to jump through to reach an objective. I mention that because young Ham's journey to finally being able to play the game wouldn't be out of place in an RPG. There were twists and turns. There were minor victories followed by heartache. There were also so many snacks.

Until *Final Fantasy 7*, I had been a casual gamer. I had a PlayStation, which I didn't use very much because the games were way too expensive. I was stuck playing the waterless jet ski simulator *Wipeout*, which came bundled for free with my console. I did like reading about video games and would occasionally pick up a copy of *PlayStation Magazine* or *Play* magazine.

Unfortunately, in Doha, a lot of the blocky character designs were deemed too provocative, and censors would black them out with a Sharpie. When we would go on summer vacation in Cairo, I would pick up bundles of old magazines for cheap from street vendors. The magazines were outdated, but I didn't care; they were Sharpie-free. That summer, I picked up a copy of a *Play* magazine that came with an entire booklet dedicated to a *Final Fantasy 7* walk-through. I put down my Christopher Pike's *The Last Vampire 2: Black Blood* and devoted all my time to reading that walk-through, cover to cover, over and over again. I was sucked in by the majestic creatures (THREE Bahamuts) that got summoned when you collected their materia. I stayed for the weird mini games based on dolphin jumping, Chocobos (cuter ostriches) racing, and squatting in a gym to get the best wig for my outfit. I could not resist that quirky group of losers trying to save the world from its impending meteor-related apocalypse.

I spent a year playing the game in my head, based on the drawings of the characters and the details in the guide. On a random mall trip, I stumbled across a discounted copy of the PC version of the game. I couldn't believe my luck and bought it immediately. Hoop number two? Cleared.

Except, when I tried to install it on the family PC, the screen delicately informed me that my graphics card was incompatible with the game.

Eventually, I did manage to find the animated videos strewn throughout the game hiding in a folder and watched them all in order, turning them into a short movie I would use to inform the game I was playing in my head.

Then hoop number three presented itself in the shape of a helpful ally. For my birthday, my one gamer friend who understood my plight got my PlayStation "chipped," which would allow it to play pirated copies of games. We picked the PlayStation up from a small dusty store after school. To peddle their wares, the store had weathered posters of old video games all over the walls and a thick booklet filled with photocopies of the front covers of countless games. I knew the first game I was going to buy.

The shop owner crammed the trio of shiny disks into an unmarked box that refused to close. I declined a bag, insisting I wanted to carry the box carefully in both hands to protect the disks from any potential scratches. I popped a disk into my PlayStation as soon as I got home, my heart thumping with anticipation as the score swelled alongside the title card. It was finally about to happen: I was going to go up against the undeniably stunning yet vicious Sephiroth.

And when it did happen, *FF7* changed how I lived my life. I'm not being glib; it's just that I literally wasn't allowed to play video games until all my homework was done. So, to maximize my precious time with Cloud Strife and the gang, I started doing all my homework during class and recess. I didn't want to give my parents reason to think that my new obsession was a problem, so I made sure my grades were better than ever. My days revolved around maximizing my gaming time. If I could sneak in a shower at the school gym, it meant that I wouldn't have to waste time on such rubbish at home, where *FF7* pulled me to the living room like a magnet.

My eating habits shifted radically. In my household, lunches were the most important meal of the day. My dad would come home from work for a few hours so we could all eat together. Dinner and snacks, however, were often left up to us. I began to plan my afternoon and evening sustenance fully around my play time.

Here is where I tell you about the snack freezer.

At this time in my childhood, my dad was a bona fide snack dealer. Technically, his job was import/export, but this meant he was always on the hunt for the next big thing to import into Doha. He constantly had samples arriving that he would test on us and a control group of trusted friends. These samples lived in an unguarded large chest freezer in the garage that, at its peak, was filled to the brim with cheese empanadas, vegetable lumpias, dulce de leche–stuffed churros, potato skins, chocolate chip and white chocolate macadamia cookies, a variety of cheesecakes, mozzarella sticks, pizza bagels, pigs in a blanket, and other random ready-to-eat treats.

So, as I crunched the numbers to maximize my *FF7* game play, it quickly became clear that this snack freezer, which was full of ready-made bites, should become my main source of fuel. I just had to make sure my dad didn't know I was stealing his limited samples. I would quietly sneak into the garage, pop the freezer open, and be sure to grab only one treat of a type at a time, enough to satisfy me but not enough for it to get noticed. It was the Ham version of the much cooler kids stealing alcohol from their parents' liquor cabinets and refilling the bottles with splashes of water.

This became my first lesson in how to be an efficient prep cook. I would creep into the kitchen, heat up the oven, then slink back to the living room to sneak in some Chocobo racing before prowling into the garage to silently grab a mozzarella stick and pizza bagel, throwing both in the oven before going back to play "Tifa's Theme" on her childhood piano. I had my timings for snacks down. And more importantly, I thought of the cook times in gameplay terms: Pizza bagels and mozzarella sticks took three random battles in the Gongaga region to be hot. Churros took one full battle tournament at the Gold Saucer.

My finest work was how I baked the frozen chocolate chip cookies. I would let the oven get ripping hot before putting a fully frozen cookie in there. The outside would get crisp, and the inside would become molten, like my own little Michel Bras's chocolate coulant (an iconic chocolate dessert that inspired the molten chocolate lava cake found in just-okay restaurants all over). The method required precision, diligence, and exact timing. If I left it in too long, it would char and turn into a puck. In my childhood oven, it took exactly seven minutes peering into the oven and one Knights of the Round Summon.

By the time I beat the game, I was a snacking savant with a list of rules.

I spent more time in the kitchen making my own snacks instead of raiding my dad's stash. I was always into food—*Yan Can Cook* was my favorite TV show—but before *FF7*, I had never thought about cooking in terms of timing. Through my snack freezer raids, I learned how to improve the quality of my snacks by breaking up longer prep projects into manageable pieces. I still take a lot of pride in my snacks, though now I have no problem sinking time into something if it's worth it.

Here's my big rule now: The ultimate snack is a flavorful dip with something crunchy. My crunchy thing is usually purchased, like a bag of Fritos, some fresh sourdough bread, or whatever flavor of potato chip I am into. But there are times when a little extra effort is necessary. The recipes for my three favorite crunchies (in increasing levels of difficulty) to make at home follow:

Bread Chips (aka Crostini)

MAKES AS MUCH BREAD AS YOU CHOOSE

These chips are great for snacking or dipping and require almost no hands-on cooking time. They're also a great way to use up stale bread. You can season the bread with whatever you're in the mood for. Use your favorite ranch powder (like the one my wife, Sohla, and I make for Burlap & Barrel) or the everything bagel seasoning from page 47.

INGREDIENTS:

- **1 loaf of bread, a baguette, several bagels, or pieces of pita**
- **Extra-virgin olive oil**
- **Kosher salt**
- **Freshly cracked black pepper**

1. Preheat the oven to 325°F. Line a sheet pan with parchment paper.

2. Cut the **bread** or bagels into even slices no thicker than ¼ inch. If using pitas, they are thin enough to cut into whichever shape you desire.

3. Transfer the bread to a large bowl and drizzle with **oil** while tossing to coat evenly. Season with a large pinch of **salt** and **black pepper.** Toss again to combine.

4. Lay out the bread in one layer on the prepared pan.

5. Bake until the bread is fully dry, crisp, and lightly golden brown, 22 to 25 minutes. (For pita chips, start to check around 15 minutes, since the pieces will be thinner.) Let the bread cool fully before serving. These chips will keep for up to 2 days in a tightly sealed container at room temperature (and up to 4 days if you store them with a desiccant, which is handy for keeping dry things fresh and can be purchased online).

Seedy Crackers

MAKES 5 OUNCES OF CRACKERS
(about a box-worth at the store)

I developed these during my healthy phase. They are packed with nutrients, last for a long time, and are easy to throw together. The base is pretty flavor neutral, so they are great for letting your dip shine, though it takes well to savory flavors like nutritional yeast, soy sauce, or a sprinkle of instant dashi.

INGREDIENTS:

- **1 cup raw whole flax seeds**
- **¼ cup raw pumpkin seeds**
- **2 tablespoons chia seeds**
- **½ cup room-temperature water**
- **1 egg white**
- **1 teaspoon Diamond Crystal kosher salt (see page 16)**
- **1 teaspoon garlic powder**

1. In a medium bowl, combine all ingredients and stir until evenly distributed. Let sit for 1 hour.

2. Preheat the oven to 375°F. Line a sheet pan with parchment paper.

3. Stir the seed mixture to loosen and spoon onto the middle of the prepared pan. Spread the mixture evenly and as thinly as possible using an offset spatula, especially pressing down in the center. The batter is sticky, so use a series of swipes and pats to smooth it out.

4. Bake until the edges curl and the center is dry and crisp, 25 to 30 minutes. Remove the pan from the oven and let the crackers cool fully before breaking into pieces. These crackers will keep for a week in a tightly sealed container at room temperature (and up to 2 weeks if you store them with a desiccant, which is handy for keeping dry things fresh and can be purchased online).

Tostones

SERVES 2 OR 3

Freshly fried tostones are one of my favorite quick crispy snacks. The ripeness of the plantain is essential. The plantain needs to be green and unripe, but I like to wait for the moment where it just starts to turn yellow, and then I pounce into tostón town. Dipping the plantain in water is key to getting it crisp on the outside and tender on the inside, while adding seasoning throughout—do not skip this step.

INGREDIENTS:

- **2 large green plantains**
- **1 tablespoon Diamond Crystal kosher salt (see page 16), plus more to season fried plantains**
- **5 garlic cloves, coarsely chopped**
- **2 green Thai chilies, stemmed and coarsely chopped**
- **Juice of 2 limes**
- **Neutral oil, for frying**

1. Trim the tops and bottoms of the **plantains** and make an incision along the sides, cutting only the skin and not the flesh. Using your thumb, pry the skin from the flesh. Cut the plantains into 1½-inch chunks.

2. In a medium bowl, combine 2 cups **water** with the **salt, garlic, chilies,** and **lime juice.**

3. Cut two 6-inch squares of parchment paper and set them next to your stovetop, side by side. Line a large plate with paper towels.

4. Fill a medium pot with about 1½ inches of **oil.** Working in batches, add half of the plantain chunks to the cold oil and turn the heat to medium. Cook until the oil reaches 350°F on an instant-read thermometer. (If you don't have one, you can tell it's roughly in range when the oil starts gently bubbling around the plantains.) The plantains should be very lightly golden brown and feel crisp. Remove the plantains from the oil with a slotted spoon and transfer them to the paper towels to drain and then move to one of the sheets of parchment paper—but be sure to maintain the temperature of the oil as you work.

5. With the plantains flat-side up, place the other sheet on top and, using a heavy skillet, press down on the plantains until they flatten into thin disks. Transfer the smashed plantains to the seasoned water and let them sit for 10 to 20 seconds.

6. Transfer the soaked plantains back into the oil and fry again, flipping occasionally, until golden-brown and crisp, 3 to 5 minutes. Gently shake off excess water. This doesn't get crazy splattery but be careful. Repeat with the rest of the plantains.

7. Transfer the fried plantains to the prepared plate and season with salt. Eat immediately.

the Simpsons

REALLY FRESH
RICOTTA
AND ZA'ATAR
p. 73
EDAMAME DIP
WITH CRISPY
ONIONS
p. 77
SHISHITO-
PISTACHIO DIP
p. 79

LAZY HUMMUS
p. 84

FOCACCIA BALADI
p. 83

TAHINI AND SILKEN TOFU DIP
p. 74

BETTER THAN BOURSIN
p. 80

Really Fresh Ricotta and Za'atar

The only way I can be convinced to eat ricotta

MAKES 1¼ CUPS

People need to relax with the ricotta. I find it in my lasagna, giving me pockets of dry, crumbly curds. It haunts my pizza, leaving the crust soggy. Unless you splurge on a fancy one, store-bought ricotta is often chalky, flavorless, and has a wide range of textures, from totally smooth to a spread reminiscent of a barrel of wet pebbles.

On the other hand, fresh ricotta made at home has an inimitable lush milkiness. And it's easy-freakin'-peasy. After simply cooking fresh milk and cream with lemon juice, you strain and hang the curds to form the cheese. If I want a looser, creamier ricotta, I hang it for 10 to 15 minutes. For a thicker, sturdier ricotta, I drain it for the full time detailed here. Occasionally, I'll even whip the drained ricotta in a food processor, with a couple of tablespoons of olive oil to produce something smoother and more luxurious.

When I feel like something sweet, I like to top fresh ricotta with everything from strawberry jam and olive oil to canned peaches and almonds. For breakfast, I'll have it with a couple of jammy eggs. When I want to change it up, I top it with confit tomatoes and fried garlic: Boom, you have a sultry little dip. And for any other time, I top it with za'atar and olive oil.

INGREDIENTS:

- **4 cups whole milk**
- **½ cup heavy cream**
- **⅓ cup freshly squeezed lemon juice (about 2 lemons)**
- **Kosher salt**
- **Zest of 1 lemon**
- **1 tablespoon za'atar, for garnish**
- **1 tablespoon extra-virgin olive oil, for garnish**

1. Fill a medium pot with 1 inch of water and bring to a simmer over medium heat.

2. In a heatproof medium bowl, add the **milk** and **cream** and whisk to combine. Place the bowl over the pot with the simmering water to make a double boiler and cook, stirring occasionally, until the milk reaches 200°F on an instant-read thermometer, 13 to 15 minutes.

3. Once the dairy reaches 200°F, add the **lemon juice** and a large pinch of **salt.** Stir occasionally, until the curds separate from the whey, about 5 minutes. The whey should start to look clear. Let the mixture cook for 5 more minutes. Meanwhile, line a fine-mesh sieve or strainer with cheesecloth and set over a large heatproof bowl.

4. Turn off the heat, then transfer the mixture to the prepared sieve. The whey should drain off, leaving the ricotta curds. Fold the corners of the cheesecloth into the center and place a plate on top as a weight to help the ricotta drain. Let the ricotta drain to your desired thickness. The longer it sits, the dryer it will be. I like to drain it for 25 to 30 minutes.

5. Transfer the ricotta to a bowl and stir in the **lemon zest.** Taste and adjust the seasoning with more salt as needed.

6. Transfer the ricotta to a serving plate, flatten with a spoon making one large divot in the middle, and garnish with the **za'atar** and **oil.**

Tahini and Silken Tofu Dip

Dare I say a potential mayo replacer, too?

MAKES 3 CUPS

As a young kid, I didn't like tahini. I always found it too bitter. Then one day, they forgot to sub my tahini for the toum on a magical shawarma. There was something about the combination of crisp, fatty lamb, coupled with the creamy tahini, that just clicked for me—bitterness be damned. My tahini aversion was over, and I haven't looked back since. This recipe is perfect for people looking to dip (get it) their toes into tahini rather than go full Ham (eating it straight from the jar with my pointer finger as a spoon). It is lighter and silkier than traditional tahini dips, adding tofu both for the body and for a subtler, nutty flavor. It's great for crudités, bagel chips, warm fluffy pita, or anything else that has a nice crisp or crunch to it. My favorite feature of this dip, though, is its versatility. I like to use it anywhere mayonnaise would be at home. It adds lusciousness to everything from chicken to tuna salad to deviled eggs.

INGREDIENTS:

- 1 **pound silken tofu, drained**
- ½ **cup tahini**
- ¼ **cup extra-virgin olive oil, plus more for garnish**
- ¼ **cup freshly squeezed lemon juice (about 1 large lemon), plus more to taste**
- 2 **garlic cloves**
- 2 **teaspoons Diamond Crystal kosher salt (see page 16), plus more to taste**
- **Smoked paprika, for garnish**

1. In the bowl of a food processor, add the **tofu, tahini, oil, lemon juice, garlic,** and **salt.** Blitz until smooth. Taste and adjust the seasoning, adding more salt and lemon juice as needed; it should taste balanced and not like salty, creamy lemonade.

2. Transfer to a serving bowl and garnish with a sprinkle of **smoked paprika** and a drizzle of oil.

Edamame Dip with Crispy Onions

Remember edamame? You haven't called or texted in years.

MAKES 3 CUPS

This dip is based on a luscious and grassy Egyptian fava bean puree known as bessara. Bessara can be found all over Egypt, in homes and served out of street stalls, hot or cold. The base is one of the staple ingredients of Egyptian cuisine, the fava bean. Unfortunately, fava beans are hard to come by in the United States, so I created a Main Character Moment for humble frozen edamame, which I use to make a similar, very herby dip. I like to let it cool in the fridge before serving so the flavors meld, but there is nothing wrong with serving it warm right out of the food processor. I usually eat this as a dip with some warm pitas or with the Focaccia Baladi (page 83), but I have also been known to eat it warm over a bed of rice with a crispy egg on top when I want to turn my dip into dinner.

INGREDIENTS:

- **1 (2-ounce) bunch of cilantro**
- **1 (2-ounce) bunch of parsley**
- **1 (2-ounce) bunch of dill**
- **⅓ cup extra-virgin olive oil, plus more for garnish**
- **1 small yellow onion, diced**
- **6 garlic cloves, coarsely chopped**
- **Kosher salt**
- **1 tablespoon ground coriander**
- **2 teaspoons dried mint**
- **1 teaspoon ground cumin**
- **1 teaspoon chili powder**
- **1 pound frozen shelled edamame**
- **⅓ cup lime juice (about 2 limes), plus more to taste**
- **½ cup French's Original Crispy Fried Onions, for garnish**

1. Trim 3 inches of the stems from the **cilantro, parsley,** and **dill** and discard. Coarsely chop the remaining leaves and stems. Set aside.

2. In a medium skillet over medium-high heat, add the **oil** and heat until shimmering. Add the **onion, garlic,** and a pinch of **salt** and cook, stirring frequently, until the onion softens and turns golden around the edges, 3 to 5 minutes. Add the **coriander, mint, cumin,** and **chili powder** and cook until fragrant, about 1 minute. Add the **edamame,** a large pinch of salt, and ⅓ cup water and bring to a simmer. Cook until the edamame is thawed and soft, 3 to 5 minutes.

3. Transfer the mixture to the bowl of a food processor and add the chopped herbs and **lime juice.** Process until smooth, scraping down the sides with a rubber spatula if needed. Taste the dip and adjust the seasoning with more salt and lime juice as needed.

4. Transfer to a serving bowl and top with a hefty glug of oil and the **fried onions.**

Shishito-Pistachio Dip

Let shishitos pretend to be muhammara for a day.

MAKES 1½ CUPS

Muhammara is one of my favorite Levantine dishes. It's a bright red dip made from roasted red bell peppers and walnuts. I never felt like red bell peppers had too much character, so I started making them with red Jimmy Nardellos instead, a kind of pepper with a much more prominent flavor, especially when roasted. It's almost like a sun-dried tomato. Unfortunately, Jimmy Nardellos have fleeting availability, so muhammara became something I only had in the summertime, but I needed more of it in my life.

I started making it year-round using different peppers and switching up the nuts to match the flavor. With grassy—and occasionally spicy—shishitos and pistachios, this variation features one of my favorite combinations. For a more traditional flavor, swap the shishitos for roasted red bell peppers and the pistachios for toasted walnuts. Or play around and make your own house mix of peppers and nuts.

INGREDIENTS:

- **2 tablespoons neutral oil**
- **8 ounces shishito peppers, stemmed**
- **½ cup shelled, unsalted pistachios**
- **1 teaspoon ground coriander**
- **½ teaspoon ground cumin**
- **½ teaspoon chili flakes, preferably Aleppo**
- **⅓ cup freshly squeezed lemon juice (about 2 lemons), plus more as needed**
- **¼ cup extra-virgin olive oil**
- **2 tablespoons nutritional yeast (optional)**
- **2 garlic cloves, chopped**
- **Kosher salt**

For the Garnish

- **Coarsely chopped toasted pistachios**
- **Extra-virgin olive oil**
- **Pomegranate molasses**

1. In a medium skillet over medium-high heat, add the **neutral oil** and heat until shimmering. Add the **peppers** and cook, stirring occasionally, until blistered and charred in spots, about 5 minutes. Add the **pistachios, coriander, cumin,** and **chili flakes** and cook until the spices are fragrant, about 1 minute.

2. Transfer the shishito mixture to the bowl of a food processor and add the **lemon juice, olive oil, nutritional yeast** (if using), **garlic,** and a large pinch of **salt.** Blitz, scraping down the sides with a rubber spatula as needed, until smooth. Taste and adjust the seasoning with more salt or lemon juice as needed.

3. Transfer to an airtight container, cover, and store in the fridge until chilled. To serve, transfer to a bowl and garnish with a sprinkle of **pistachios,** a few glugs of **olive oil,** and a heavy drizzle of **pomegranate molasses.**

Better Than Boursin

You'll never pry open that foil again.

MAKES 2 CUPS

My mom never indulged in many treats for herself. Once a week, though, she would buy a quarter pound of a nice cheese for dinner along with some seedy crackers. A sharp aged Cheddar with big crunchy, salty crystals was always her favorite. She would eat it after my sister and I were in bed, when the house was calm and serene.

When I got older, I also developed a love for cheese, and I would join her meditative cheese dinners. Luckily for me, my wife, Sohla, also shares my deep love for fancy cheese dinners, but sometimes, we don't want to explore the fancy cheese section—sometimes, we want something simpler. Sometimes, I want to turn my brain off to the soothing sounds of All Elite Wrestling *instead of the latest movie from A24.*

Enter garlic and herb Boursin, the perfect cheese drawer pairing for watching two grown men in singlets perform choreographed acts of aggression. I can't tell you how many nights Sohla and I have demolished a container of Boursin (which is glorified cream cheese with dried herbs running through it) with a fresh baguette. It really is the best dinner, but it's an even better snack. Make a bowl of this recipe and keep it tightly wrapped in the fridge for up to four days for when the urgent need to dip a cracker strikes.

INGREDIENTS:

- **½ cup heavy cream**
- **½ cup labneh, room temperature**
- **¼ cup chopped parsley leaves**
- **¼ cup chopped dill**
- **¼ cup chopped chives**
- **1 garlic clove, finely grated**
- **Kosher salt**
- **Extra-virgin olive oil, for garnish**

1. In a medium bowl, add the **cream** and whisk until you have soft peaks (when the peaks of the cream droop only at the tip when you lift your whisk). Be careful not to overwhip. Gently whisk the **labneh** into the cream in three additions, until fully combined. Using a spatula, fold in the **parsley, dill, chives, garlic,** and a pinch of **salt** until evenly distributed. Taste and adjust the seasoning with more salt as needed.

2. Transfer to a bowl to serve and garnish with a drizzle of oil on top.

PS:
If herbs aren't your thing, you can season the whipped labneh in any direction. You can even sweeten it with honey or maple syrup and fold in some vanilla and lemon zest. Serve it with graham crackers for an instant cheesecake-ish dip. The pro wrestling, however, is not optional.

Focaccia Baladi

Taste of Egypt with a lot less effort

MAKES 1 LOAF

Bread is called different things throughout the Middle East; most call it khubz. *In Egypt, bread is called* aish, *which translates to "life."*

Aish baladi is a flatbread found throughout Egypt; it's like a pita but is made from whole wheat flour and often rests on wheat germ to prevent sticking. It also has the slight tang of sourdough that other pitas do not possess—that sucks for other pitas. What sucks for me, though, is that this bread is nearly impossible to find in New York City, and I am never in the mood to get a sourdough starter going and then form and bake a dozen aish.

So, I created this focaccia recipe to satisfy even my wildest aish baladi cravings. A caveat: Focaccia recipes are often sold to home cooks as a bread that comes together quickly and easily. This focaccia is definitely easy, but it is not quick. The long fermentation is essential because it gives this focaccia its sourdough texture and allows the proper amount of gluten to develop. Whole wheat flour takes longer to develop gluten, so the high-hydration (aka large volume of water) dough, the multiple folds, and the long proof time all ensure that the focaccia has a nice chew. I cannot brag enough about the perfect, almost custardy crumb texture of this focaccia. It is at its peak 20 minutes after it comes out of the oven, slathered with quality butters and topped with flaky salt. Make sure to try some then. Any leftovers are great alongside dips or as bread for a sandwich.

INGREDIENTS:

Scant 3 cups / 350g all-purpose flour
1⅔ cups / 200g whole wheat bread flour
1 tablespoon / 15g extra-virgin olive oil
4½ teaspoons / 15g Diamond Crystal kosher salt (see page 16)
Scant 2½ teaspoons / 8g instant yeast

For baking

⅔ cup / 160g extra-virgin olive oil
4 tablespoons / 55g wheat germ
Flaky salt, for sprinkling

1. In a large container with a tight-fitting lid or in a large bowl, combine the **flours, oil, kosher salt, yeast,** and 2⅔ cups / 630g room-temperature water. Stir with a spatula until no dry spots of flour remain. Cover the container with the lid or the bowl with plastic wrap and let sit for 20 minutes.

2. After 20 minutes, uncover the dough. Rub some of the oil on your fingers and place them underneath one corner of the dough. Lift and pull the dough to the opposite corner. Repeat with all four corners. (See illustration to the right.) Repeat the process with all four corners one more time. Cover the dough again and let it sit for 20 minutes. Repeat this process (folding all the corners twice every 20 minutes) three more times for a total of five complete rounds (the total rest time is 1 hour 40 minutes).

3. Place the dough in the fridge and let it sit for 2 whole days. (I know. I'm sorry. Come on this focaccia journey with me.)

4. Pour ½ cup of the **oil** into a 9 × 13-inch metal baking pan and swirl to coat, making sure to get all the edges. Sprinkle 2 tablespoons of the **wheat germ** along the bottom of the pan and slide the cold dough on top. Press the dough down and outward with stiff fingertips to fill the pan as much as possible. (There may be some empty corners.) Cover the pan with a towel and leave it in a warm place to proof until it is slightly poofy and has filled the pan, 1 to 1½ hours.

5. Preheat the oven to 500°F.

6. Use stiff fingers to press into the dough, creating uniform dimples across the surface. Top with the remaining oil and the remaining 2 tablespoons wheat germ. Season with a sprinkle of flaky salt. Bake the focaccia until the top is deeply golden brown, charred in spots, and crunchy all along the base, about 30 minutes.

7. Transfer to a wire rack to rest for at least 20 minutes before slicing and serving.

PS:
You should double this recipe and keep some focaccia in the freezer, wrapped in plastic wrap and stored in a resealable freezer bag for up to 1 month. Reheat in a 350°F oven until warm in the center. That's it. That's the tip.

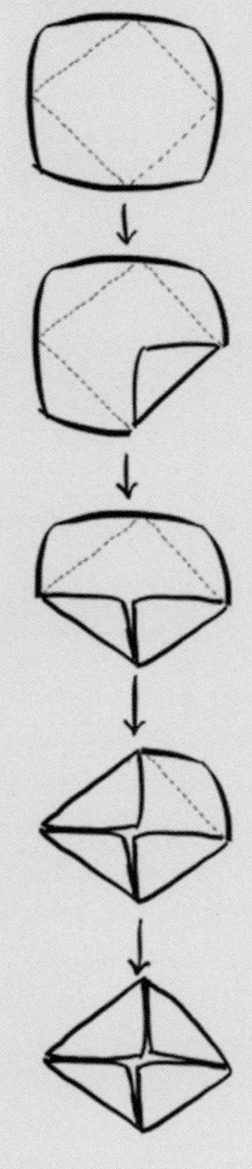

Lazy Hummus

One pot, one bowl, one whisk, and no heavy lifting

MAKES 2 CUPS

Our home food processor is an impressive commercial Robot Coupe. It was one of the only pieces of equipment that we saved from our old restaurant. It can turn nuts into smooth butter and whips chicken liver into a mousse luscious enough to frost cakes. Its processing potential is measured in horsepower. It is the food processor she told you not to worry about. And it makes the silkiest hummus I've ever had.

The Robot Coupe is also, like, incredibly heavy. And I rarely can muster up the strength to lug it from my closet into an empty space on the kitchen counter. So, I almost never do. Enter this hummus, which requires no special equipment to make. It is the one I end up eating in front of the television several times a week, while avoiding eye contact with the cabinet that contains Sir Robot Coupe.

You just simmer the canned chickpeas with baking soda first to make them extremely soft and remove any "can" flavor. Whisking an ice cube into your dips is a classic Middle Eastern technique to give your dips some fluff. The ice cube helps incorporate air, giving you a lighter end result. Try it out the next time you whip up a batch of baba ghanouj or some French onion dip. If your food processor is more… accessible… then you can also use this same recipe for silky, smooth hummus.

INGREDIENTS:

- **1 (15.5-ounce) can chickpeas, drained**
- **½ teaspoon baking soda**
- **¼ cup freshly squeezed lemon juice (about 1 large lemon), plus more to taste**
- **¼ cup tahini**
- **3 tablespoons extra-virgin olive oil**
- **1 teaspoon Diamond Crystal kosher salt, plus more to taste** **(see page 16)**
- **1 garlic clove, grated**
- **1 ice cube**

For the Garnish

Extra-virgin olive oil
Hot paprika
Flaky salt

1. In a medium pot over medium-high heat, combine the **chickpeas, baking soda,** and 2 cups water. Bring to a simmer, then turn down the heat to maintain a simmer and cook for 20 minutes. After cooking, drain chickpeas well.

2. In a medium bowl, combine the **lemon juice, tahini, oil, salt,** and **garlic.** Add the chickpeas and **ice cube** to the bowl. Use a whisk to mix everything vigorously, until the chickpeas have broken down and the texture is mostly smooth with some small, coarse bits of chickpeas running throughout. Taste and adjust the seasoning with more salt and lemon juice as needed. Transfer to the fridge and wait until fully cooled before serving.

3. Garnish the hummus with a few glugs of **oil,** sprinkles of **hot paprika,** and some **flaky salt.**

Crunchy Greeny-Beany Fritters

Move aside, falafel.

MAKES 20 TO 25 FRITTERS

The green chickpea fritters known as falafel have been embraced by vegetarians and nonvegetarians worldwide. The (let's be honest, superior*) Egyptian version, ta'ameya, is much less known. They share many similarities but have two main differences: ta'ameya is made with fava beans instead of chickpeas and is often rolled in cracked coriander and sesame seeds before frying. The pops produced by the crust are my favorite part; they add another depth of crunch and an incredible amount of flavor.*

If you can find dried fava beans, follow this method to make a more authentic version; just be sure to soak your beans for twenty-four hours before processing. I usually make my fritters with white navy beans because they soak quickly and are easy to find. Their neutral flavor also really lets the other elements shine. You can use this recipe as a template for any bean fritter; if the dried beans are sufficiently soaked so they are tender enough to be broken down into a paste, they will work! I like eating these as a quick snack or in a pita with tahini and a salad accompaniment for a meal.

INGREDIENTS:

- **8 ounces dried white navy beans (or any dried beans)**
- **Kosher salt**
- **1 (2-ounce) bunch of cilantro**
- **1 (2-ounce) bunch of parsley**
- **¼ cup extra-virgin olive oil**
- **1 bunch of scallions (white and green parts), coarsely chopped**
- **8 garlic cloves**
- **1 small bunch of mint, leaves picked**
- **2 tablespoons ground coriander**
- **2 teaspoons ground cumin**
- **1 teaspoon chili powder**
- **1 teaspoon baking soda**
- **2½ tablespoons coriander seeds**
- **⅓ cup white sesame seeds**
- **Neutral oil, for frying**

1. Place the **beans** in enough cold water to cover them by 2 inches, add a large pinch of **salt,** and soak for at least 12 hours and up to 48 hours in the fridge.

2. Line a sheet pan with parchment paper. Line a plate with paper towels.

3. Thoroughly drain the beans, discard any liquid, and pat the beans dry with a paper towel.

4. Trim 3 inches of stems from the **cilantro** and **parsley** and discard. Coarsely chop the remaining leaves and stems.

5. In the bowl of a food processor, add the soaked beans, **olive oil, scallions, garlic, cilantro, parsley, mint, coriander, cumin,** 1 teaspoon **salt, chili powder,** and **baking soda.** Process the mixture until it becomes a homogeneous green paste with no discernible bits, scraping down the sides with a rubber spatula if needed.

6. In a spice grinder, add the **coriander seeds** and pulse once or twice to crack them. You are not looking for a fine powder; some whole seeds are also okay. Mix them with the **sesame seeds** in a shallow bowl and set aside.

7. Divide the bean mixture into 2-tablespoon portions and roll each portion into a ball. Pat them each into a disk. Dip the flat sides of the fritter into the sesame seed mixture and re-form them into disks with your hands if they get deformed. Lay them on the prepared sheet pan until ready to fry.

8. Heat about ½ inch of **neutral oil** in a medium skillet over medium heat until it reaches between 325°F and 350°F on an instant-read thermometer. In batches, fry the fritters until they are deep brown and crisp on one side, 2 to 3 minutes. Flip them and continue to fry until the other side is a deep golden brown, another 2 minutes. Transfer to the prepared plate and immediately season with salt.

SHRIMP TOAST
p. 90

ZA'ATAR AND LABNEH CRESCENT ROLLS
p. 92

Shrimp Toast

With the soul of lahm bi ajeen

SERVES 6 TO 8

My first real job was as an English as a Second Language teacher in Doha, while I was studying to be a chemical engineer. At first, I taught the ABCs to a bunch of kids a few times a week, but soon, I spent eight hours a day instructing corporate classrooms on meeting vocabulary and how to order a pizza.

All day long a Lebanese coffee shop in the lobby of that gig served lahm bi ajeen, a flatbread baked with a thin layer of tomatoey spiced ground meat spread thinly on top. It was perfectly seasoned, with the crisp edge along the perimeter that I craved. They didn't have an oven or a kitchen, but somehow it was always fresh. I don't know how they did it.

This shrimp toast—a kind of shrimp "sausage" smeared onto bread and then pan-fried crisp—is an ode to the snack that kept me going through those bizarre workdays. It comes together quickly and captures many of the same flavors found in a classic lahm bi ajeen: a hint of tomato, a touch of warm spices, and pops of bright parsley and lemon all surrounded by a crispy perimeter. Delicate shrimp are the perfect canvas to let the warm spices and bright pomegranate molasses shine, whether or not you're expected back upstairs in ten minutes to explain the concept of "circling back" to many bored adults.

INGREDIENTS:

For Dry-Brining the Shrimp

- **1 pound shrimp (any size), peeled and deveined**
- **1 teaspoon Diamond Crystal kosher salt** **(see page 16)**

For the Shrimp Paste

- **3 tablespoons extra-virgin olive oil**
- **2 tablespoons tomato paste**
- **1 small yellow onion, diced**
- **3 garlic cloves, thinly sliced**
- **1 teaspoon hot paprika**
- **½ teaspoon ground cinnamon**
- **½ teaspoon ground allspice**
- **1 teaspoon Diamond Crystal kosher salt**
- **1 egg white**
- **1 tablespoon cornstarch**
- **¼ cup coarsely chopped parsley**
- **1 tablespoon pomegranate molasses**

For Assembling and Frying

- **Neutral oil**
- **6 to 8 slices of white bread**
- **Kosher salt**

For the Garnish

- **1 lemon, cut into wedges**
- **1 small yellow onion, diced**
- **½ cup coarsely chopped parsley**
- **Pomegranate molasses**

1. ***To dry-brine the shrimp:*** In a medium bowl, toss the **shrimp** with the **salt** and let sit for at least 10 minutes.

2. ***To make the shrimp paste:*** In a small nonreactive skillet over medium heat, warm the **olive oil** until shimmering. Add the **tomato paste** and cook, stirring frequently, until the color deepens and it no longer smells metallic, about 3 minutes. Add the **onion** and **garlic** and cook until slightly softened and fragrant, 3 more minutes. Add the **paprika, cinnamon, allspice,** and **salt** and stir to combine. Cook until the spices are fragrant, about 1 minute. Turn off the heat and set aside.

3. In the bowl of a food processor, add three-quarters of the shrimp, the onion mixture, **egg white,** and **cornstarch.** Process until a smooth paste forms, scraping down the sides with a rubber spatula if needed. Transfer to a medium bowl.

4. Coarsely chop the remaining shrimp and fold into the shrimp paste, along with the **parsley** and **pomegranate molasses.**

5. ***For assembling and frying:*** Line a wire rack with paper towels.

6. Heat about ½ inch of **neutral oil** in a medium skillet over medium heat until the oil reaches between 325°F and 350°F on an instant-read thermometer—no hotter.

7. Using a butter knife or offset spatula, evenly spread ½ cup of the shrimp mixture onto each slice of **bread,** making sure to go all the way to the edge. Use more shrimp paste if needed to get an even ¼- to ½-inch-thick layer.

8. Fry the toasts a few at a time, shrimp-side down, until the shrimp are puffed and golden-brown, 1 to 2 minutes. Flip the bread over and fry until golden-brown and crisp all the way through, 3 to 4 minutes. Transfer to the prepared rack, shrimp-side up, to drain. Lightly season both sides with salt. Repeat with the remaining bread.

9. Garnish the toasts with a squeeze of **lemon,** a sprinkle of **onion** and **parsley,** and a drizzle of **pomegranate molasses.**

Za'atar and Labneh Crescent Rolls

Pillsbury, beware.

MAKES 16 SMALL OR 8 LARGE CRESCENT ROLLS

Every grocery store in Doha sold "croissants" filled with za'atar and labneh in plastic clamshells. We always had them at home, and I liked warming them up and having them with… more labneh and za'atar. (I never said I was a minimalist.)

As I got older and became familiar with French croissants, I realized that my childhood "croissants" were closer to crescent rolls than the French version; that is, less flake, more… bread.

This recipe is my ideal version of the croissants from my memory. They're light, fluffy, and buttery throughout. I like to serve them warm with a side of labneh and za'atar; I also like to serve them with a heap of tempered salted butter, as if I were some sort of renaissance prince. For different crescent roll adventures, I've also switched out the filling for other combos like ranch powder and cream cheese or plain butter.

INGREDIENTS:

For the Croissants

- **2⅓ cups / 280g bread flour, plus more as needed**
- **½ cup / 120g whole milk, warm**
- **3 tablespoons / 52g warm water**
- **3 tablespoons / 33g sugar**
- **2 teaspoons / 6g instant yeast**
- **1½ teaspoons / 6g Diamond Crystal kosher salt (see page 16)**
- **1 large egg**
- **¼ cup unsalted butter, cut into tablespoon-sized chunks, room temperature**

- **½ cup labneh**
- **¼ cup za'atar**
- **Kosher salt**
- **1 large egg**
- **2 tablespoons whole milk**
- **¼ cup melted unsalted butter, for topping**
- **Flaky salt, for topping**

1. ***To make the "croissants":*** In the bowl of a stand mixer fitted with the dough hook, combine the **flour, milk, water, sugar, yeast, kosher salt,** and **egg** and knead on medium until the dough is homogeneous and a thick rope forms that slaps the side of the bowl, about 10 minutes. Stop the mixer every 2 minutes and use a rubber spatula to scrape down the bowl and hook to ensure everything gets mixed evenly. If, after 10 minutes, the dough still seems too wet, add another tablespoon of flour and mix again until the right texture is achieved. Do not add more than 2 tablespoons of flour.

2. Add the chunks of **butter** and mix on medium speed until fully incorporated and a small ball of dough can be stretched into a square with a thin film that doesn't break (aka the windowpane test), about 10 minutes more.

3. Remove the dough from the mixer bowl and use your hands to form a tight ball with a smooth surface. Place it in a lightly oiled bowl and cover tightly with plastic wrap. Do not use a towel. Let the dough proof in the fridge or in a very cold spot for 12 to 24 hours for maximum flavor, or you can put it in a warm place for 2 hours; it should double in size and feel firm.

4. Lightly flour a clean surface and place the dough on top. Flour the top of the dough. Using a rolling pin, roll the dough into a 13-inch disk. Using an offset spatula or butter knife, spread an even layer of the **labneh** across the surface and evenly scatter the **za'atar** on top. Season the surface with **kosher salt.**

5. Line a sheet pan with parchment paper.

6. Cut the dough into sixteen even slices (like a pizza) or into eight slices if you want bigger rolls. (Make sure to clean your knife with a warm dishcloth after each slice to prevent the dough from sticking to the knife.) Remove a triangle, pull it lightly to elongate it, and then roll it from the wider end to the skinny, pointed end to form a crescent roll. Transfer to the prepared pan and repeat until all the rolls are formed. Cover with a kitchen towel and let rise again until almost doubled in size and very poofy and jiggly, about 2 hours.

7. Toward the end of the rise, preheat the oven to 375°F.

8. In a small bowl, whisk the **egg** with the **milk** until no random bits of egg remain. Using a brush, brush each roll with the egg wash. Bake until fully golden brown and cooked through, 15 to 20 minutes. Remove the pan from the oven and immediately brush each roll with melted **butter** and top with some **flaky salt**.

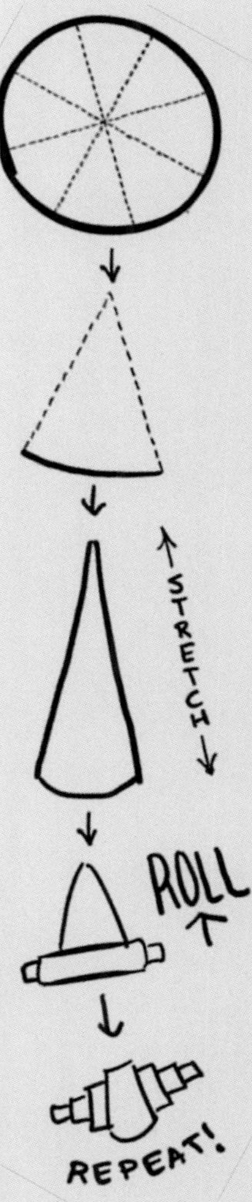

PS:
This rich bread dough can be turned into anything from pigs in a blanket to donuts to burger buns. All you need is to remember the bread mantra: proof, form, proof, bake. After making the dough, let it proof in a cold place overnight. Form it into the shape you desire, then let it proof again. Finally, after the second proof, it is ready to bake or fry!

Cheese Empanadas

Puffy, crispy, and cheesy

MAKES 6 EMPANADAS

My mom loved making empanadas. They were one of the few things she could make with local Doha ingredients that would taste like home. Whenever she fried up these light, flaky pastries filled with milky cheese, I knew it was because she felt homesick. In my Bolivian family, teatime was a big deal. Lunch was technically the main meal; everybody would come home from school or work to have a big meal together before continuing their day. But then, around five o'clock, they would break to have coffee and horneados, *which translates to "baked goods" but encompasses baked and fried snacks. We used to go to the local bakery and watch* pan de arroz, *fermented rice bread made of pounded rice and yuca then wrapped in blistered banana leaves, coming out of the hearth, along with lightly charred* sonzo, *yuca and cheese mash coming off the grill. Those things were harder for my mom to replicate back in Doha, but empanadas were always within reach. She still had to make some adjustments, though. She couldn't find lard, so she would make them with butter. And the key part to Bolivian cheese empanadas is the local cheese. Luckily, the readily available Palestinian cheese Akkawi was an almost perfect substitute and that's what I now use. Mozzarella makes a fine alternative if you don't have access to Akkawi.*

INGREDIENTS:

- **1½ cups / 190g all-purpose flour, plus more for dusting**
- **1 teaspoon / 3g Diamond Crystal kosher salt, plus more for seasoning (see page 16)**
- **⅛ teaspoon baking soda**
- **3 tablespoons / 40g lard or butter, room temperature**
- **½ cup / 120g hot water**
- **2 cups / 240g crumbled Akkawi or shredded mozzarella cheese**
- **Neutral oil, for frying**

1. In a medium bowl, combine the **flour, salt,** and **baking soda** and whisk for a full minute to ensure everything is fully combined.

2. Add the **lard** and rub it into the flour between your fingers until it feels evenly coated and there are no pebbles of lard. Add the hot water and combine using stiff, rigid fingers.

3. Transfer to a clean, lightly floured surface and knead until the dough is fully homogeneous and smooth, 3 to 5 minutes. Cover with a kitchen towel and let the dough rest for at least 20 minutes or wrap it well in plastic and let it rest overnight in the fridge. (Make sure the dough comes back to room temperature before rolling.)

4. Divide the dough into six portions (about 50g each). Form each portion into a ball. Cover with a kitchen towel and let the balls rest for 20 minutes. Roll the balls into thin 5½-inch rounds, using a lightly floured rolling pin. Fill the centers with ¼ cup (about 40g) of the cheese and fold over, forming half-moon shapes. Using a fork, crimp the edges to seal.

5. Line a plate with paper towels.

6. In a medium skillet over medium heat, add ½-inch of oil and heat until it reaches 325°F to 350°F on an instant-read thermometer. When you drop the empanada in the oil, the oil should bubble rapidly but should not be smoking. Fry the empanada until golden-brown on one side, about 3 minutes, then flip and fry the other side until puffed and golden-brown, another 3 minutes. Transfer to the prepared plate and season with salt. Repeat with the remaining empanadas. Serve hot.

PS:
Many bakeries in Santa Cruz dust their cheese empanadas with sugar for a little sweet and salty action.

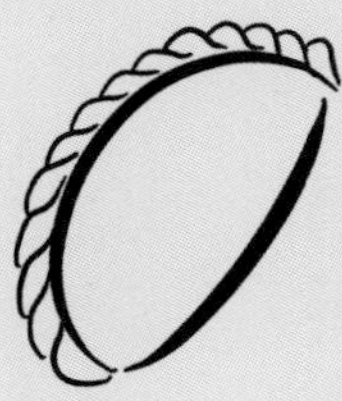

GARLIC BREAD CHEWY BUNS p. 98

CHEESE EMPANADAS p. 95

6
4
2

Garlic Bread Chewy Buns

Garlic bread with a mochi-esque chew

MAKES 6 TO 8 BUNS
Countries all over South America make chewy, cheesy bread made from tapioca starch. In Brazil, they call it pão de queijo*; in Colombia, it's* pandebono*; in Argentina, it is* chipas. *The Bolivian version I am most familiar with is called* cuñapes.

On trips to Santa Cruz, Bolivia, my grandfather would always bribe us to wake up at 6:00 a.m. with a thermos filled with café con leche, a plate of freshly cut ripe papaya, and a basket of steaming, just-baked cuñapes.

In this version, I take cuñapes on a field trip to my local pizzeria, seasoning the batter with a blend of garlic, oregano, and Parmesan, while keeping that characteristic moist, chewy center. Everything comes together in a blender, making it an easy bread to pull together as a quick snack, as a side to any weeknight plate of pasta, or at 6:00 a.m., if you need to cajole someone out of bed before they're ready, though I wouldn't know anything about that.

INGREDIENTS:

- **1 cup / 240g whole milk**
- **¼ cup / 55g unsalted butter**
- **1¾ cups / 210g tapioca starch (or tapioca flour—it's the same thing!)**
- **1 large egg**
- **1 garlic clove**
- **4¼ ounces / 120g Parmesan cheese, coarsely grated**
- **1½ teaspoons garlic powder**
- **1½ teaspoons dried parsley flakes**
- **1 teaspoon Diamond Crystal kosher salt** **(see page 16)**
- **1 teaspoon dried oregano**
- **½ teaspoon chili flakes**
- **Neutral oil, for greasing**

1. Preheat the oven to 400°F. Place a muffin pan in the oven as it preheats.

2. In a small saucepan over low heat, combine the **milk** and **butter** and warm until the butter has melted. Transfer to a blender and add the **tapioca starch, egg,** and **garlic.** Blend on high until a smooth batter forms, about 1 minute.

3. Add the **Parmesan, garlic powder, parsley flakes, salt, oregano,** and **chili flakes** and blend on low until the batter is well mixed and there are flecks of Parmesan and seasonings evenly speckling the batter, no more than 30 seconds.

4. Carefully remove the muffin pan from the oven and lightly grease six cups. Fill each one almost to the brim with the batter, adding more oil to additional divots as needed. You should have six to eight filled divots. Transfer the pan to the oven and bake until the buns are puffed and the tops are crackling with splotches of golden-brown, 30 to 35 minutes. Carefully remove the buns from the pan and transfer them to a rack to cool. They are best eaten the same day but freeze well (in a resealable freezer bag, they will keep for up to 3 months). To reheat, warm them in a 325°F oven until hot.

CHAPTER 3

Vegetables

Beet, don't kale my vibe

SPICY ROASTED POTATO
p. 141

GREEN BEANS BRAISED IN TOMATO
p. 119

ZUCCHINI POACHED IN YOGURT
p. 112

STEWED KALE WITH TOASTED GARLIC
p. 116

BROCCOLI AND CHAMOMILE SOUP
p. 120

KALE PESTO PASTA
p. 134

BAKED TOMATOES WITH HALLOUMI
p. 159

EGGPLANT AND TOFU RAGÙ
p. 130

SAUTÉED COLLARD GREENS
p. 145

TOMATO DRESSED IN TOMATO (ON TOAST)
p. 156

CARAMELIZED CAULIFLOWER PUREE
p. 124

GREEN BEANS WITH DILL BUTTER
p. 128

BREAD-AND-BUTTER PICKLED CAULIFLOWER
p. 123

ROASTED CAULIFLOWER WITH RAISIN-CAPER SAUCE
p. 127

CABBAGE, APPLE, AND FISH SAUCE SLAW
p. 155

WARM BUTTON MUSHROOMS AND RADISHES
p. 151

I HAVE SOME strong opinions on vegetables, probably because I come from a long line of vegetable despots. When my dad ran a grocery store, he would hand-pick seasonal produce from the vegetable aisle and bring some home every day. My sister and I would wait in the kitchen for his car to pull up and then help him carry warm bags that had been gently roasting in the desert sun from the trunk of his car. Depending on the time of year, there would be large peaches juicy with nectar, deeply red watermelon, or peppery rocket with its bite of fresh horseradish. As we helped put the produce away, he would tell us what he looked for in each piece. Melons, he instructed us firmly, should have a dry and wrinkly stem, be weighty, and have the faint aroma of sweet flowers. Cabbage should be dense, have a compact head, and be a vibrant green.

My mom often prepared peak vegetables very simply. When zucchini were at their best, she would just sauté them in garlic and olive oil. Hearty fresh spinach—the stuff that comes in a bunch encrusted in soil and is tied together by woven string, not the leaves from the plastic box that have been power-washed into oblivion—was stewed with toasted cumin and seared ground lamb and finished with parsley, finely grated raw garlic, and lemon. Even salads were simply dressed, using a drizzle of lemon juice and olive oil and a few pinches of salt and sumac instead of a more elaborate dressing.

I might have taken my dad's lessons on produce for gospel, had my Bolivian grandfather not also had his own lessons about produce. When I visited in the summers, he would occasionally wake me up at 5:30 to have a cup of coffee and a wedge of fresh papaya. He would then grab a tote bag made from weathered woven plastic and slowly walk the four blocks it took to get to the local mercado, with me holding his hand and then later, trailing behind. He had to get there right when it opened so he could have first pick from the vendors. He would get a warm loaf of crackly pan francés before heading over to the produce section, where he would look for a couple of crisp cucumbers and a perfectly ripe avocado. (The way to tell? The perfect amount of give when you squeeze it.)

He would then head back home to have his favorite breakfast, a sandwich of salted softened butter, ripe avocado, sliced cucumbers, and more hefty sprinkles of salt. ("Enough with the salt! You're going to KILL YOURSELF!" my grandmother would yell.) After breakfast, he would discuss lunch with her before heading back to the market to get produce for the rest of the day.

FARM
NORWICH MEADOWS FARM
CERTIFIED ORGANIC

We used to visit my grandparents every two years, and I never missed a trip to the market, starting from when I was a little Ham and had to grip his hand on the way to when I was a broody teen hiding behind my oversized Korn hoodie.

My grandfather was especially particular about picking plantains. Every day, before his afternoon siesta, he had a roasted plantain with a glass of cold milk for dessert after lunch (just like on page 254!). My grandfather insisted on having only the ripest plantains (fully blackened and gooey) for roasting, so he always had multiple stalks of plantains ripening so he would never be without the ideal roasting plantain.

Unsurprisingly, my wife, Sohla, and I have developed our own rituals around produce. We're fortunate to live within walking distance of New York City's Union Square Greenmarket and try to go there on market days. We wake up early, shackle the dogs, saddle up the baby, and walk over. We've developed a set of rules to get the most out of the market:

1. Don't be a produce hoarder. The real magic of a farmers' market is its freshness, so make sure to take advantage of that valuable quality. If you aren't preserving, only get enough for a few days.

2. Store the produce at room temperature if you can. When you get home, wash and dry all the produce, then put it on a lined tray on the kitchen counter (with the exception of salad greens and delicate herbs, which you should wrap in a paper towel and store in the fridge). This keeps the products front of mind, so you make sure to use them before they spoil. More importantly, there are so many nuances that get lost when exceptional produce goes in the fridge.

3. Reveal—don't conceal. Let the quality produce shine; don't do too much.

Obviously, getting your produce from the supermarket is fine, but don't fear the farmers' market. It's a good way to support your local farmers, reduce your carbon footprint, and get quality produce at the same time.

Over the years, I've discovered my favorite preparations that I keep returning to when specific produce is in season. I've compiled them in a chart (see page 106). I think of vegetables as either hearty (best cooked) or tender (best raw). There are some vegetables that are equally good both ways. Thinking of them in this way helps me organize myself, based on how much time I have to cook or on how much effort I'm willing to put in.

Pansies
$4 pack
2pack $7
Pansies
$5
2/$9

The Produce Chart

TENDER VEGETABLES

Tomatoes
Mix mayo with garlic powder, Knorr tomato bouillon powder, and smoked paprika. Spread the mayo on a plate. Slice tomatoes and season on both sides with salt. Place slices on top of mayo. Top with finely chopped parsley, olive oil, and chunks of good crusty bread fried in olive oil.

Lettuce
Separate heads of Little Gem lettuce into individual leaves. Wash and dry. Slice a ripe avocado into wedges and season with salt and lime. Make a pot of rice (see page 163). Crush some toasted peanuts and cut some cucumbers into spears. Make a lettuce cup with rice, ripe avocado, peanuts, cucumbers, and a dollop of chili crisp.

Cucumbers
Cut Persian cucumbers into rings and season with salt. Toss with lemon zest and juice, sumac, sliced olives, olive oil, and pieces of pita fried in olive oil. Serve with labneh on the side or a poached egg on top.

Celery
Peel and cut celery on a bias (aka diagonal slices). Toss with salt, lemon zest and juice, finely grated garlic, olive oil, toasted walnuts, finely chopped anchovies, cracked Castelvetrano olives, and freshly grated horseradish if you have it (finely grated Parm works, too).

VEG THAT GO BOTH WAYS

Cabbage
Thinly shave a head of cabbage (that's been cut in half and cored) on a mandoline. In a heavy-bottomed pot over medium-high heat, add some oil and half the shaved cabbage. Add a pinch of salt and cook until charred in spots. Add bone broth and bring to a simmer and reduce by half. Season with soy sauce and sesame oil. Add some cooked noodles and top with raw cabbage, cilantro, and thinly sliced scallions. Top with chili crisp if you're feeling it.

Summer Squash
Cut squash into rings. Add olive oil to a hot pan. Add thinly sliced garlic and cook until lightly golden brown. Add squash and cook until just tender. Season with salt and lemon juice. Toss basil leaves with the squash right before serving.

Corn
Cook corn in boiling salted water for 1 minute. Cut kernels off the cob and toss in salt, lime zest and juice, hot sauce, grated Cotija cheese, cilantro, and a dollop of mayo. Top with crushed corn nuts.

Spinach
Bring a pot of dashi or bone broth to a boil. Add spinach and kill the heat. Ladle into a bowl, add a poached egg, and top with furikake.

Snow Peas / Snap Peas
Cook peas in boiling salted water for 1 minute. Soak in cold, lightly salted water until cool. Drain. Slice peas very thinly lengthwise. Toss with the vegan nutritional yeast dressing on page 152, watercress, croutons, and Parmesan cheese.

HEARTY VEGETABLES

Potatoes

Simmer new potatoes in salted water until tender. Split in half while hot, immediately top with flaky salt, finely grated garlic, slabs of butter, and finely sliced chives or scallions.

Sweet Potatoes

Poke an Okinawan (or any other small sweet potato) with a fork all over, rub with oil, season with salt, wrap in aluminum foil, and bake in a 400°F oven until softened. Split in half, drizzle with molasses, toasted pecans, a pat of butter, and flaky salt.

Winter Squash

Split a honeynut squash in half, take out seeds with a spoon, and rub in neutral oil. Season cut side with salt, brown sugar, cinnamon, smoked paprika, cayenne, and cubes of butter. Roast in a 375°F oven until soft.

Parsnips

Peel parsnip and cut into rings. Add to a saucepan with a garlic clove and simmer in milk until tender. Strain, saving the milk, and season with salt and white pepper. Blend with a pat of butter and enough milk to make a smooth puree.

Brussels Sprouts

With a fine-tipped knife, cut the core out of the brussels sprouts and cut in half. Toss in olive oil and salt, place on a sheet pan cut-sides down and roast in a 450°F oven until tender and charred. Meanwhile, slice bacon into small chunks and cook on low heat until fat is rendered and bacon is crisp. Turn off the heat and add a couple of splashes of apple cider vinegar and a glug of maple syrup. Taste and adjust with more cider or maple as needed.

Toss the brussels sprouts in a bowl with sliced apples and the bacon dressing.

Beets

Toss beets with olive oil and salt and wrap in aluminum foil. Bake in a 375°F oven until softened, about 55 minutes. While warm, rub with a paper towel to remove skin. Cut into slices and toss with more olive oil, red wine vinegar, finely grated garlic, finely chopped parsley, and a dollop of sour cream or mayo.

Onions

Cut onions in half and put in a dish cut-side down. Cover halfway with bone broth and season with salt, black pepper, and small cubes of butter. Cover with foil and bake in a 400°F oven until tender. Top with finely grated Pecorino cheese and freshly cracked black pepper and serve with slices of crusty bread.

Carrots

Toss carrots in olive oil and salt. On a sheet pan lined with foil, broil the carrots, turning often, until charred all over and tender. Cut in half lengthwise and serve on top of yogurt seasoned with lemon zest, finely grated garlic, and finely chopped cilantro. Drizzle with some pomegranate molasses and extra-virgin olive oil.

Broccoli

Cut the head in half. Toss with olive oil and salt. Lay out on a sheet pan, cut-side down, and broil until the florets are charred and the stalks are tender. Toss with lemon juice, olive oil, sliced almonds, dried cranberries, thinly sliced Thai bird's-eye chili, and salt.

Mushrooms

Get a cast-iron skillet hot. Cut oyster mushroom clusters in half lengthwise. Toss with neutral oil and salt. Place cut-side down in skillet and place a weight on top. Cook until the cut side of mushrooms is deeply golden brown before turning and repeating until the other side is browned as well. If the skillet is too dry, add more oil. If the mushrooms start to get too dark before they are tender all the way through, add a splash of water. Toss mushrooms with finely grated garlic, finely chopped anchovy, finely chopped mint and parsley leaves, lemon zest, olive oil, and salt as needed.

Green Beans

Get a cast-iron skillet hot. Toss green beans with neutral oil and salt. Add to skillet and cook until tender and charred in spots. Transfer to a bowl and toss with crushed peanuts, fish sauce, lime juice, cilantro, and honey.

Cauliflower

Cut cauliflower into florets and fry in olive oil until golden-brown. Transfer to a bowl and season with lemon juice, minced Calabrian chilies, parsley, and Parmesan cheese.

Asparagus

Trim the woody parts of the asparagus. Add to a pan with a glug of water and a pinch of salt. Simmer, turning asparagus, until each stalk is tender. Turn off the heat and, while swirling the pan, add pats of butter until it emulsifies into the water and thickens. Transfer to a plate and top with lemon juice, minced chives, and a jammy egg.

Peppers

Roast Hatch or Cubanelle peppers over an open flame until charred all over. Transfer to a bowl and cover. Let steam for 20 minutes. Peel peppers, cut a slit, and remove the seeds and ribs. Stuff with grated mozzarella tossed with diced Calabrian chilies, diced pepperoni, garlic powder, and a pinch of salt. Drizzle olive oil and roast in a 400°F oven until the cheese is melted. Top with some toasted bread crumbs if you have them.

THE DRIED BEAN TECHNIQUE

1. Soak beans overnight in water with a pinch of salt.
2. Drain and place the beans in a pot with water, a pinch of salt, and a bay leaf.
3. Simmer until the beans are tender. Season with salt.
4. In a small pan, sauté finely chopped onion and garlic until golden-brown.
5. Season with ground cumin and smoked paprika, if you want, or season just with salt.
6. Kill the heat and add a ladleful of beans to the pan. Mash the beans into a sauce and add back to the whole beans. Stir to combine, taste, and adjust the seasoning as needed.

How to Salad

There is no wrong way to salad, but following a formula can turn your sad salad into a dream dinner.

Greens		Bonus Veggies / Protein		Crunchies and Chewies		Dressing
Iceberg	+	Jammy egg	+	Croutons	+	Surprise! The only dressing I use on a salad like this is a simple vinaigrette of olive oil and an acid like vinegar or lemon juice. I don't even premix it. I just toss my salad in salt, a drizzle of extra-virgin oil, and whatever acid I'm feeling. Taste and adjust the seasoning as needed. If I want a little more pucker and don't want to add more liquid acid, I throw in a sprinkle of sumac.
Romaine	+	Chicken of choice	+	Nuts	+	
Green/red leaf	+	Canned fish	+	Potato chips	+	
Little Gem	+	Beans	+	Pretzel sticks	+	
Endive	+	Cucumber	+	Dried fruit	+	
Radicchio	+	Tomato	+	Seeds	+	
Treviso	+	Radish	+	Cheese	+	
Arugula	+	Celery	+	Olives	+	
Frisée	+	Avocado	+	Rendered & crispy bacon bits	+	
Watercress	+	Tender herbs (such as cilantro, dill, or chives)	+	Corn nuts	+	
Spinach	+	Sliced apple/pear/jicama	+	Thinly sliced cured meat	+	
Kale *(massaged with salt)*	+	Cut citrus	+	Dates	+	

GREEN BEANS BRAISED IN TOMATO p. 119

ZUCCHINI POACHED IN YOGURT p. 112

ROASTED EGGPLANT WITH CHICKPEAS AND YOGURT
p. 115

STEWED KALE WITH TOASTED GARLIC
p. 116

Zucchini Poached in Yogurt

A different way to yogurt

SERVES 2–4

Yogurt is much more versatile than as just a component of a breakfast granola bowl. I grew up eating a lot of Lebanese home cooking at friends' houses and was blown away by all the different ways yogurt can be used in savory cooking. Hung and drained into luscious labneh, it's then rolled in spices and stored as shanklish. It's also turned into a brothy sauce for lamb-filled dumplings known as shish barak or for kibbeh. I liked that brothy yogurt sauce so much I started using it to poach everything from vegetables to fish. Zucchini takes especially well to this tangy, creamy sauce.

INGREDIENTS:

- **2 large zucchini (about 10 ounces each)**
- **Kosher salt**
- **2 tablespoons extra-virgin olive oil**
- **2 tablespoons cornstarch**
- **½ cup heavy cream or water**
- **2 cups whole milk plain yogurt**
- **2 tablespoons unsalted butter**
- **4 garlic cloves, minced**
- **1 tablespoon dried dill weed**
- **¼ cup fresh dill, coarsely chopped**

1. Trim and cut the **zucchini** into thirds, then in half lengthwise. Season the cut side with a pinch of **salt** and let sit for at least 10 minutes.

2. In a large Dutch oven over medium-high heat, add the **oil** and heat it until it shimmers. Pat the zucchini dry and cook it in an even layer (in two batches if needed), cut-sides down, until it's golden-brown, 5 to 8 minutes. Kill the heat and transfer the zucchini to a plate.

3. In a medium bowl, whisk the **cornstarch** into the **cream** until no flecks remain. Add the **yogurt** and whisk until fully incorporated.

4. In a large pot over medium heat, add the cream mixture and cook, whisking constantly, until the yogurt simmers and thickens, 6 to 8 minutes. Season the yogurt with a pinch of salt, turn down the heat to low, and add the zucchini, cut-side up. Cover and cook until the zucchini is tender but not mushy, 6 to 8 minutes, then transfer to a serving bowl.

5. While the zucchini cooks, in a small skillet over medium heat, add the **butter, garlic,** and a small pinch of **salt** and cook until the garlic starts to sizzle, is fragrant, and starts to turn golden-brown along the edges, 2 to 3 minutes. Add the **dill weed** and **fresh dill** and stir. Spoon the garlic mixture on top of the zucchini and serve immediately alongside some rice.

Roasted Eggplant with Chickpeas and Yogurt

The superior fattah

SERVES 4

Fattah, a bread based layered casserole found throughout the Middle East, is a celebration classic. This Palestinian inspired version is light, easy to assemble, and the most convincing way to get people to eat a bunch of eggplant that isn't called eggplant parm. The extra yogurt-tahini sauce makes an excellent spread for sandwiches or a dip for vegetables and pita crisps.

INGREDIENTS:

- **2 pitas (preferably the thin kind), cut into ¼-inch cubes**
- **½ cup extra-virgin olive oil, divided**
- **Kosher salt**
- **2 medium Italian eggplants, cut into ¼-inch slices**

For the Chickpeas

- **1 tablespoon extra-virgin olive oil**
- **1 garlic clove, minced**
- **½ teaspoon ground cumin**
- **1 teaspoon ground coriander**
- **1 (15.5-ounce) can chickpeas, drained and rinsed**
- **Kosher salt**

For the Sauce

- **1 cup whole milk plain yogurt**
- **¼ cup tahini**
- **¼ cup freshly squeezed lemon juice (about 1 large lemon), plus more to taste**
- **2 tablespoons extra-virgin olive oil**
- **1 garlic clove, finely grated**
- **Kosher salt**

For the Topping

- **2 tablespoons unsalted butter**
- **¼ cup slivered almonds**
- **¼ cup parsley leaves, coarsely chopped**

1. Arrange a rack in the center of the oven. Preheat to 325°F. Line a sheet pan with parchment paper.

2. Put the **pita cubes** on the prepared sheet pan and toss with ¼ cup of the **oil** and a large pinch of **salt.** Bake until golden-brown, dry, and crisp, 20 to 30 minutes. Remove the pan from the oven and transfer the pitas to a plate.

3. Increase the oven temperature to 450°F. Pop the **eggplant** in one even layer on the same baking sheet you cooked the pita on. Brush each eggplant slice on both sides with the remaining ¼ cup oil and season each slice with salt. Roast until golden-brown and tender, 25 to 35 minutes, flipping after 15 minutes. If the eggplant is not deeply golden brown, then turn the broiler on high and broil for about 5 minutes more.

4. In a medium pot over medium heat, add the **oil, garlic, cumin,** and **coriander** and cook, stirring constantly, until the garlic is fragrant, 1 to 2 minutes. Add the **chickpeas** and ¼ cup water and stir, then simmer until all the water has evaporated and the chickpeas start to sizzle, about 6 minutes. Season with salt to taste. Remove the pot from the heat.

5. In a medium bowl, add the **yogurt, tahini, lemon juice, oil,** and **garlic.** Season with a large pinch of **salt** and whisk until everything is homogeneous. Taste and adjust the seasoning with more salt and lemon juice as needed. If it is too thick, adjust by adding water; it should be thick but still pour in a constant stream and not glop.

6. In a small pan over medium heat, add the **butter** and melt until foaming. Add the **almonds** and stir until lightly toasted, 2 to 3 minutes. Add the **parsley**, kill the heat, and toss to combine.

7. On a serving platter, spread a layer of the eggplant, top with the chickpeas, and if there is any leftover eggplant, pop it on top, too. Spread the pita chips on top. Drizzle on the sauce and spoon the almond mixture over the sauce, serving any extra sauce on the side. Serve immediately.

Stewed Kale with Toasted Garlic

Molokhia without the molokhia

MAKES A LITTLE MORE THAN 1 QUART

Molokhia was one of the first Egyptian dishes my mom learned to make. It is my dad's and many other Egyptians' favorite dish. Molokhia, *or "jute mallow," is both the name of the green and the dish of finely chopped greens, simmered in broth and seasoned with toasted garlic and coriander. Molokhia thickens stews similarly to okra; the slime is what gives molokhia its charm. There are variations of this dish throughout the Middle East: In the Levan, it is made with larger pieces of leaves, but in Egypt, the leaves are finely chopped to enhance the natural okra-esque slime. It is often eaten with poached chicken, but my favorite version is one made with the rabbits my grandmother reared on the roof of her clay house. Aside from a very small window in the summertime, fresh molokhia is nearly impossible to find in New York City. While not as thick, using the same technique on a hearty green like kale makes a silky stew with many of the same flavors and none of the slime.*

INGREDIENTS:

- **2** **bunches of lacinato kale (about 1½ pounds), stripped from the stems**
- **¼** **cup unsalted butter**
- **1** **small yellow onion, minced**
- **8** **garlic cloves, minced**
- **Kosher salt**
- **1** **tablespoon ground coriander**
- **1** **teaspoon ground cumin**
- **½** **teaspoon chili powder (cayenne or Kashmiri)**
- **4** **cups chicken bone broth**
- **White rice or pitas, for serving**

1. Use a knife or a food processor to *very* finely mince the **kale leaves** until there are no large chunks; they should resemble that finely chopped curly parsley you used to find around the rims of plates in restaurants in the nineties.

2. In a medium saucepan over medium-high heat, add the **butter, onion, garlic,** and a pinch of **salt.** Cook until the onions soften and brown along the edges, about 5 minutes. Add the **coriander, cumin,** and **chili powder** and cook until fragrant, about 1 minute more. Add the chopped kale and another pinch of salt and stir to combine.

3. Add the **bone broth** and bring it to a simmer. Once simmering, turn the heat down to medium-low, cover, and cook until the kale is silky and the flavors meld, 50 to 55 minutes. Taste the soup and adjust the seasoning with salt as needed. Serve ladled on top of **white rice** or alongside warm **pitas.**

PS:
Traditionally, the garlic and spices are fried in a separate pan, then poured on top of the stew at the end, right before serving. You can do that for a more pronounced flavor, but I usually prefer to wash one less pan.

Green Beans Braised in Tomato

Soft beans deserve love, too.

SERVES 2

My favorite way to have green beans is how my Tante Hosna makes them. She braises them in large aluminum pots for hours in a delicately spiced tomato sauce that bubbles under a thin layer of glistening olive oil. When they are in season in the summertime, I always use Romano or fresh pole beans from Norwich Meadows Farm. Those beans turn impossibly silky and luscious when braised. During the hot season, try to find great string beans near you, but this dish will be delicious even if you're using winter grocery store beans. If you have any leftovers in the fridge, don't bother heating them. Serve them cold alongside a dollop of labneh and some warm pitas.

INGREDIENTS:

- **1 large ripe tomato**
- **¼ cup extra-virgin olive oil, plus more for drizzling**
- **1 medium yellow onion, minced**
- **5 garlic cloves, smashed**
- **Kosher salt**
- **2 tablespoons tomato paste**
- **2 teaspoons ground coriander**
- **1 teaspoon ground cumin**
- **½ teaspoon hot paprika**
- **½ teaspoon ground cinnamon**
- **8 ounces green beans, tops and bottoms trimmed**
- **1½ cups chicken bone broth**
- **1 bay leaf**
- **½ cup parsley leaves and tender stems, coarsely chopped**

1. Trim a thin slice off the bottom of the **tomato,** revealing the flesh. Grate the cut side of the tomato into a bowl using the large holes of a box grater. The pulp will fall into the bowl, leaving you with a handful of skin. Discard the skin and save the pulp.

2. In a medium pot over medium heat, add the **oil** and heat until it is very lightly smoking. Add the **onion, garlic,** and a pinch of **salt** and cook, stirring frequently, until the onion has softened slightly and is turning brown along the edges, about 5 minutes. Add the **tomato paste** and cook, stirring constantly, until the color deepens and it smells less like a can and more like roasted tomato, 3 to 5 more minutes. Add the **coriander, cumin, paprika,** and **cinnamon** and cook until fragrant, about 1 minute. Add the tomato pulp and **green beans** and stir to coat, then add the **bone broth, bay leaf,** and a large pinch of salt. Turn the heat to medium-high. When the liquid comes to a simmer, turn down the heat to medium-low and cover. Cook until the beans are fully tender, stirring occasionally, and the sauce has thickened, 40 to 45 minutes. Stir parsley into the beans and drizzle with oil. Serve with rice or bread.

Broccoli and Chamomile Soup

A different vehicle for eating cheese

SERVES 2

Tea is a very underrated cooking liquid. People will talk your ear off about how great bone broth is (I am "people") but will neglect to mention tea, which is versatile and affordable. I like pairing chamomile with green vegetables; the light floral tones really play off the deep vegetal notes that those vegetables bring. Chamomile is delicate enough not to overpower a dish, while still imparting some astringency. Use tea anywhere you would use a vegetable broth or a light chicken stock (other more intense teas, like Assam or hojicha, can also pack a robust punch); just make sure it isn't a recipe that calls for a reduction. Reducing teas can turn your dish very bitter and give it a pucker that will instantly dry your mouth out. Try tea out the next time you boil a batch of potatoes or season tea with bay leaves, salt, and citrus peels to poach shrimp.

INGREDIENTS:

- **4 chamomile tea bags**
- **1 large head broccoli (about 18 ounces)**
- **2 tablespoons extra-virgin olive oil, plus more for serving**
- **2 garlic cloves**
- **Kosher salt**
- **½ cup grated Parmesan cheese**

1. In a medium pot over high heat, bring 2¼ cups water to a boil. Add the **tea bags,** turn off the heat, and cover with a tight-fitting lid. Let steep for 5 minutes, then remove the tea bags.

2. Cut the florets off the **broccoli,** coarsely chop, and set aside. Peel the tough skin from the stalks and dice into small cubes.

3. In a medium pot over medium heat, add 1 tablespoon of the **oil,** the **garlic,** a large pinch of **salt,** and the broccoli florets. Cook until the florets turn bright green, about 2 minutes. Add the chamomile tea and simmer until the florets have softened, 5 to 8 minutes.

4. Transfer the broccoli to a blender along with the chamomile tea and blend until smooth.

5. In the same medium pot over medium heat, add the remaining 1 tablespoon oil and the diced stalks. Season with a pinch of salt and cook, stirring occasionally, until the stalks are tender, about 5 minutes.

6. Add the blended soup to the stalks and cover.

7. In a small nonstick skillet over low heat, add ¼ cup of the **Parmesan.** Be sure to sprinkle it in one even layer. Cook until the cheese is lightly golden brown, 3 to 5 minutes. Flip the cooked cheese onto a paper towel and allow it to cool. Repeat with the remaining cheese.

8. Ladle the soup into bowls and top with a broken shard of crispy Parmesan; drizzle some oil on top and serve hot.

PS:
A poached egg on top takes this to another level.

Bread-and-Butter Pickled Cauliflower

It's kind of a big dill.

MAKES ABOUT 4 CUPS

The word on the street is that bread-and-butter pickles got their name during the Great Depression because of what they were used for: bread, butter, and pickle sandwiches. I don't know about you, but a good pickle sandwich is enough to put me in a great mood. I like the sweetness that a bread-and-butter pickle brings, with its gentle jabs of mustard seeds and peppercorns. I use this brine to bread-and-butter-ify any vegetable into a sandwich-ready pickle (or one you'll eat right out of the jar). You can use this method for any vegetable if you keep the following tip in mind: If it is a vegetable you enjoy eating raw (like cucumbers, tomatoes, or radishes), let the brine cool completely before pouring it on top of the vegetable. This method is called cold pickling (because the brine is… cold). If, like cauliflower, the vegetable is better off cooked, apply the hot pickling method used here. Hot brine helps soften a tough vegetable, while maintaining some crunch. Once you've eaten the pickles, the strained leftover brine makes a great marinade for fish, chicken, or pork.

INGREDIENTS:

- **½ head cauliflower, cut into ½-inch florets (about 3 cups)**
- **1 tablespoon Diamond Crystal kosher salt** **(see page 16)**

For the Brine

- **1¼ cups apple cider vinegar**
- **⅓ cup sugar**
- **2 tablespoons Diamond Crystal kosher salt**
- **½ teaspoon turmeric**
- **1 teaspoon coriander seeds**
- **1 teaspoon celery seeds**
- **1 teaspoon mustard seeds**
- **1 teaspoon black peppercorns**
- **2 garlic cloves, lightly smashed**
- **1 small yellow onion, sliced into ¼-inch slices**
- **1 bay leaf**
- **1 sprig of dill**

1. In a medium bowl, toss the **cauliflower** with the **salt** and let it sit for 15 minutes. Rinse under cold running water and drain well. Transfer to a heatproof container with a tight-fitting lid. While the cauliflower sits in salt, prepare the brine.

2. ***To make the brine:*** In a medium pot over medium-high heat, combine 2 cups water, the **vinegar, sugar, salt, turmeric, coriander seeds, celery seeds, mustard seeds, peppercorns, garlic, onion, bay leaf,** and **dill** and bring to a boil. Immediately pour the hot brine over the cauliflower and tightly cover it. Let it sit at room temperature for 1 hour before transferring it to the fridge. Let it sit overnight before using.

Caramelized Cauliflower Puree

I'm just a man, standing before a home cook, asking them to love cauliflower harder.

MAKES 3 CUPS

Only one vegetable can dominate the collective consciousness at a time. Kale had its moment (enter the kale Caesar), brussels sprouts (always with bacon) had their chance to shine, and cauliflower (especially roasted whole as a vegetarian alternative to a roast) was revered for a blip. Cabbage is the current champion, but I'm simply begging you to give cauliflower more time in the sun. It has a glorious crunch and soaks up flavors beautifully. It has the virtuousness of an Erewhon Market smoothie but the luxurious silkiness of the most extravagant mashed potato. When roasted, it holds on to deep, savory Maillard notes. By caramelizing and pureeing the cauliflower, you are left with an intensely buttery puree that goes well with all kinds of fish, pork, and poultry. My favorite garnishes for a hunk of roasted cauliflower are capers, lemon zest, and parsley, so I adopt those here to give it some zip.

INGREDIENTS:

- **3 tablespoons neutral oil**
- **1 head cauliflower, coarsely chopped**
- **Kosher salt**
- **⅔ cup whole milk**

For the Garnish

- **2 tablespoons capers**
- **2 tablespoons coarsely chopped parsley leaves and tender stems**
- **1 tablespoon extra-virgin olive oil**
- **Zest of 1 lemon**

1. In a medium pot over medium-high heat, add the **oil, cauliflower,** and a large pinch of **salt.** Stir frequently until the cauliflower is tender and deeply golden-brown, 15 to 18 minutes.

2. Add the **milk,** bring to a simmer, and season with another pinch of salt. Transfer to a blender and blend on high until smooth. Taste and adjust with more salt as needed. Transfer to a serving bowl.

3. Garnish with the **capers, parsley, oil,** and **lemon zest.** Serve hot.

Roasted Cauliflower with Raisin-Caper Sauce

An easy way to Jean-Georges

MAKES 1 CUP

I once worked at a restaurant that often paid homage to influential chefs: a lobster terrine for Marco Pierre White, eggs benedict for Wylie Dufresne, head cheese and lentils for Fergus Henderson. My favorite homage was a scallop and cauliflower taco, inspired by a timeless Jean-Georges Vongerichten dish. This recipe gets rid of my least favorite part of the dish, the scallops, and turns it into a roasted cauliflower extravaganza. The sauce is a luscious and briny raisin, caper, and butter emulsion and is the knockout part of the dish. It is great served alongside any seafood or deeply roasted brassicas like cabbage or broccoli.

INGREDIENTS:

- 1 **medium head cauliflower, halved**
- ¼ **cup extra-virgin olive oil**
- **Kosher salt**

For the Sauce

- 2 **ounces non-pareil capers (about ½ cup), drained**
- ½ **cup golden raisins**
- ¼ **cup unsalted butter, cut into tablespoon-sized chunks**
- 1 **tablespoon freshly squeezed lemon juice, plus more for seasoning**
- **Kosher salt, as needed**

For Topping

- ¼ **cup parsley leaves and tender stems, coarsely chopped**
- ¼ **cup toasted slivered almonds**
- 2 **tablespoons golden raisins**

1. Preheat the oven to 450°F. Line a sheet pan with parchment paper.

2. Lay the **cauliflower** cut-side down on the prepared pan. Using your hands, rub the **oil** evenly onto the cauliflower, getting it into the crevices and on the cut sides. Season all over with **salt.** Roast until charred along the outside and tender, 40 to 45 minutes. While the cauliflower roasts, prepare the sauce.

3. ***To make the sauce:*** In a small saucepan over medium heat, combine the **capers, raisins,** and ½ cup water and bring to a simmer. Cook until the **raisins** have softened and the water has reduced by half, about 5 minutes.

4. Transfer the mixture to a blender and blend on high until smooth; add 2 tablespoons water and the **butter** and continue blending until the butter has fully melted and blended into the sauce. Add the **lemon juice,** stir, and taste and adjust the seasoning with salt or more lemon juice as needed. If the sauce seems too thick, add splashes of water until it is thick but pourable.

5. Transfer the cauliflower to a serving plate, drizzle with the sauce, and top with the **parsley, toasted almonds,** and **raisins.** Serve with any extra sauce on the side for dipping.

Green Beans with Dill Butter

A simple recipe packed with lessons

SERVES 2 TO 3

Green beans tossed in butter may seem like a nonsense recipe at first glance. Still, if you look deeper, there are three separate lessons to learn here: how to make compound butter, how to steam vegetables, and how to emulsify butter and water to make a creamy, luxurious sauce.

Compound butter, a fancy term for butter with stuff mixed into it, is versatile and can be used to finish anything from steaks to grains to vegetables (not to mention it is great on a hot piece of toast) for a boost of flavor and richness. Here are the rules: (1) The flavoring needs to be ready to eat (yes to finely diced country ham; no to finely diced raw shrimp); (2) it needs to have a relatively low moisture content (yes to lemon zest; no to lemon juice); and (3) it needs to be cut small (finely mince everything). If you tightly wrap compound butter in plastic and transfer it to a resealable freezer bag, it can be stored in the freezer for months.

The method used here for cooking the green beans is how I steam most vegetables. It works especially well with quick-cooking vegetables like broccoli, peas, and greens because you are left with a flavorful liquid that is great for emulsifying butter.

I always add cold butter to hot liquid, because the melting allows a small amount of butter to be introduced at a time, increasing the emulsion success rate. It's the same thought process behind slowly drizzling in oil when making a mayonnaise.

INGREDIENTS:

5 tablespoons unsalted butter, room temperature
1/3 cup finely chopped dill
2 garlic cloves, finely grated
1/4 teaspoon chili flakes
Zest of 1 lemon
Kosher salt
1 pound green beans, tops and bottoms trimmed
Juice of 1 freshly squeezed lemon

1. In a medium bowl, mix the **butter, dill, garlic, chili flakes, lemon zest,** and a large pinch of **salt** until everything is evenly combined. Set aside.

2. In a large pot over medium-high heat, add 1 cup water and bring to a boil. Add the **green beans** and a large pinch of salt and cover. Cook the beans, stirring occasionally, until they are tender but still have a bite to them, 3 to 4 minutes.

3. Add the butter to the beans and stir to combine. Let the water and butter simmer until they emulsify into a creamy sauce, about 2 minutes. Season the beans with **lemon juice** to taste and serve immediately.

Eggplant and Tofu Ragù

Here I disrespect Italians yet again.

SERVES 4 TO 6

Eggplant doesn't get enough respect for its versatility. Sure, people will happily scarf down breaded and fried slabs of it without hesitation, but there is a texture of eggplant that is often overlooked: the braised eggplant. Braising finely chopped eggplant and tofu gives it a luscious, silky texture that complements the thick, chewy paccheri pasta I recommend you serve it with. Taken together, the dish is just as satisfying as, dare I say, a traditional Bolognese. This recipe makes a big batch, since you'll be eating leftovers of this anywhere you can fit it: with eggs, toast, rice, steamed greens, leftover cardboard. The flavors deepen even further as it cools, making it the perfect meal-prep pasta sauce. Keep a batch in your freezer for up to three months so you are never without this showstopping ragù. And if a nonna rolls through, just claim it's your riff on pasta alla norma to save face. What tofu?

INGREDIENTS:

- **1 pound firm tofu, drained and cut into 1-inch chunks**
- **1 pound eggplant (2 medium), cut into 1-inch chunks**
- **Kosher salt**
- **⅓ cup extra-virgin olive oil, plus more for drizzling**
- **1 large onion, diced**
- **8 garlic cloves**
- **2 tablespoons tomato paste**
- **1 teaspoon chili flakes**
- **1 cup sake or white wine**
- **2 cups chicken bone broth or water**
- **1 (28-ounce) can crushed tomatoes**
- **3 tablespoons white miso**
- **Freshly cracked black pepper**
- **1 pound paccheri, rigatoni, or any dried pasta of your choice**
- **½ cup parsley leaves and stems, coarsely chopped**
- **½ cup Parmesan cheese, grated, plus more for garnish**

1. Place the **tofu** in the bowl of a food processor and pulse until it has broken down into small chunks. (You could also crush it by hand if you prefer not to clean a food processor.)

2. Transfer the tofu to a large bowl and repeat the process to break down the **eggplant.**

3. Transfer the eggplant to the same bowl as the tofu, season with 2 tablespoons **salt,** and toss to combine. Let the mixture sit for 10 minutes before transferring to the center of a large kitchen towel. Bring the corners together and, over a sink, wring out as much moisture from the eggplant and tofu as possible, then return them to the bowl.

4. In a large pot over medium-high heat, add the **oil** and heat until shimmering. Add the tofu and eggplant mixture and cook, stirring frequently, until lightly browned, with bits of both beginning to stick to the pan, 12 to 15 minutes.

5. Add the **onion, garlic, tomato paste,** and **chili flakes** and sauté, stirring frequently, until the tomato paste deepens in color and the onion is fragrant and has softened, about 5 minutes.

6. Add the **sake** and scrape up any bits stuck to the bottom of the pot using a wooden spoon or firm spatula. Simmer, stirring frequently, until the sake has fully reduced and the mixture seems dry, about 5 minutes.

7. Add the **bone broth** and **tomatoes** and simmer, uncovered, for 15 minutes to allow the flavors to meld. Add the **miso** and stir until fully melted into the sauce. Taste and adjust the seasoning with more salt and **black pepper.**

8. While the ragù cooks, cook the **pasta** for 1 minute less than the instructions on the package. To test for doneness, cut a noodle in half: You are looking for a very thin ring of white in the center, as though just the very core is undercooked. Reserve 1 cup of the pasta water before draining.

9. Add the **parsley** to the ragù, taste again, and adjust the seasoning as needed with more salt and black pepper.

10. In the pot the pasta was cooked in, over medium-high heat, return the drained pasta and the reserved pasta water. Add as much ragù as you'd like once the water has begun to simmer. Simmer until the sauce is thickened and coats the pasta, about 2 minutes. Add the **Parmesan** and stir vigorously, until it melts into the sauce and becomes glossy.

11. To serve, divide the pasta into bowls and top with a generous oil drizzle and a final Parmesan flurry.

Kale Pesto Pasta

Please, don't use jarred pesto.

MAKES ABOUT 7 CUPS

Like George Costanza, it took me a long time to get pesto. It wasn't until I started making it at home out of anything but basil that I learned to love it. I like the coarser texture of pesto made with a heartier green like kale. Unfortunately, this usually means you need to steam the green to soften it enough to blend. If you are using a tender herb, like the traditional basil, the leaves are tender enough that no cooking is necessary. Using frozen kale is how I skip the need to blanch; freezing and thawing soften the once-leathery leaves. If you must use fresh kale, steam (or microwave!) it until it wilts, transfer it to the fridge to cool, then proceed with the recipe. You can swap out the greens and nuts for any other combo. Mustard greens and hazelnuts make for a great pesto alongside some seared pork chops, and a parsley, tarragon, and almond one is delicious when folded into a chicken salad.

INGREDIENTS:

- **Kosher salt**
- **1 pound gemelli pasta or any dried pasta of your choice**
- **1 (10-ounce) package frozen kale, thawed**
- **¾ cup Parmesan cheese, grated, plus more for topping**
- **5 garlic cloves**
- **½ cup shelled, roasted, salted pistachios**
- **½ cup extra-virgin olive oil, plus more for drizzling**
- **1 teaspoon chili flakes**
- **Zest of 1 lemon**

1. Bring a medium pot of water to a boil. Season it like a slightly salty soup. Cook the **pasta** 1 minute less than the instructions on the package. To test for doneness, cut a noodle in half: You are looking for a very thin ring of white in the center, as though just the very core is undercooked. Reserve 1 cup of the pasta water before draining.

2. Meanwhile, place the **kale, Parmesan, garlic, pistachios, oil, chili flakes,** and **lemon zest** in a food processor and blitz until the kale is fully broken down into a paste, scraping down the sides with a rubber spatula if needed. Taste the pesto and adjust with salt as needed.

3. In the pot the pasta was cooked in, over medium-high heat, return the drained pasta and the reserved pasta water. Once the water has begun to simmer, add the pesto and stir vigorously to combine. Simmer until the sauce thickens and coats the pasta, about 2 minutes.

4. To serve, divide the pasta into bowls and top with a generous oil drizzle and a Parmesan sprinkle.

Zucchini Ribbons and Feta

Just call it the Juicy Couture salad.

MAKES 7 CUPS

Like Korean wings executed perfectly—which stay shatteringly crisp despite being glazed in sauce—there's something extremely satisfying about a salad that is both crisp and juicy. This is that salad. Asian pears maintain their crispness in most situations, and their subdued sweetness makes them a perfect candidate for salad additions. Salting the thin slices of zucchini ahead of time turns them from stiff to tender. Slicing vegetables thinly and tossing them with salt can make many tough vegetables palatable to eat raw. Try thinly slicing anything from brussels sprouts to butternut squash and tossing them in salt to turn them into new salad elements: crisp, yet so very juicy.

INGREDIENTS:

- **2 large zucchini (about 20 ounces)**
- **⅓ cup dried cranberries**
- **1 teaspoon Diamond Crystal kosher salt (see page 16), plus more as needed**
- **1 Asian pear, cut into ¼-inch matchsticks**
- **3 ounces feta cheese, crumbled**
- **1 small bunch of mint, leaves picked and roughly torn**
- **¼ cup freshly squeezecd lemon juice (about 1 large lemon), plus more as needed**
- **2 tablespoons extra-virgin olive oil**

1. Trim the tops and bottoms of the **zucchini.** Use a peeler to peel the zucchini into strips lengthwise, turning it around with each slice to whittle it down evenly. Stop when you get to the seeds and discard the remaining cores.

2. In a medium bowl, combine the zucchini ribbons with the **dried cranberries** and toss with the **salt.** Let sit for 10 minutes.

3. Add the **pear, feta, mint,** and **lemon juice** to the zucchini. Toss to combine. Taste and adjust the seasoning with more salt and lemon juice as needed.

4. Transfer to a serving bowl and drizzle with the **oil**—the juicier, the better.

Labneh Mashed Potatoes

One-pot mash

MAKES 3 CUPS

This is the fastest, most efficient way to get a pot of mashed potatoes on the table. Whenever my wife, Sohla, feels a little blah, the only thing that will make her feel better is a bowl of mashed potatoes and gravy. I always make sure I have gravy in the freezer, and I perfected this one-pot mash to go from raw potato to a bowl in Sohla's hands as quickly as possible. The labneh adds a little tang, but if you are looking for something more buttery, double the amount of butter and swap out the labneh for hot heavy cream.

INGREDIENTS:

- **1½ pounds Yukon gold potatoes, cut into ¼-inch cubes**
- **1½ cups whole milk**
- **Kosher salt**
- **3 tablespoons cold unsalted butter, cut into tablespoon-sized chunks**
- **⅓ cup labneh**

1. In a medium pot over medium-high heat, combine the **potatoes** and **milk.** Season with a large pinch of **salt.** Bring to a simmer, then turn down the heat to low. Cook the potatoes, stirring frequently, until they are fall-apart tender, 13 to 15 minutes.

2. Once the potatoes are tender, turn off the heat and go to town on them with a masher or whisk until they are fully mashed. Turn the heat to low and mix in the cold **butter** and **labneh.** Keep stirring until the butter has fully melted into the potatoes. Taste and adjust the seasoning with more salt as needed. Serve immediately.

Spicy Roasted Potato

A spicy gratin without the dairy

SERVES 4 TO 6

My Aunt Hosna used to make giant trays of shingled sliced potatoes, slathered in a fiery tomato sauce. The edges would lightly char and get crisp, and the insides would be fluffy and soft. This dish is inspired by those memories, but I turn up the heat even further. The Korean chili paste gochujang adds more depth and earthiness to the tomato liquid, but you can skip it if you don't have any around. I don't usually like cold potatoes unless they're in salad form, but a slab of this cold in a warm pita with a swipe of mayo is the ultimate carb-on-carb midnight snack.

INGREDIENTS:

- **1 cup chicken bone broth**
- **¼ cup sliced jarred hot cherry peppers, plus 1 tablespoon cherry pepper liquid**
- **2 tablespoons gochujang**
- **2 tablespoons tomato paste**
- **1 teaspoon ground cumin**
- **1 teaspoon ground coriander**
- **8 garlic cloves**
- **2 tablespoons extra-virgin olive oil, plus more for drizzling**
- **4 medium russet potatoes, cut into ¼-inch-thick slices**
- **1 large yellow onion, halved and cut into ¼-inch-thick slices**
- **Kosher salt**
- **Flaky salt, for topping**
- **½ cup coarsely chopped parsley leaves and tender stems, for topping**

1. In a blender, combine the **bone broth, cherry peppers** and liquid, **gochujang, tomato paste, cumin, coriander**, and **garlic** and blend on high speed until smooth.

2. Add the **oil** to a 10-inch cast-iron or oven-safe skillet and swirl to coat.

3. Preheat the oven to 450°F.

4. Layer the **potatoes** and **onion** in the skillet, alternating between potato and onion, drizzling with oil and seasoning each layer with a pinch of kosher salt. Pour the blended liquid on top. Drizzle more oil on top and cover tightly with a layer of aluminum foil.

5. Bake until the potatoes are tender when poked with a skewerlike object, about 1 hour. Uncover and broil on the middle shelf until charred in spots, 13 to 16 minutes. Remove the skillet from the oven and let rest for 5 to 10 minutes before drizzling with oil and sprinkling **flaky salt** and **parsley** on top. Serve hot, room temperature, or cold.

Boiled Potatoes with Green Cream

Boiled potatoes are all that and a bag of chips.

SERVES 4

Boiled potatoes are criminally underrated. In Bolivia, boiled potatoes are a common side to many braises and stews. Like plain white rice, boiled potatoes are excellent vehicles to transport an intensely flavored sauce… straight to your mouth. When freshly dug potatoes are in season, I always snap up the smaller-sized ones to boil until meltingly tender, crack them open while still steaming hot, and fill them with a slice of salted butter. I make this roasted pepper cream when I feel like doing a little more work. (It also makes for a great dip for potato chips.) The avocado may seem like overkill, but it brings another layer of richness to the party, and the potatoes can take it.

INGREDIENTS:

- **1½ pounds miniature Yukon gold potatoes (aka creamer potatoes)**
- **Kosher salt**
- **1 poblano pepper**
- **2 jalapeño peppers**
- **½ cup sour cream**
- **2 garlic cloves**
- **Juice of 1 freshly squeezed lemon, plus more as needed**
- **½ cup parsley leaves, coarsely chopped**
- **1 avocado, pitted and flesh removed, diced into ¼-inch cubes**

1. In a medium pot over medium-high heat, add the **potatoes** and cover with cold water by ½ inch. Add a giant sprinkle of **salt** and cook until the potatoes are fully tender, 35 to 40 minutes. Pierce the largest potato with a skewer or something skewer-esque to check doneness; it should go in and out without much resistance and not feel crunchy. Drain the potatoes, crack them open with a knife when cool enough to handle, season the opening with salt, and transfer them to a serving bowl.

2. While the potatoes cook, turn one burner on medium-high (this only works with a gas stove, not induction; see Note). Place the **poblano** and **jalapeños** over the flame, resting on the stovetop grates, and cook, rotating as one side chars, until all sides are blackened, 6 to 8 minutes. (Use tongs or tweezers to avoid burning your fingers.) Immediately transfer the peppers to a sealable bag and seal tightly (or a bowl wrapped in plastic wrap). Let sit and steam for about 10 minutes. After 10 minutes, use your finger to scrape off the skin. Cut the peppers open and remove all the seeds with a knife or spoon. Transfer what's left of the peppers to a blender.

3. To the blender, add the **sour cream, garlic, lemon juice,** and a large pinch of salt. Blend on high until smooth. Taste and adjust the seasoning with more salt and lemon juice as needed.

4. Spoon some pepper cream on top of the potatoes. Season the avocado with salt and a hit of lemon juice. Garnish with the **parsley leaves** and **avocado.** Serve with any remaining pepper cream on the side.

Note:
If you are without a gas stove, hit the peppers under your broiler, turning them as one side blackens, until they are charred all over, then proceed with popping them into a bag.

Sautéed Collard Greens

A nod to couve

MAKES ABOUT 2 CUPS

Feijoada, the rich Brazilian stew of black beans and porky bits, has started to gain some notoriety through cooking competitions, where people get sent home for making it poorly (like that one person who ladled meatless, unseasoned beans over blown-out rice). I love a pot of porky beans, but my favorite part of a feijoada is the sides. I'm crazy! Feijoada is often flanked by garlicky sautéed collard greens called couve, orange slices, white rice, and a toasted tapioca crumb called farofa. Farofa is easily one of my favorite side dishes of all time. The satisfyingly crunchy toasted tapioca flour is often seasoned with some combination of smoky bacon, garlic, scrambled egg, banana, or plantain. Farofa is also a common side dish at Brazilian grill sessions. As a kid, I would go nuts over farofa, liberally showering it over any pile of beans, rice, or meat I ate. Everything became a vehicle for farofa. Alas, the right tapioca flour is tough to find, so I cook fine bread crumbs to achieve a similar texture. This dish reminds me of my favorite feijoada-sides combo, a plate of couve showered in an irresponsible amount of farofa.

INGREDIENTS:

For the Bread Crumbs

- **4 slices of thick-cut bacon, cut into ¼-inch strips**
- **1 tablespoon unsalted butter**
- **½ cup plain bread crumbs**
- **1 garlic clove, finely grated**
- **¼ cup parsley leaves, coarsely chopped**
- **Kosher salt**

- **2 bunches of collard greens, stripped from the stems**
- **2 tablespoons neutral oil**
- **4 garlic cloves, thinly sliced**
- **Kosher salt**

1. ***To make the bread crumbs:*** Line a plate with paper towels.

2. In a medium skillet over medium heat, add the **bacon** and ½ cup water. Cook, stirring frequently, until the bacon has rendered its fat and is crisp, 8 to 10 minutes. Using a slotted spoon, remove the bacon from the pan and transfer it to the prepared plate. Add the **butter, bread crumbs,** and **garlic** to the bacon fat. Cook, stirring frequently, until the bread crumbs are crisp and light golden brown, 6 to 8 minutes. Kill the heat, add the bacon back into the bread crumbs along with the **parsley,** and stir to combine.

3. Line the plate with fresh paper towels. Transfer the bacon and bread crumb mixture to the prepared plate. Taste for seasoning, adjust with **salt** as needed, and set aside.

4. Stack all the **collards** on top of each other and tightly roll them into a fat cigar. Slice the collard cigar very thinly, as if you were making confetti.

5. Place a large cast-iron pan or stainless steel skillet over medium-low heat until lightly smoking. Turn the heat to medium-high and add the **oil.** Swirl to coat. Add the **garlic** and cook until fragrant and lightly browned, 1 to 2 minutes.

6. Add the collard greens, season with a large pinch of **salt,** and cook, stirring constantly, until the greens are tender but still have a little bite and some have crisped and are lightly charred, 6 to 8 minutes. If the pan feels too hot and the greens or garlic start to burn, add ¼ cup water and simmer until the water evaporates.

7. Transfer to a serving bowl and top with a layer of the toasted bread crumbs. Serve any extra in a small bowl on the side.

Steamed Shiitakes with Ginger-Garlic-Scallion Sauce

A microwave recipe from a not-microwave guy

MAKES ABOUT 4 CUPS

David Chang, I'm not trying to encroach on your territory, but this is a microwave recipe. This is my one *and only microwave trick. Look, it's a great tool for steaming vegetables. If you toss vegetables with a splash of water in a sealed container, the microwave becomes a fast, easy way to steam. Just do it in bursts so you don't overcook them. My favorite vegetable to use for this technique is the mushroom, which is, in general, a very underrated steamed veggie. I love what steaming does to the texture of shiitakes, making them juicy and tender with a hint of chew. This recipe is a side dish, but it is also a deeply flavorful condiment for soups, noodles, and rice. It lasts in the refrigerator for five days, so I like to make a batch at the beginning of the week and dip into it whenever I eat something that needs a savory umami boost.*

INGREDIENTS:

- 1 **pound shiitake mushrooms, stems removed**
- 1 **bunch of scallions (green and white parts), thinly sliced**
- **2-inch piece of ginger, finely grated**
- 6 **garlic cloves, finely grated**
- 1 **Thai chili, thinly sliced**
- 3 **tablespoons soy sauce**
- 1 **tablespoon white miso**
- 1 **tablespoon sesame oil**
- 1 **tablespoon rice wine vinegar**
- ¼ **cup neutral oil**

1. Place the **shiitake caps** in a microwave-safe container that has a tight-fitting lid.

2. In a medium bowl, combine the **scallions, ginger, garlic, Thai chili, soy, miso, sesame oil,** and **vinegar.** Then, whisk until the miso is fully incorporated and no lumps remain. Add the neutral oil and whisk again.

3. Dump the sauce onto the shiitakes and cover with the lid, leaving one corner popped, as if it's winking at you (it is!). Microwave in 1-minute bursts until the shiitakes are fully tender, 5 to 6 minutes. Let rest with the lid closed for 5 minutes before serving.

PS:
If you want to make just the ginger-scallion sauce, you can microwave the sauce in 1-minute bursts until the scallions have wilted and the garlic is fragrant, about 3 minutes. Store in your fridge in a container with a tight lid for up to a week.

Warm Button Mushrooms and Radishes

Cute as a button . . . mushroom

SERVES 2 OR 3

I grew up eating canned mushrooms, since they were the most affordable and readily available option in Doha. On the most special of occasions—like birthdays, Christmas, or the infrequent but extremely thrilling 4.1 GPA report card days—my mom would splurge on a plastic container of button mushrooms. Button mushrooms may have fallen out of favor, especially when competing for your cart/heart with slender shiitakes, exotic oysters, or sexy trumpets. But let me vouch for my guys the buttons: They possess a deep umami flavor that rivals any other fancy fungi when cooked properly. I cook button mushrooms for a long time over medium heat because they have a lot of moisture in their fibers, so I cook them long enough to release all that liquid, let it evaporate, and then really brown them. I no longer get report cards, but I still like to blow up some balloons, light some sparklers, and celebrate a long weekend with these buttons.

INGREDIENTS:

- **1 cup ¼-inch cubes of quality crusty bread (the kind of bread you buy whole, not presliced)**
- **1 tablespoon extra-virgin olive oil**
- **Kosher salt**
- **Freshly cracked black pepper**
- **8 ounces button mushrooms (preferably petite)**
- **1 tablespoon neutral oil**
- **1 bunch of radishes**
- **½ cup sake or white wine**
- **3 garlic cloves, peeled**
- **1 cup chicken bone broth**
- **2 tablespoons unsalted butter**
- **Zest of 1 lemon**
- **1 bunch of chives, thinly sliced**

1. Preheat the oven to 325°F.

2. In a medium bowl, toss the **bread** with the **olive oil** and season with a pinch of **salt** and a few cracks of **black pepper.** Spread out the bread on a sheet pan and bake until dry and crisp, 15 to 20 minutes.

3. In a medium bowl, add the **mushrooms** and fill the bowl with cold water. Keep rinsing them until there are no bits of dirt stuck to them. Drain well. If the mushrooms are larger than the radishes, cut each one in half.

4. In a medium pot over medium heat, add the mushrooms, **neutral oil,** and a large pinch of salt. Cook, stirring occasionally, until the mushrooms are deeply browned and tender, 10 to 12 minutes. The mushrooms should release a bunch of liquid; that liquid will evaporate, and the mushrooms will continue brownin'.

5. Meanwhile, trim off the tops and bottoms of the **radishes** and cut each one in half.

6. Once the mushrooms have browned, add the **sake** and **garlic** and let simmer until the liquid is almost fully evaporated, 5 to 7 minutes. Add the **bone broth** and simmer to reduce to about ¼ cup of liquid, 6 to 8 minutes. Add the radishes, **butter,** and **lemon zest** and simmer until the butter melts and the sauce has thickened and emulsified, about 2 minutes. Be careful not to over-reduce because the butter will break from the broth and the sauce will appear greasy. If this happens, add a splash of water and simmer to re-emulsify. Taste and season with more salt and black pepper as needed.

7. Toss the croutons into the pot and stir until fully coated in the sauce. Transfer to a serving bowl and top with the **chives.** Serve immediately.

Charred Broccoli with Nutritional Yeast Dressing

Fine, you can call it a vegan Caesar.

SERVES 4

You know what? I changed my mind; don't call it a vegan Caesar. Because that implies that this—a dish of blistered broccoli and punchy, deeply savory dressing—needs a PR campaign to make it fun. Like it needs to borrow from the canon of Caesar, implying some sort of swaps for anchovies and Parm. But this dressing is perfect and memorable as it is, without those show-stealers. In fact, I often prefer it over a Caesar because it's easier to make, feels a lot lighter, and somehow feels more savory than the sounds Italian, but really is Mexican *salad I won't be referring to from here on out.*

INGREDIENTS:

- **2 medium heads broccoli**
- **2 tablespoons neutral oil**
- **Kosher salt**
- **Freshly squeezed lemon juice, for drizzling**

For the Bread Crumbs

- **½ cup panko bread crumbs**
- **2 tablespoons extra-virgin olive oil**
- **1 garlic clove, finely grated**
- **Kosher salt**
- **Freshly cracked black pepper**

For the Dressing

- **½ cup raw cashews**
- **⅓ cup nutritional yeast**
- **2 tablespoons extra-virgin olive oil**
- **2 tablespoons freshly squeezed lemon juice, plus more as needed**
- **1 tablespoon white miso**
- **1 garlic clove**
- **Freshly cracked black pepper**
- **Kosher salt**

1. Preheat the oven to 450°F. Line a baking sheet with parchment paper.

2. Peel the stalks of the **broccoli** with a peeler and trim ¼ inch from the bases. Quarter the heads of broccoli lengthwise. Place on the baking sheet and toss using your hands (wash them if you pick your nose; I don't judge, I just advise) with the **neutral oil** and a large pinch of **salt.** Roast until the broccoli is charred in spots and the stalks are tender, 17 to 20 minutes. Remove the pan from the oven, season with a drizzle of lemon juice, and transfer to a serving plate.

3. ***To prepare the bread crumbs:*** In a small bowl, toss the **panko** with the **olive oil** until evenly coated.

4. In a medium skillet over medium heat, add the panko and **garlic.** Cook, stirring frequently, until the bread crumbs are golden-brown and crisp, 8 to 10 minutes. Transfer to a small bowl and season with **salt** and **black pepper.**

5. ***To make the dressing:*** In a blender, add the **cashews,** ½ cup water, the **nutritional yeast, olive oil, lemon juice, miso, garlic,** a few grinds of **black pepper**, and a large pinch of **salt.** Blend until smooth. Taste and season with more salt or lemon juice as needed. If it is too thick, thin it with water until it is the thickness of bottled C**s*r dressing.

6. Spread a thin layer of dressing all over the broccoli and top with the bread crumbs. Serve any extra dressing on the side.

Cabbage, Apple, and Fish Sauce Slaw

For when you kinda want som tam

MAKES 6 CUPS

I freaking love som tam, the pounded Thai green papaya salad that perfectly balances crunch with funk, sweetness, acidity, and heat. It's hard to find fresh green papaya near me, so I leave my som tam–ing to the professionals at Thai restaurants. When I want to have a hint of it at home, though, I make a slaw of cabbage and apple using all the same flavors. I get a similar crunch, with an added sweetness from the apple that plays with the fish sauce like they've been best friends all along.

INGREDIENTS:

For the Dressing

- **3 tablespoons fish sauce**
- **¼ cup freshly squeezed lime juice, plus more as needed**
- **3 tablespoons sugar, dissolved in 3 tablespoons hot water, plus more as needed**
- **1 tablespoon dried shrimp, finely chopped (optional)**
- **1 garlic clove, thinly sliced**
- **2 Thai bird's-eye chilies, thinly sliced**
- **Kosher salt**

- **1 small head green cabbage (¾ to 1 pound), quartered and cut as thinly as possible (preferably with a mandoline)**
- **1 apple (ideally Fuji or Honeycrisp), cut into ¼-inch matchsticks**
- **8 ounces cherry tomatoes, cut in half**
- **⅓ cup dry-roasted salted peanuts, coarsely chopped**
- **½ cup (packed) cilantro leaves and tender stems, coarsely chopped**

1. ***To make the dressing:*** In a medium bowl, combine the **fish sauce, lime juice, dissolved sugar, dried shrimp** (if using), **garlic,** and **chilies.** Whisk to combine. Taste the dressing and add more lime juice, salt, or sugar if it tastes flat.

2. In a medium bowl, combine the **cabbage, apple,** and **tomatoes** and toss with the dressing until evenly coated. Top with the **peanuts** and **cilantro** and toss again. Serve with rice and grilled meat or anywhere you would have coleslaw.

Tomato Dressed in Tomato (on Toast)

Pan con tomate con tomate

MAKES 2 SLICES

I fully recognize that if I owned a pool, I might feel different, but: There are few things better in the summertime than pan con tomate. The tomato juice soaks into the bread, making it an instant savory bread pudding. It may be gilding the lily a bit, but topping pan con tomate with more tomate (aka tomato—keep up!) brings another texture to the party and celebrates summer better than any burger grill session can. This grated tomato dressing is a great tool to keep in your back pocket when tomatoes peak. Use it to top labneh for an instant summery dip. Turn the heat up with Thai chilies, thinly sliced shallots, and fish sauce and have it on a crispy egg with rice. Fold it into hot pasta with a pat of butter, some torn basil leaves, and fresh, coarsely grated Parm. Its versatility knows no bounds. I'll grate a few tomatoes and keep them in the fridge for a couple of days, so it's never too far away. Let it come to room temperature before using it; cold tomato is not a summer vibe.

INGREDIENTS:

- **2 large ripe tomatoes**
- **1 garlic clove, finely grated**
- **1 tablespoon extra-virgin olive oil, plus more for drizzling**
- **½ teaspoon sherry vinegar, plus more as needed**
- **⅛ teaspoon smoked paprika**
- **Kosher salt**
- **2 slices of 1-inch-thick crusty bread**
- **Flaky salt, for topping**

1. Trim a thin slice off the bottom of one **tomato,** revealing the flesh. Using the large holes of a box grater, grate against the cut side of the tomato into a bowl. The pulp will fall into the bowl, leaving you with a handful of skin. Discard the skin. Season the tomato pulp with the **garlic, oil, vinegar, paprika,** and a pinch of **kosher salt.** Taste the mixture and adjust with more vinegar or salt as needed.

2. Thinly slice the remaining tomato and season each slice with a pinch of kosher salt.

3. Toast the **bread** however you like—I'm not the toast police. You need to make sure the bread is crisp and hot.

4. Immediately transfer the toasted slices to a serving plate and evenly divide the tomato mixture between the two pieces of bread; it should sizzle upon contact. The heat from the toast is essential to waking up the tomato dressing. Top with the slices of tomato, season with some **flaky salt,** drizzle with oil, and serve.

PS:
This is one of the best ways to utilize in-season tomatoes and an even better base for a summer BLT. Top the toast with a swipe of mayo before adding the tomato sauce and slices, then add a few slices of crisp bacon, and a heap of lettuce. I do not support open-faced sandwiches, but I always make an exception for this dialed-up BLT.

Baked Tomatoes with Halloumi

A tomato Provençale I actually want to eat

MAKES 6 TOMATOES

My apologies to Jacques Pépin; every tomato Provençale I've ever had has been bland. The ratio of bread crumb to tomato is always off. You know what it's missing? Cheese. Adding crisp Halloumi tossed in bright herbs facilitates a punchy bite that complements the juicy roasted tomato, ensuring that every bite is seasoned with… cheese. Peeling the tomatoes may seem like a buzzkill, but it is necessary. This dish is all about textures; I do not want tough tomato skin to get in the way. Make this dish when tomatoes are in season and ripe; roasting dry tomatoes will give you a sad, dry dish.

INGREDIENTS:

- **6 medium ripe tomatoes**
- **4 tablespoons extra-virgin olive oil, plus more for drizzling**
- **Kosher salt**
- **⅓ cup bread crumbs**
- **6 ounces Halloumi cheese, diced in ¼-inch cubes and patted dry**
- **¼ cup mint leaves, roughly torn**
- **¼ cup parsley, coarsely chopped**
- **⅓ cup whole, shelled, roasted, salted pistachios, coarsely chopped**
- **2 garlic cloves, finely grated**
- **1 tablespoon honey**
- **½ teaspoon chili flakes, plus more as needed**

1. Fill a medium pot halfway with water and set over high heat until it comes to an angry boil.

2. Cut a shallow X at the bottom of each **tomato** and place them in the boiling water. Cover and boil for 1 minute. Kill the heat and carefully dump as much water as possible into the sink. Run the pot under cold water until the tomatoes are cool enough to handle. Drain the rest of the water. Using a paring knife, peel the tomatoes and then pat them dry with paper towels. Trim the stem sides of the tomatoes so they are flat.

3. Turn the oven to a high broil.

4. Lay the tomatoes cut-sides up in a casserole dish. They should fit in one layer without too much extra space. Drizzle each tomato with **oil** and season with small pinches of **salt.** Broil the tomatoes on the middle shelf until charred and softened, 30 to 35 minutes.

5. In a medium bowl, toss the **bread crumbs** with 2 tablespoons of the oil and a pinch of salt until evenly coated. Use more oil if needed.

6. While the tomatoes char, place a medium skillet over medium-high heat until, if you squint, you can see a bit of smoking (like when you know the table next to you is vaping but you can't quite catch them in the act). Drizzle oil on top of the cut **Halloumi** and toss to coat. Transfer to the skillet and cook, flipping each piece as it browns, until all pieces are golden-brown on both sides, 8 to 10 minutes. Drizzle more oil on the cheese if it sticks too much. Kill the heat and transfer the cheese to a bowl. Add the **mint, parsley, pistachios, garlic, honey, chili flakes,** and the remaining 2 tablespoons oil. Toss to coat. Taste a piece of cheese (poor you) and adjust the seasoning with salt or chili flakes as needed.

7. Once the tomatoes are charred, remove them from the oven and lower the heat to 375°F. Cover the tomatoes with a thin layer of the bread crumbs and drizzle oil on top. Return them to the oven and bake until the bread crumbs are golden-brown, 12 to 15 minutes. Turn off the oven.

8. Top the tomatoes with the Halloumi cheese mixture and let it ride in the oven for 5 minutes to warm the cheese through. Serve immediately.

CHAPTER 4

Rice, Grains & Pasta

Helping you grain confidence

GIARDINIERA
RICE
p. 169

RICE WITH CARAMELIZED
ONIONS AND BLACK PEPPER
p. 170

MOM'S (RAIN OR SHINE)
PERFECT POT OF RICE
p. 163

SPAETZLE
AND CHEESE
p. 188

RICE
PORRIDGE
p. 182

CENCIONI
WITH SAUSAGE
p. 192

HAM AND
CHEESE LASAGNA
p. 173

MACARONA
BÉCHAMEL
p. 174

MY NAME IS Ham, and I'm a… pro-wrestling fan. Like many kids who grew up in the nineties, I used to tune in every week to watch the violent soap opera that was the World Wrestling Foundation (WWF), now World Wrestling Entertainment (WWE). I was intrigued by the incredible feats of athleticism and the irreverent storylines but kept watching for the sheer bravery of the performers. Nobody embodied that more than Mick Foley.

Mick Foley wasn't the most technical or athletic wrestler, but he was definitely the bravest. (As the kid who was always picked last in gym class, that's exactly what I related to.) He didn't even win all that often—just like me, he usually lost. But he made sure to create memorable moments with every loss. One such moment occurred during a Hell in a Cell match against The "undead" Undertaker. Hell in a Cell matches were saved for only the most bitter of feuds, had no rules, and took place in a twenty-foot-high, fully enclosed steel cage. Mick Foley, as Mankind, instead of going through the door, immediately climbed to the top of the cage, and The Undertaker followed him. The cage wasn't constructed to hold that much weight, so you could see the support clips that held the frames of the roof together flying off as they battled. I held my breath, waiting for them to fall through the drooping metal cage. Then, out of nowhere, The Undertaker threw Mankind from the top of the cage, through the wooden Spanish announcer's table (it's ALWAYS the Spanish announcer's table) below. There was a moment of silence during which everybody was in shock, before the crowd exploded into cheers. I had never seen anything like it before. Watching the reaction from the crowd after a stunt like that had me hooked on Foley's style of wrestling. As Mankind was being wheeled out of the building for a surely dislocated shoulder, he fought his way back to the cage and *climbed it again.* The Undertaker followed him up there, and after some back-and-forth, he wrapped his hand around Mankind's throat and lifted him up for his signature choke slam. As soon as Mankind hit the top of the cage, there was a loud clunk as the cage gave way. Mankind fell to the center of the ring with a thud.

"That's it. He's dead," the commentator, Jerry "The King" Lawler, said matter-of-factly.

As I sat cross-legged on my quintessentially nineties shag-carpeted living room floor, two feet from the television, I felt the crowd erupt around me. The ring filled with paramedics and officials. That *still* wasn't the end of the match. Fighting through a concussion and a hole in his lip made by an errant loose tooth, Mankind insisted on doing a thumbtack spot, where The Undertaker tossed him onto hundreds of thumbtacks that Mankind had theatrically dumped onto the floor minutes earlier. It took more punishment for Mankind to finally accept defeat, even though there were signs of life in him, as his leg feebly tried to kick out before the count of three. And after everything Mankind had gone through, he rejected a stretcher and walked out of the arena to a thunderous standing ovation.

The next day, everybody at school was talking about the Hell in a Cell, but I was the only one who had found Mankind's performance, even in defeat, to be the star of the show. Mankind commanded an entire arena and had the audience on the edge of their seats, based on the gutsiness of his performance instead of his physique and athleticism.

And that's what inspired me to start my ruthless rivalry with my mom's twenty-five-pound burlap sack of basmati rice.

My mom had to have a pot of basmati rice with every meal. She didn't feel like the table was complete without it. Since we went through so much rice, we bought it in bulk. We always had a burlap bag of it in a cupboard. One particular bag had been taunting me with its Adonis physique for weeks. Tripping me as I tried to put away dishes. Gently whispering "Loser" in my ear whenever I closed the panini press.

I (tried to) make that bag pay.

While my mom was distracted, I channeled Mankind, and I dragged that burlap sack and dropped it by the trunk of her Toyota Corolla. I climbed onto the trunk and jumped off, mimicking Mick Foley's trademark elbow drop—only I missed. Luckily, I got off with a badly scraped elbow, but I yelled loudly enough that my mom found us in the middle of our blood feud. To the surprise of no one, she sided with the bag of rice. She was distraught that I had potentially damaged the delicate grains. The commissioner had spoken. That was the end of my biggest rivalry, and like Mick Foley, I lost in a blaze of glory.

Mom's (Rain or Shine) Perfect Pot of Rice

1. Rinse 2 cups of basmati rice in cold water until the water is almost fully clear.

2. Cover it with cold water and let sit for 20 minutes.

3. Set a heavy-bottomed pot with a heavy lid over medium heat. Add a pat of butter, a finely minced garlic clove, and a couple of tablespoons of minced onion and sweat until translucent. Add a bay leaf.

4. Drain the rice well and add to the aromatics. Cook, stirring constantly, until the rice is coated in fat and feels dry.

5. Add 3 cups of water to the rice and a large pinch of salt, bring to a simmer on high heat, stirring occasionally, turn down the heat to low, and cover. Cook for 18 minutes.

6. Remove the lid, stir rice with a fork, then cover again. Let it rest for 10 minutes before serving.

Bolivian Cheesy Rice

Nostalgic arroz con queso

MAKES 5 CUPS

Arroz con queso is a dish that instantly teleports me to the backyard of my Bolivian uncle, Victor Hugo. We would have joyous, raucous churrascos in that backyard. It was where I learned to start a charcoal fire. It was where I had my first blood sausage, deliciously iron-y, custardy, and studded with chewy rice grains. It was where I learned to cook beefy picanha skewers a su punto, *"perfectly." It was where I learned the importance of slicing a steak properly,* always *against the grain. It was also where I had arroz con queso the most often. It would turn my plastic plate molten as I balanced it on my knees. In Santa Cruz de la Sierra, no plate of grilled meat is complete without a scoop of luscious, creamy arroz con queso. The local cheese makes it special; it melts, but not all the way, so you get a stretchy bite of chewy, squeaky cheese. Akkawi, a Palestinian cheese found in many Middle Eastern specialty stores, is the perfect substitute, since it melts similarly. Mozzarella also works, although it tends to fully melt into the rice; this is not bad, just not backyard-canon.*

INGREDIENTS:

- **1 cup short grain rice (like sushi rice)**
- **3 tablespoons unsalted butter, cut into tablespoon-sized chunks**
- **1 small yellow onion, diced**
- **2 garlic cloves, minced**
- **Kosher salt**
- **½ cup milk, plus more as needed**
- **6 ounces Akkawi cheese or low-moisture mozzarella, cut into thin slices**
- **4 scallions (white and green parts), thinly sliced**

1. In a medium bowl, add the **rice** and rinse under cold water until the water is mostly clear but still a hint cloudy, 3 to 4 rinses. Cover the rice with water and let it soak for 20 minutes. Drain well.

2. In a medium pot over medium heat, add the **butter, onion, garlic,** and a pinch of **salt.** Cook, stirring frequently, until the onion has slightly softened and is fragrant, 4 to 5 minutes. Add the rice and cook, stirring frequently, until the grains turn white and are evenly coated in fat, about 2 minutes. Add 4 cups water and turn the heat to medium-high. Cook until the water simmers, then turn down the heat to medium-low, maintaining a gentle simmer. Cook, stirring frequently, until the rice is tender and the water mostly evaporates, 18 to 22 minutes. There should be a thin layer of sputtering liquid above the tender rice.

3. Add the **milk,** stir to incorporate, and then simmer. Taste and adjust the seasoning with more salt as needed. Add the **cheese** and **scallions** and stir well until the cheese melts and starts to pull. The consistency should be loose, like a well-made risotto. It should flatten on a plate, not mound; adjust it with milk if needed to loosen it. Serve immediately.

GIARDINIERA
RICE
p. 169

BOLIVIAN CHEESE RICE p. 164

RICE WITH CARAMELIZED ONIONS AND BLACK PEPPER p. 170

Giardiniera Rice

An ode to Shebestan

MAKES 5 CUPS

When I was a kid, there was a Persian restaurant called Shebestan in Doha that served dill rice with pickles (instead of the traditional favas). The cornichon-esque pickles were finely diced and provided little pops of briny crunch throughout. It paired perfectly with grilled seafood, almost like a tartar sauce in rice form. I took that spin further and made dill rice with my favorite spicy pickled vegetable blend, giardiniera. It is as outrageous as it sounds, and if you feed it to a child, I hope it inspires them to develop an utterly chaotic riff one day. In the meantime, make this the next time you need a side to some cooked fish or shrimp.

INGREDIENTS:

- **1½ cups basmati rice**
- **3 tablespoons unsalted butter**
- **2 garlic cloves, minced**
- **Kosher salt**
- **2 teaspoons dried dill weed**
- **1 cup giardiniera, coarsely chopped and drained of extra liquid**
- **¼ cup fresh dill, coarsely chopped**

1. In a medium bowl, add the **rice** and rinse under cool running water until the water is almost clear, 3 to 4 rinses. Cover the rice with water and let it soak for 20 minutes. Drain well.

2. In a medium pot with a tight-fitting lid over medium heat, add the **butter** and **garlic** and cook until the butter has fully melted and the garlic is fragrant, 1 to 2 minutes. Add the rice, a large pinch of **salt,** and the **dill weed** and cook, stirring constantly, until the rice is dry and coated in fat, 2 to 3 minutes. Add 2¼ cups water and stir well. Turn the heat to medium-high. Cook until the water simmers, then cover and turn the heat to low. Cook for 18 minutes.

3. Uncover, add the **giardiniera** and **fresh dill,** and stir quickly to distribute. Cover again and let the rice rest for 10 minutes before serving.

Rice with Caramelized Onions and Black Pepper

Caramelized onions aren't just for soup.

MAKES 4 CUPS

There was a seafood restaurant near the port city of Alexandria, Egypt, that my family used to visit anytime we were in town. You would go up to a long, iced counter filled with the freshest of fish, with their crystal-clear eyes and glittering scales. You could pick your seafood of choice and then pick how they would prepare it: fried, grilled, or roasted. While the seafood was impeccable, I always looked forward to the sides that graced the table alongside the seafood—like the banchan at a Korean BBQ spot. My favorite was the rice that they served, stained brown with caramelized onions and seasoned with aggressive cracks of black pepper. It was the perfect foil for fresh fish.

INGREDIENTS:

- 1½ **cups short grain rice (like sushi rice)**
- 2 **tablespoons neutral oil**
- 1 **large yellow onion, diced**
- 4 **garlic cloves, minced**
- 1 **teaspoon freshly cracked black pepper**
- **Kosher salt**
- 1 **teaspoon ground coriander**
- 1 **teaspoon ground cumin**
- ¼ **teaspoon hot paprika**
- ¼ **teaspoon ground turmeric**

1. In a medium bowl, add the **rice** and rinse under cold running water. Rinse until the water runs almost clear, 3 to 4 rinses. Cover the rice with water and let it soak for 20 minutes. Drain well.

2. In a medium pot over high heat, add the **oil** and **onion** and cook, stirring frequently, until the onion turns dark brown along the edges. Add a splash of water and continue cooking, stirring frequently and adding splashes of water whenever the bottom of the pan starts to get too dark (make sure your previous addition has fully evaporated first). Continue cooking until the onion has fully softened and is a very dark brown, 15 to 20 minutes. Add the **garlic, black pepper,** a large pinch of **salt,** the **coriander, cumin, paprika,** and **turmeric** and cook until fragrant, about 1 minute. Add the rice and cook, stirring frequently, until the rice is dry and evenly coated in fat, 2 to 4 minutes.

3. Add 1½ cups water, stir to combine, then turn down the heat to medium-high until the water simmers. Cover, then turn down the heat to low, and cook for 18 minutes. Uncover, fluff the rice with a fork, then cover again. Let sit for 10 minutes before serving. Season to taste.

Ham and Cheese Lasagna

Put the ragù away.

SERVES 6

Brazilians love a good lasagna for any occasion, from New Year's Eve to chill weeknight potlucks. There was a version made with sliced ham that, if I'm being honest, I like better. There is no ricotta, which exemplifies my very hottest take: Ricotta has NO place in a lasagna. Not taking questions at this time. Okay, fine; I'll answer one question: Yes, you can use this as a template for your own dream lasagna… swap out the ham for your favorite ragù or for sautéed finely chopped greens mixed with cheese—just so long as you leave the ricotta out of it.

INGREDIENTS:

For the Béchamel

- **10 tablespoons unsalted butter**
- **10 tablespoons all-purpose flour**
- **6 cups whole milk**
- **Kosher salt**
- **1 whole clove**
- **1 bay leaf**
- **¼ large yellow onion, peeled but with root intact**
- **1 garlic clove, smashed**
- **⅛ teaspoon freshly grated nutmeg**

- **2 tablespoons extra-virgin olive oil, plus more as needed**
- **3 garlic cloves, thinly sliced**
- **1 (28-ounce) can passata**
- **1 pound dried lasagna noodles**
- **1 pound sliced ham (such as jambon de Paris or prosciutto cotto)**
- **1 pound fresh mozzarella, thinly sliced**
- **5 ounces Parmesan, grated**

1. ***To make the béchamel:*** In a medium pot over medium heat, add the **butter** and melt until lightly foaming. Add the **flour** and cook, whisking constantly, until the flour no longer smells raw and is very foamy, 2 to 3 minutes. Add the **milk** in ½-cup increments while whisking, adding the next addition once the previous one has been fully incorporated. Add a large pinch of **salt** and keep whisking until the milk comes up to a simmer.

2. Use the **clove** to stud the **bay leaf** to the outside of the **onion.** This will make it easier to pull out.

3. Turn down the heat to medium-low, add the studded onion and **garlic** to the milk mixture, and simmer, stirring occasionally, until the flour has fully cooked out and the sauce has thickened to the consistency of thick pudding, 8 to 10 minutes. Taste the sauce and add more salt as needed. Remove the onion and discard. Kill the heat, add the **nutmeg**, and whisk to combine. Taste the sauce again and add more salt as needed. Cover and set aside.

4. In another medium pot with a lid over medium heat, add the **oil** and **garlic** and cook until the garlic is fragrant and turns golden-brown along the edges, 3 to 5 minutes. Add the **passata** and bring to a simmer. Cover with a lid three-quarters of the way through and cook until slightly reduced and the flavor concentrates, 10 to 15 minutes. Taste again and add more salt as needed, then set aside.

5. Bring a large pot of water to a boil. Season it like a slightly salty soup. Cook the **lasagna** for 1 minute less than the instructions on the package. Drain well, then toss the lasagna sheets in some oil.

6. Preheat the oven to 375°F. Rub a 9 × 13 × 2-inch metal pan or a casserole dish with oil.

7. Put a layer of tomato sauce at the bottom of the pan, add a layer of **ham,** then noodles, followed by some béchamel, **mozzarella,** and finally some **Parmesan.** Repeat the layering in the same order.

8. Cover the pan with aluminum foil and bake for 45 minutes, until the sides are bubbly. Remove the foil, turn the broiler on high, and broil until the top is golden-brown and charred in spots, 3 to 5 minutes. Let the lasagna rest for at least 20 minutes before slicing and serving.

Macarona Béchamel

How I learned to béchamel

SERVES 6

The macaroni (or macarona *in Arabic) béchamel was my first introduction to béchamel, the velvety French mother sauce of milk thickened with a cooked butter and flour paste known as a roux. It quickly became a staple of my early cooking, with a satiny texture and buttery, milky flavor. I would slather it on top of large chunks of roasted vegetables to broil, mix it with cheese to toss with boiled potatoes, and use it as a sauce for roasted chicken for an instant potpie vibe. It was my Egyptian Tante Hosna who first showed me the ways of the macaroni béchamel, a layered casserole of macaroni, spiced ground beef, and a thick layer of béchamel, baked until the top is golden and the inside molten. I use a 9 × 13-inch pan here, but when feeding just our family of three on a weeknight, I cut the recipe in half and bake it in a loaf pan.*

INGREDIENTS:

For the Béchamel

- **7 tablespoons unsalted butter, cut into tablespoon-sized chunks**
- **7 tablespoons all-purpose flour**
- **5 cups whole milk**
- **Kosher salt**
- **¼ teaspoon freshly grated nutmeg**

For the Beef

- **2 tablespoons extra-virgin olive oil, plus more for greasing**
- **1 pound ground beef**
- **Kosher salt**
- **2 tablespoons tomato paste**
- **1 small yellow onion, diced**
- **3 garlic cloves, minced**
- **1 teaspoon ground cinnamon**
- **1 teaspoon ground allspice**
- **2 teaspoons hot paprika**
- **1 (28-ounce) can crushed tomatoes**
- **¼ cup parsley leaves, coarsely chopped**
- **4 ounces Parmigiano-Reggiano cheese, cut into chunks**
- **1 pound ditalini**

1. ***To make the béchamel:*** In a medium pot over medium heat, add the **butter** and let it melt. Add the **flour** and whisk until the butter is foamy and the flour no longer smells raw, 3 to 5 minutes. Add the **milk** ½ cup at a time, whisking to incorporate the milk into the flour fully before adding the next addition. Add a large pinch of **salt** and cook, whisking frequently, until the sauce has thickened and no longer tastes of raw flour, 13 to 15 minutes. Kill the heat, add the **nutmeg,** and whisk to combine. Taste the sauce and adjust with salt as needed. Cover and set aside.

2. In a Dutch oven over medium-high heat, warm the **oil** until shimmering. Add the **beef** and a large pinch of **salt.** Smash the meat into smaller pieces with a whisk. Cook, stirring occasionally, until the beef is a deep crusty brown, 15 to 18 minutes. Add the **tomato paste** and cook, stirring occasionally, until the color deepens, 3 to 5 minutes.

3. Add the **onion, garlic,** and a pinch of salt and cook until the onion slightly softens, about 5 minutes. Add the **cinnamon, allspice,** and **paprika** and cook until fragrant, about 1 minute. Add the **tomatoes** and bring to a simmer, then cover and turn down the heat to medium-low. Cook until the onion has fully softened, the beef is tender, and the flavors have melded and deepened, 20 to 25 minutes. Kill the heat, add the **parsley,** and stir to incorporate. Taste and adjust with more salt as needed.

4. While the meat sauce is simmering, transfer the **Parmesan** to a food processor or blender and pulse until ground into small, fine pebbles. Set aside.

5. Preheat the oven to 375°F. Rub a 9 × 13 × 2-inch metal pan or a casserole dish with oil.

6. Bring a large pot of water to a boil. Season it like a slightly salty soup. In the last 10 minutes of the meat sauce's simmering, cook the **ditalini** for 2 minutes less than the instructions on the package. Drain well, reserving ½ cup of the pasta water.

7. Add the drained pasta and the pasta water to the meat sauce and stir well to incorporate. Taste and adjust the seasoning with more salt as needed.

8. Put the beef and noodle mixture in one even layer in the bottom of the prepared dish. Top with the béchamel and smooth out the top, sprinkle with the cheese, and bake, uncovered, until bubbly and starting to brown, about 45 minutes. Increase the heat to 450°F and continue baking until the top is a golden-brown with darker splotches and the sides show some signs of bubbling, 5 to 10 minutes more. Remove the pan from the oven and let it rest for at least 20 minutes before scooping and serving.

The Everything Nippon Travel Guide Series
THINGS
I WISH I KNEW
BEFORE
GOING TO
JAPAN
UPDATED
+
EXPENDED

Chicken and (Mochi) Dumplings

A comforting bowl of textures

MAKES 10 CUPS

This is what I picture chicken and dumplings becomes after spending a semester abroad in Japan. It starts listening to anime soundtracks. It dresses up for every occasion in an ill-fitting kimono. It swaps out classic doughy dumplings for chewy mochi ones. It uses sake for acidity and sweetness, and white miso for an umami boost. (It's sure to tell you alllllll about that umami boost.) Be sure to get the variety mushroom pack; every mushroom brings a different texture to this Dragon Ball Z *convention.*

INGREDIENTS:

- **1 pound boneless, skinless chicken breasts, diced into ½-inch cubes**
- **2 teaspoons Diamond Crystal kosher salt** **(see page 16)**
- **Freshly cracked black pepper**

For the Soup

- **¼ cup unsalted butter, cut into tablespoon-sized chunks**
- **3 tablespoons all-purpose flour**
- **1 medium yellow onion, diced**
- **2 stalks celery, diced**
- **6 garlic cloves, thinly sliced**
- **1 bunch of scallions (white and green parts), thinly sliced, with whites and greens separated**
- **1 pound assorted mushrooms (such as oyster, shiitake, and king trumpet), stemmed and cut into ½-inch chunks**
- **Kosher salt**
- **½ cup sake or white wine**
- **4 cups chicken bone broth**

For the Dumplings

- **1½ cups mochiko flour**
- **½ teaspoon Diamond Crystal kosher salt**
- **¾ cup warm water, plus more as needed**

- **2 tablespoons white miso**
- **½ cup parsley leaves, coarsely chopped**
- **1 lemon, cut into wedges**

1. In a medium bowl, toss the **chicken** with the **salt** and **black pepper.** Transfer to the fridge uncovered.

2. ***To make the soup:*** In a large pot over medium heat, add the **butter** and melt until it is lightly foaming. Add the **flour** and cook, stirring frequently, until the flour no longer smells raw, about 1 minute. Add the **onion, celery, garlic, scallion whites, mushrooms,** and a large pinch of **salt.** Stir until the mushrooms are coated in the flour. Add the **sake** and **bone broth,** increase the heat to medium-high, and bring to a simmer. Turn down the heat to medium-low, cover most of the way with a lid, and cook until the mushrooms and celery are as tender as you were on the last night of study abroad, about 20 minutes.

3. ***To make the dumplings:*** Bring a medium pot of water to a boil over high heat. Season with a large pinch of salt.

4. In a medium bowl, combine the **flour** and **salt,** then stream in the **water.** Whisk with stiff fingers until all the flour is moist. Knead in the bowl until a smooth dough forms, adding more water if needed, about 3 minutes.

5. On a clean surface, divide the dough into tablespoon-sized portions and roll each portion into a ball.

6. Add the dumplings to the boiling water. When they start to float, cook for 3 more minutes. Drain the dumplings, then rinse them under cold running water until cool to the touch. Drain again, then set aside.

7. Stir the **miso,** chicken, and (mochi) dumplings into the soup. Gently simmer until the chicken is fully cooked, 8 to 10 minutes. Finish the soup with the scallion greens, black pepper, and **parsley** and stir to combine. Taste and adjust the seasoning with more salt and pepper as needed.

8. Divide the soup among bowls and hit each one with a squeeze of **lemon** before serving.

Quinoa Chicken Salad with Ham (Me, Not the Meat) Ranch

Your home can become a Sweetgreen if you let it.

SERVES 4

Grain bowls are great. They're an easy, reliable meal to order when you're too busy to cook or when you're trying to feed a group of people you're working with but don't know their culinary preferences. They're a safe choice, but let's be honest… they rarely result in an exceptional meal. This grain bowl does, and it is all thanks to the dressing. As with a Caesar salad, the dressing is the real star. This one is a spin on the Peruvian ají verde, but I swap out the herbs and chilies for things that are more easily accessible (love you). I'm not going to be militant about it, but it'd be super cool if we could start calling it Ham Ranch! I'll go first: Ham Ranch is great on top of everything from grilled meats to crispy fried eggs to plain white rice. This recipe makes more than you need, but you will be happy to have more Ham Ranch lying around. Change up the base, depending on what you are in the mood for. Have fun with the herb variety or use up whatever looks unwell in the fridge. For the full experience, feel free to Venmo yourself $21 every time you make one.

INGREDIENTS:

For the Chicken

- **4 boneless, skinless chicken thighs (about 18 ounces)**
- **1 teaspoon ground cumin**
- **1 teaspoon ground coriander**
- **1 teaspoon hot paprika**
- **2 teaspoons Diamond Crystal kosher salt (see page 16)**
- **2 tablespoons neutral oil, plus more as needed**

For the Quinoa

- **1 tablespoon neutral oil**
- **1 cup quinoa, rinsed**
- **Kosher salt**

For the Ham Ranch

- **1 cup cilantro leaves and tender stems**
- **1 cup assorted tender herb leaves (such as parsley, chives, tarragon, dill, or more cilantro)**
- **½ cup buttermilk**
- **¼ cup mayonnaise**
- **1 garlic clove**
- **1 large jalapeño**
- **¼ cup grated Parmesan cheese**
- **Zest and juice of 1 freshly squeezed lemon, plus more as needed**
- **Kosher salt**
- **Freshly cracked black pepper**

For Topping

- **½ cup toasted peanuts**
- **2 Persian cucumbers, cut into ½-inch pieces**
- **6 red radishes, quartered**
- **1 avocado, cut into ½-inch pieces**

1. ***To prepare the chicken:*** In a medium bowl, toss the **chicken thighs** with the **cumin, coriander, paprika, salt,** and **oil** until evenly coated.

2. Set a wire rack inside a baking sheet.

3. Transfer the chicken to the wire rack and let the pan sit in the fridge, uncovered, for at least 12 hours and up to 24 hours.

4. ***To prepare the quinoa:*** Place a medium pot with a tight-fitting lid over medium heat until hot, about 3 minutes. Add the **oil** and **quinoa** and toast, stirring frequently, until the quinoa is dry and turns white, 3 to 5 minutes. Add 2 cups water and a large pinch of **salt** and increase the heat to high. Once the water boils, cover, turn down the heat to low, and cook for 12 minutes more. Uncover, fluff with a fork, cover again, and let the quinoa rest for 15 more minutes.

5. In another medium pan over medium heat, add enough oil to coat the bottom of the pan. When hot,

add the chicken. Cook until golden-brown on both sides and cooked through, about 4 minutes per side. Remove the pan from the heat and set aside to rest.

6. ***To make the Ham ranch:*** In a blender, combine the **cilantro, assorted herbs, buttermilk, mayo, garlic, jalapeño, Parmesan,** and **lemon zest** and **juice** and blend on high until smooth. Taste and adjust the seasoning with more salt, lemon juice, and **black pepper** as needed.

7. Slice the chicken. Divide the quinoa among your serving bowls and top with the chicken slices, **peanuts, cucumbers, radishes,** and **avocado.** Serve with the Ham Ranch on the side to drizzle on as you eat.

Soba Sharkaseya

Some good ol'-fashioned Egyptian-Japanese fusion. The kids are begging for it!

SERVES 2 TO 4

Chicken sharkaseya, a regal Egyptian dish with roots in the Ottoman Empire, is made with delicately poached chicken and a luscious walnut sauce, perfumed with warm spices like cinnamon, cardamom, and cloves. It is usually served over buttery rice with toasted vermicelli running throughout. I simplify the stew into its essence—a fragrant walnut gravy—and serve it tossed with soba. The walnuts play off the natural nuttiness of the buckwheat in the soba the same way a traditional sesame seed dressing would. The sauce keeps for up to four days in the refrigerator and is as delicious cold as it is right out of the pot. I don't need any chunks of chicken in this dish, but if you have any leftover chicken in the fridge, this is a good way to use it up; just shred and toss into the sauce.

INGREDIENTS:

- **3 tablespoons unsalted butter**
- **1¼ cups untoasted walnuts**
- **2 tablespoons neutral oil**
- **8 garlic cloves, smashed**
- **1 medium onion, diced**
- **1 bay leaf**
- **1 teaspoon freshly cracked black pepper, plus more as needed**
- **½ teaspoon ground cinnamon**
- **¼ teaspoon ground cardamom**
- **¼ teaspoon ground allspice**
- **2 whole cloves**
- **2 cups chicken bone broth**
- **4 sheets nori**
- **3 tablespoons toasted white sesame seeds**
- **Kosher salt**
- **1 (8.8-ounce) package dried soba**
- **⅓ cup tahini**

1. In a medium pot over medium heat, add the **butter** and melt until foaming. Add the **walnuts** and cook until lightly toasted, 3 to 5 minutes. Transfer the walnuts to a plate. Take ½ cup of the walnuts and coarsely chop. Set aside to mix in at the end.

2. Add the **oil** to the same pot and heat until shimmery. Add the **garlic** and **onion,** turn down the heat to medium, and cook until the onion is opaque and softened with some browning along the edges, 6 to 8 minutes.

3. Add the **bay leaf, black pepper, cinnamon, cardamom, allspice,** and **cloves** and cook until fragrant, about 1 minute.

4. Add the **bone broth** and the remaining whole walnuts. Simmer over medium-high heat until the broth has reduced by half and the walnuts begin to soften, 15 to 20 minutes.

5. Crush the **nori** into small pieces with your hands over a small bowl. Use this as an opportunity to let out any pent-up aggression. Transfer the villainous pulverized nori to a spice grinder along with the **sesame seeds** and blitz until a fine powder forms. Season with a large pinch of **salt** and return to the small bowl. Set aside.

6. Cook the **soba** according to the instructions on the package. Once cooked, run them under cold water until cool, then place them in a strainer over a bowl to allow excess water to drain.

7. Discard the bay leaf from the walnut mixture and transfer the rest to a blender with the **tahini.** Blend on high until smooth (it should be the consistency of a melted milkshake). If the sauce is too thick, add water a tablespoon at a time as you blend.

8. Return the walnut sauce to the same pot. Add the chopped walnuts, then taste and adjust the seasoning with more salt and pepper as needed. Toss with the prepared soba and divide among bowls. Top with a generous sprinkle of the nori-sesame powder (and serve any extra on the side). Eat immediately.

PS:
Only dress the amount of soba that you know you will eat. Cooked soba and sauce keep much longer when they are stored separately in airtight containers for up to 4 days.

Rice Porridge

With the flavors of chicken arsia

MAKES 6 CUPS OF PORRIDGE AND 1 CUP OF CONDIMENT

On the first day of every Ramadan in Doha, our next-door neighbor would come by an hour before iftar and bring us some chicken arsia—it was the perfect thing to break our daylong fast, with its long-simmered burst grains of rice, warm spices, and comforting chicken broth. After the rice was cooked, the mixture was beaten until the rice fully broke down into a paste that thickened the broth. My favorite part was the zippy tarsha condiment on top. It took the soothing, warming bowl of rice porridge into a dynamic direction that I looked forward to every year.

INGREDIENTS:

- **1 cup short grain rice (such as sushi)**
- **4 cups chicken bone broth**
- **2 boneless, skinless chicken breasts**
- **¼ teaspoon ground cardamom**
- **¼ teaspoon ground cinnamon**
- **¼ teaspoon ground ginger**
- **1 bay leaf**
- **Kosher salt**

For the Tarsha

- **¼ cup raisins**
- **6 Medjool dates, pitted**
- **2 tablespoons tamarind concentrate**
- **Kosher salt**
- **Freshly cracked black pepper**
- **3 to 4 Thai bird's-eye chilies, thinly sliced (optional, but strongly recommended)**

- **4 tablespoons butter, cut into tablespoon-sized chunks, for serving**

1. In a medium bowl, add the **rice** and rinse under cold running water until the water runs almost clear, 3 to 4 full rinses. Drain well.

2. In a large pot over high heat, combine the **bone broth** and 4 cups water and bring to a boil. Add the **chicken,** cover, then turn off the heat. Let the chicken sit in the hot liquid until almost fully cooked (it should register around 150°F on an instant-read thermometer), 25 to 30 minutes. Remove the chicken from the broth and transfer to a plate. Once cool, shred the chicken into strands using two forks.

3. Add the rice, **cardamom, cinnamon, ginger, bay leaf,** and a large pinch of **salt** to the broth and cook over medium heat, stirring frequently, until the rice bursts and looks porridgey, 45 to 55 minutes. If at any point the porridge looks too dry before the rice is cooked, add more water. Return the chicken to the pot and stir to warm through. Season to taste.

4. ***To make the tarsha:*** While the rice cooks, in a medium pot over medium heat, combine the **raisins, dates,** and ½ cup water and cook until the fruit has softened and absorbed most of the water, 6 to 8 minutes.

5. Transfer to a blender, add the **tamarind,** and blend on high speed until smooth (it should be the consistency of A.1. Sauce). Adjust with water as needed. Taste and adjust the seasoning with **salt** and **pepper**. Add the **chilies** (if using) and stir.

6. Remove and discard the bay leaf from the porridge. Divide among bowls, top with a spoonful of the tarsha, a pat of **butter,** and a sprinkle of black pepper, if desired. Serve immediately.

Note:
Tarsha keeps in an airtight container in the fridge for up to 2 weeks. Use it as a condiment for soups, stews, or as a sauce for seared meats.

Toasted Thin Spaghetti, Black Beans, and Parm

Pasta e fagioli meets sopa seca.

SERVES 2

I love pasta e fagioli. I eat it at least once a week. I love the texture of the creamy beans and al dente pasta; throw some weird greens in there, and I'm over the freakin' moon. This takes the combo of pasta and beans and flies it (coach—sorry, but I used miles) to Mexico. When I was working at Empellón Cocina in New York, there was always some version of sopa seca on the menu. Sopa seca, *which literally means "dried soup" in Spanish, is a dish of noodles cooked in a broth until the noodles are fully hydrated and the water in the broth has almost completely evaporated. It results in flavorful noodles coated in a luscious sauce. The key to this recipe is getting the proper toast on the noodles first; this adds a deep, nutty flavor to the dish while allowing the noodles to maintain their texture and chew. This recipe is a great fridge cleaner. Use it as a template and throw in whatever cooked veggies or leftovers you have.*

INGREDIENTS:

- **8 ounces thin spaghetti or angel hair pasta**
- **3 tablespoons neutral oil**
- **6 garlic cloves, thinly sliced**
- **1 teaspoon chili flakes, plus more as needed**
- **2 cups chicken bone broth or water**
- **Kosher salt**
- **1 (15.5-ounce) can black beans, drained and rinsed**
- **1 bunch of Swiss chard, stems stripped and coarsely chopped**
- **⅓ cup parsley leaves, coarsely chopped**
- **1 cup grated Parmigiano-Reggiano cheese**
- **3 tablespoons sour cream**
- **Zest of 1 lemon**
- **Juice of 1 freshly squeezed lemon, plus more as needed**
- **Freshly cracked black pepper**

1. Place the **pasta** in a large bowl. Have any lingering Italians avert their eyes and snap the pasta into roughly 1-inch pieces. There is no need to be super precise.

2. In a large heavy-bottomed pot over medium heat, add the **oil.** Once it's shimmering, add the mutilated pasta. Toast, stirring constantly, until it turns a light golden brown, about 2 minutes. Add the **garlic** and keep toasting, stirring frequently, until the noodles are a deep golden brown, about 2 minutes more.

3. Add the **chili flakes** and toast until fragrant, about 1 minute.

4. Add the **bone broth** and a large pinch of **salt** and bring to a simmer while stirring frequently. Continue to simmer until the liquid is fully absorbed and the noodles are cooked, about 6 minutes. If the liquid dries up and the noodles aren't yet cooked, add water by the ¼ cup until the noodles are tender.

5. Add the **beans** and **chard** and cook, stirring frequently, until the greens are fully wilted, 3 to 4 minutes.

6. Add the **parsley, Parmesan, sour cream, lemon zest** and **juice** and stir vigorously until everything is incorporated. Give it a taste and adjust the seasoning with more salt, black pepper, and lemon juice as needed. Serve right away.

SPAETZLE
AND CHEESE
p. 188
CENCIONI
WITH SAUSAGE
p. 192

PARISIAN GNOCCHI WITH BROWN BUTTER AND CRISPY SAGE
p. 191

Spaetzle and Cheese

Move over mac 'n' cheese, there's a new sheriff in town.

SERVES 4

The first time I had spaetzle was in culinary school. I had never heard of it before and was intrigued by the scraggly dumplings that didn't require any special equipment to make. The instructor of the class was especially excited to teach us his spaetzle method. He had clearly made it a bunch and was very good at it. According to him, the key to good spaetzle is making sure that the dough is mixed enough to fully develop the gluten (which is also aided by an overnight rest). The dough should stretch and fight you as you mix it. These steps will give you perfectly chewy dumplings to float in a classic mac 'n' cheese sauce. If you don't feel like making spaetzle, the sauce below works just as well on elbows for a classic stovetop mac 'n' cheese.

INGREDIENTS:

For the Spaetzle

- 3¼ **cups / 390g bread flour**
- 4 **large eggs**
- 1 **cup / 240g whole milk**
- 1 **teaspoon Diamond Crystal kosher salt (see page 16)**
- ¼ **teaspoon freshly grated nutmeg**
- **Extra-virgin olive oil**

For the Sauce

- 1¾ **cups whole milk**
- 9 **ounces sliced American cheese, roughly torn**
- 1 **teaspoon Dijon mustard**
- ¼ **teaspoon cayenne powder**
- 9 **ounces shredded melty cheese of your choice (such as Muenster, Cheddar, Gruyère, or more American)**
- **Kosher salt**
- **Freshly cracked black pepper**

1. ***To make the spaetzle:*** In a large bowl, combine the **flour, eggs, milk, salt,** and **nutmeg** and vigorously whisk until stretchy, about 6 minutes. Cover the bowl with plastic wrap and let rest in the refrigerator for at least 1 hour and up to 24 hours.

2. Fill a large pot three-fourths of the way with water, season with a large pinch of salt, and bring to a boil.

3. Using a rubber spatula, mix the spaetzle batter; it should be stretchy and fight you.

4. Hold a box grater sideways, with the large holes facing down and the bottom opening toward you, 6 inches above the boiling water. Using a plastic bench scraper, scoop some spaetzle batter into the box grater and push the batter through the holes into the water. (Alternatively, a colander with similar holes can also work.) Repeat with half the batter. Stop, stir the spaetzle, and cook until they float and inflate slightly, about 1 minute. With a slotted spoon, pull the spaetzle out and drop them onto a baking sheet to cool. Toss the spaetzle in **oil** as they cool so they don't stick. Proceed with the rest of the batter.

5. Place a large pan over medium heat until lightly smoking. Add just enough spaetzle to form one even layer in the pan (you may have to do this in two batches), drizzle some oil on top, and cook until one side of the spaetzle is golden brown and crisp, 3 to 5 minutes, then transfer to a plate and repeat with the rest.

6. ***To make the sauce:*** In a medium pot over medium heat, add the **milk, American cheese, mustard,** and **cayenne** and stir to incorporate. Cook, stirring frequently, until the cheese melts into the milk. Add the **shredded cheese,** turn down the heat to low, and stir until it melts into the sauce (it will be the consistency of heavy cream). Taste and adjust the seasoning with salt and pepper as needed. Drizzle half of the cheese sauce on the spaetzle and toss to coat. Add more sauce as needed. Serve immediately.

PS:
Top your spaetzle and cheese with whatever you're feeling. Most of the time, I enjoy the chewy texture of the spaetzle in the luscious goo, but if I put something on top, it is the bread crumbs from page 145. You can use anything from thinly sliced chives and freshly shaved white truffle to a fistful of hand-crushed Fritos.

PPS:
Save any extra cheese sauce for a batch of mac and cheese or for draping on top of steamed broccoli.

Parisian Gnocchi with Brown Butter and Crispy Sage

The only time the potato version of something loses

SERVES 2

For the longest time, I was familiar only with potato gnocchi. They are always sold as light, delicate pillows… and I've had a lot of gnocchi made by fancy-pants Italian chefs… but they are never light enough to be pillows. The first time I tried Parisian gnocchi, at a small French bistro in Soho run by my friend Matt Conroy, I was stunned. These were the gnocchi of my dreams. These were in fact light, and pillowy, and buttery, and dreamy. They are also much simpler to make. The dough is a traditional pâte à choux, piped into boiling water, then seared until crisp in a pan of foaming butter. I like to dress them simply in some sage leaves and Parm, but you can use them anywhere you use potato gnocchi

INGREDIENTS:

- **8 tablespoons unsalted butter, cut into small chunks**
- **1 cup all-purpose flour**
- **Kosher salt**
- **4 large eggs**
- **Extra-virgin olive oil**
- **10 large sage leaves, torn in half**
- **Zest of 1 lemon**
- **Freshly cracked black pepper**
- **2 ounces finely grated Parmigiano-Reggiano cheese**

1. In a medium pot over low heat, add 6 tablespoons of the **butter** and cook until the butter melts. Add 1 cup water, increase the heat to medium, and bring to a simmer. As soon as the water simmers, add the **flour** and 1 teaspoon **salt** and stir vigorously with a spatula. Your arms will get tired, but you can do this. Keep stirring until a smooth dough forms. Cook until a thin film of flour paste forms at the bottom of your pot, 3 to 4 minutes. If you poke the dough, it should feel greasy and won't stick to your fingers. Turn off the heat and let the flour mixture cool for 2 minutes while stirring.

2. Once cooled, add the **eggs** one at a time, whisking vigorously until the egg incorporates fully into the dough, then switch back to a spatula to scrape the dough from the whisk and stir until you have a smooth dough again. Continue until all the egg is incorporated. Transfer to a piping bag and let cool in the fridge for at least 1 hour.

3. Fill a large pot three-fourths of the way with water and bring to a boil over high heat. Season with a large pinch of salt and turn down the heat to a simmer. Cut a 1-inch opening in the piping bag. Working in batches, hold the piping bag about 6 inches above the simmering water and push out 1 inch of dough before cutting it (with scissors) flush against the piping bag so a cylindrical dumpling falls into the water. Cook until the dumplings float, about 3 minutes. Transfer the dumplings to a baking sheet and coat in **oil.** Repeat with the remaining dough.

4. Place a large skillet over medium-high heat until lightly smoking. Add the dumplings and a drizzle of oil and cook until one side is golden-brown. Add the remaining 2 tablespoons butter and the **sage** and cook, tossing frequently, until the dumplings are golden-brown on most sides, slightly puffed, and the sage has browned, 8 to 10 minutes. Remove the pan from the heat. Add the **lemon zest** and a few cracks of **black pepper** and toss to distribute.

5. Transfer to a serving dish and top with the **Parmesan.**

Cencioni with Sausage

Tasty "little rags"

SERVES 4 OR 5

New York City is a haven for lovers of Italian food. A chef trained by his or her nonna makes fresh pasta on almost every block. I worked for one of them, Frank Prisinzano; under Frank, I learned about the intricacies of regional Italian cuisine and how to run a true neighborhood restaurant (the secret is always being open, always*—holidays, blizzards, the apocalypse . . .).*

Beyond all that, there is one more thing I will always be grateful to Frank for: introducing me to cencioni. I had never even seen this pasta shape—like flatter, larger orecchiette—and when I tasted it, I was hooked on its chewy texture and its ability to cling to a meaty ragù. This is a great handmade pasta to try if you've never made pasta before. You don't even need a rolling pin. Since the pasta shape is so large, each noodle is relatively forgiving to form; just be sure you are pressing down firmly enough to flatten its center; if it isn't thin enough, the pasta will taste unpleasantly doughy instead of delicate and chewy. Be warned: As these noodles come out of the water and you toss them in olive oil, keep them away from potential snackers. Otherwise, they'll be gone before you know it. (Though, Frank, if you're reading this, I still maintain my innocence in all matters of missing cencioni.)

INGREDIENTS:

For the Dough

- **2⅓ cups / 290g durum flour, plus more for dusting**
- **¾ cup / 175g lukewarm water**
- **½ teaspoon Diamond Crystal kosher salt (see page 16)**

For the Sauce

- **8 hot Italian sausages, removed from the casing**
- **¼ cup extra-virgin olive oil**
- **8 garlic cloves, thinly sliced**
- **1 medium yellow onion, diced**
- **Kosher salt**
- **½ cup sake or white wine**
- **2 teaspoons chili flakes**
- **1 bay leaf**
- **1 (28-ounce) can crushed tomatoes**
- **Freshly cracked black pepper**
- **⅓ cup parsley leaves, coarsely chopped**
- **Extra-virgin olive oil, for drizzling**
- **½ cup finely grated Parmigiano-Reggiano cheese**

1. ***To make the dough:*** In a medium bowl, combine the **flour, water,** and **salt.** Using stiff fingers, whisk to combine until all the flour is moist. Transfer the dough to a clean surface dusted with flour and knead for 5 minutes. Dust the surface with flour again and knead for another 5 minutes. The dough should be smooth, not sticky, and bounce back when poked. Roll the dough into a ball and cover it with a moist kitchen towel. Let it rest at room temperature for about 30 minutes. While the dough rests, make the sauce.

2. ***To make the sauce:*** In a large pot over medium-high heat, add the **sausage** and **oil** and, using a whisk, break up the pieces of sausage into smaller chunks. Cook, stirring frequently and making sure to scrape the corners of the pot, until the sausage gets bits of brown, about 5 minutes. Jab at the sausage with the whisk again to break it into smaller, more even pieces. Cook for another 5 minutes, until the sausage is evenly browned, then add the **garlic, onion,** and a large pinch of **salt.** Cook, stirring frequently, until some of the garlic turns a deep golden brown, about 5 minutes.

3. Add the **sake,** stir to combine, then cook until the liquid has completely reduced and the sausage starts frying in the fat again, 4 to 6 minutes. Add the **chili flakes** and **bay leaf,** stir to incorporate, and cook for 1 minute.

4. Add the **tomatoes.** Season with a large pinch of

Recipe continues →

PS:
This is the same dough and process as you—the bravest pastaiolo around!—would use to make orecchiette. All you need to do is make a rope ¼ inch thick and cut it into ¼-inch pieces, then proceed as written.

PPS:
This amount of sausage makes a very meaty ragù; if you want a saucier, tomato-forward one, use 4 links instead.

Cencioni with Sausage

Continued

salt and a few grinds from the peppermill. Stir to combine. Put the lid most of the way on, then let the sauce come to a simmer. Stir again, turn down the heat to low, and cook for 20 minutes, stirring frequently to avoid scorching. Taste and adjust the seasoning with more salt and black pepper as needed. Stir in the **parsley.** If the sauce is done before you are done making the pasta, hold on low heat until the pasta is ready.

5. ***To form and cook the cencioni:*** Divide the dough into four balls and roll each piece into a 1-inch rope. Cut a 1-inch piece. Using a butter knife or metal bench scraper, place the knife jagged-side down on the top of the dough portion. Press firmly, flatten the dough, then drag it to the opposite side. The dough should curl around itself. Pick up the pasta, unroll it, pull it into an oval, and stretch it slightly to form a definitive flat interior with a ridge. Transfer to a sheet pan lightly dusted with flour. Repeat with all the dough.

6. Bring a large pot of water to a boil. Season it like a slightly salty soup. Boil the cencioni until they are cooked through (they should be chewy but not doughy), about 3 minutes. Taste them to make sure. Transfer the cencioni to a large heatproof bowl, drizzle with olive oil, and toss to coat.

7. ***To serve:*** Add the pasta to the sauce and stir to combine. Make sure that the cencioni are not stuck together. Divide among bowls, and top with a fistful of **Parmesan** and a drizzle of **oil.** Eat while the cencioni are still steaming hot. (Don't eat the bay leaf, though. Just pull that out when you come across it.)

CHAPTER 5

Meat, Poultry & Seafood

Become a cut above the rest

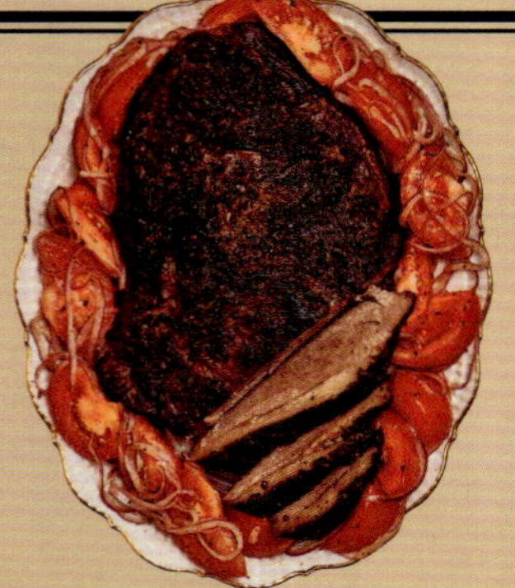

CHICKEN
AND RICE
p. 212

STRIP STEAK, BAKED
POTATO, AND WEDGE SALAD
p. 208

GINGER-GARLIC-SCALLION
SHRIMP SCAMPI
p. 239

PIMPI'S
CHILI CON CARNE
p. 226

BRAZILIAN
HOT DOG PARTY
p. 227

KINDA SHISH
TAWOOK SPREAD
p. 215

CRISPY SALMON AND
BULGUR SALAD
p. 242

PORK CHOPS AND
TOMATILLO NAM PLA PRIK
p. 223

A ROASTED
CHICKEN DINNER
p. 219

FROM THE AGES of six to fourteen, I struggled with chronic immune thrombocytopenia (ITP). ITP is a rare autoimmune disorder where your body decides to attack and destroy its own platelets. When my platelet count was low, which was often, minor bumps resulted in large, purple bruises and my gums and nose would bleed like I was auditioning for Fight Club. The care I got in Doha was great, but there were no long-term solutions. I would just need to go in for treatment whenever my platelets dropped below a certain level. I spent a lot of time in a hospital hooked up to an IV during those years.

After three years of constant fluctuations in my platelet count and various internal bleeding close calls, my parents had had enough. They put together enough money to take me to Johns Hopkins Hospital in Baltimore for a couple of weeks. They had heard that there were new developments for treatment, and I qualified as one of the potential candidates to try it out. We couldn't afford to all go, so I went just with my dad. This was the first time I had ever gone to the United States, and the only time I ever spent any amount of time alone with my dad.

We stayed in the studio apartment of a friend of my dad's who was on vacation. I didn't know what to expect, and I was pretty terrified of this unknown treatment. On our first night there, we went to a steakhouse that was a few blocks away from the apartment. I'd never been to a steakhouse. I ordered a New York Strip (medium-rare), a fully loaded baked potato, and a wedge salad. I still remember the perfect hints of char on the blushing steak. The fluffy baked potato could barely contain all the sour cream it was filled with, and it was showered with finely minced chives. It was everything I had hoped it would be. (Now, after working in steakhouses, I know that the meat was painstakingly brushed in butter as it was roasted in one of those big commercial broilers, and the potato was probably cooked on a bed of salt.)

It was over this dinner that my dad and I had a rare conversation about his life. I learned about his childhood in Qalyub, and his experiences after he moved to Washington, DC. It began to flesh out a person I felt I barely knew.

We spent all our time either at the hospital or at the apartment eating Oscar Mayer turkey bologna and American cheese on Ritz crackers while watching reruns of *The Fresh Prince of Bel-Air*. By the end of the trip, we had the Jazzy-Will handshake down. We went to the theater one night and happened upon the greatest Disney movie of all time: *A Goofy Movie*. Similar to the very journey we were on, Max and his dad, Goofy, go on a road trip and develop a relationship that hadn't existed before. My dad spent so much time on work trips (he was away almost six months of the year) that he sometimes felt like a stranger. Spending all this time

THE BEEF CHART

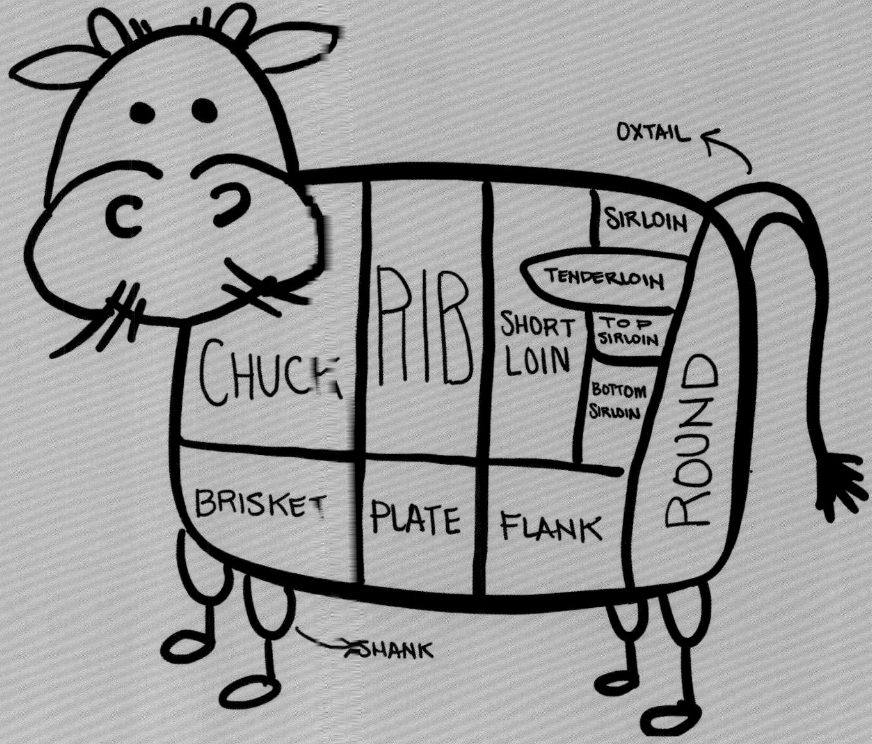

with just him and learning about his experiences as a kid made me see him in a completely different light. I found out about all his secret hiding places for beer as a kid, how he got hepatitis from swimming in the Nile, and how his older sister, Hosna, made sure he and his siblings were fed. I found out that he knew jokes and had a vibrant sense of humor. And most importantly, we could both spend all day watching *The Fresh Prince*

Ultimately, the treatment didn't work (years later, the ITP magically disappeared as my body went through puberty). But we cheered ourselves up by going to the same steakhouse on our last night in Baltimore.

I knew what I was going to order without even looking at the menu

BEEF TEMPERATURE CHART

Here is a chart of final internal temperatures for desired doneness. Take into account the resting time for meat; it always causes the temperature to creep up a few degrees. The larger the piece of meat, the more the temperature creeps up during resting.

RARE
120°F

MEDIUM-RARE
130°F

MEDIUM
140°F

MEDIUM-WELL
150°F

WELL
160°F

STEAKS

Seasoning

Be sure to season steak liberally with kosher salt on all sides, then give it a tap against the cutting board to knock off any excess salt.

Black pepper first or last

There is much debate about whether to pepper your steak before cooking or right after it comes out of the pan. Pre-pepperers like the deeply toasted flavor you get from the charred peppercorn as the steak sears. Post-pepperers prefer the more delicate burn of a peppercorn gently warmed from the residual heat of the steak. It really comes down to my mood; there is no right or wrong method. Experiment with both and choose your go-to method.

Resting

Anything with meat fibers needs to rest after cooking, ideally for half the time it took to cook (unless we're talking long braises and low and slow roasts; 30 minutes is plenty for those). This is even more important for steaks. A well-rested steak is more tender and doesn't leech its precious juices all over your cutting board instead of in your mouth. What is resting? Just do nothing. After cooking, transfer your steak to a cutting board and let it sit. Don't bother tenting with aluminum foil; the steak will still be warm after resting.

Filet (from the tenderloin)

This expensive cut is very lean and a great choice to use raw as tartare or carpaccio. To cook, sear, then baste in a bunch of butter until rare or medium-rare. If you are in the mood for a little peppercorn-sauce action or a hit of au poivre, go with a filet to accompany it. Its nuanced flavor really lets the sauce shine.

Flank (from the flank)

This is another beefy steak but more fibrous and less tender. It's best cooked medium-rare to medium and must be cut against the grain.

Flat Iron (from the chuck)

Similar to a flank, this is a beefy, relatively lean steak that is best seared or grilled to medium-rare to medium and must be cut against the grain.

Hanger (from the plate)

This cut is so flavorful that it used to be known as the butcher's cut because butchers hoarded it for themselves. It has a very prominent grain that needs to be cut against. It's best cooked over medium-high heat, flipping every minute, until it's medium-rare to medium.

New York Strip (from the short loin)

Leaner than a rib eye but richer than a filet, this is my ideal steak. Start with searing the fat cap (the strip of fat along one side) to render it a bit. It's best served medium-rare and seared in a cast-iron skillet over medium-high heat in neutral oil or grilled.

Picanha (Coulotte) (from the sirloin)

My second-favorite cut of steak, picanha is very popular in Brazil and amazing on the grill. It has an intense beef flavor similar to a strip but also has a thick fat cap. Sear it, starting with the fat cap, in a cast-iron pan, then roast it in a 300°F oven until it's medium-rare to medium.

Rib Eye (from the rib)

This is a very beefy, rich steak with streaks of fat running throughout. The best part is the band of meat surrounding the center, known as the deckle or the cap. Since rib eyes are so fatty, cook to medium so some of the fat gets a chance to render. Sear in a cast-iron skillet over medium-high heat in neutral oil or grill. I don't butter-baste these steaks, since there is plenty of fat that renders out as it cooks.

Skirt (from the plate)

A long, thin steak with thick, distinctive fibers, this is another steak that needs to be sliced against the grain. These steaks are great candidates for deep, crusty sears, whether in a roaring cast-iron pan or on a hot grill. The wide surface area and loose structure of the meat fibers mean this steak takes to marinades really well.

T-Bone and Porterhouse (from the short loin)

These have a filet and a strip attached to a T-shaped bone. I'm not a fan of these two cuts of steak, because they need different treatments to be at their best. I always end up having to choose which side I want cooked better. Cook them on a grill, so even if they are overcooked, the meat will get great flavor from the charcoal. They are solid candidates for sauce as well.

NON-STEAK CUTS

Beef Shank (from the shank)

This is what I use when I want a rich ragù for some paccheri or tagliatelle. Liberally season the beef shank with salt and pepper and let it rest on a rack in the fridge, uncovered, for 24 hours. In a Dutch oven, sear the beef shank on all sides until deeply golden brown. Remove and set aside. Add finely minced onion, garlic, celery, and carrot. Cook on medium-high heat until the vegetables are soft and the onions start to get some color. Add a large dollop of tomato paste and cook until it deepens in color. Add a few glugs of red wine and the beef shank. Cover halfway with bone broth and bring to a simmer. Cover and transfer to a 350°F oven and cook until the beef shank is tender (depending on the size, it can take 3½ to 4½ hours). Let it rest, covered, for 30 minutes. Remove the meat from the bones, lightly chop, and return to the braising liquid. Finish with finely sliced red Thai bird's-eye chili, parsley, mint, lemon zest, and a clove of finely grated garlic. Taste and adjust the seasoning with salt.

Cook the pasta 1 minute less than the instructions on the package. Drain the pasta, saving some cooking water, and add to the beef shank along with a glug of pasta water. Bring to a simmer and cook, stirring frequently, until the sauce coats the pasta. Transfer to bowls and garnish with a drizzle of good extra-virgin olive oil and a few shaves of Parm if you want it.

Bone Marrow

Bone marrow (aka bovine butter or mammal margarine) is easy to prepare. Get a butcher to split it in half lengthwise, not as pipes. Soak in a 2 percent brine (2 grams of salt for every 100 grams of water) for 24 hours. Pat dry and roast in a 450°F oven until the marrow starts bubbling along the sides, without fully melting. Serve with slabs of toasted quality bread; lemon wedges; flaky salt; freshly cracked black pepper; thinly shaved shallots tossed in red wine vinegar, salt, freshly cracked black pepper, and olive oil; and a fistful of picked parsley.

Brisket (from the brisket)

This packs a lot of flavor but takes a long time to break down. Rub the brisket with Knorr bouillon powder and lots of black pepper and let it sit on a rack in the fridge, uncovered, for at least 24 hours. From there, put some bone broth or water at the bottom of the roasting pan, put a rack on top, then place the brisket on top. Wrap it tightly in aluminum foil and roast in a 325°F oven until tender and the meat easily breaks apart when poked with a fork; this can take up to 4 hours. Refill the bottom of the pan with water if it dries up. Once tender, uncover and broil the brisket until it's a deep golden brown. Remove the rack, slide the brisket into the drippings in the pan, and let it rest for 30 minutes. After resting, slice against the grain in ½-inch slices and serve with the drippings.

Note: You can add whatever aromatics you want to the water at the bottom of the roasting rack. A bunch of thinly cut yellow onions and whole garlic cloves are some of my favorite additions.

Cheek

Beef cheek is the ultimate braising meat. I treat it the same way as the beef shank (see page 201), only instead of serving it with pasta, I serve it whole on top of creamy mashed potatoes seasoned with a large dollop of grainy mustard and freshly grated horseradish on top.

Chuck (from the chuck)

This is the ideal cut for a pot roast. Season liberally with black pepper and Knorr bouillon powder and let it sit on a rack, uncovered, in the fridge for 24 hours. Sear it hard in a Dutch oven on all sides. Add any aromatics you'd like. I like to keep it tradish with onions, garlic, carrots, and sprigs of thyme and rosemary. Fill the pot halfway with bone broth or water, bring the liquid to a simmer, cover, then transfer to a 350°F oven to finish cooking. Cook until it's tender enough to pull apart with a fork. Depending on the size, it can take 3½ to 4½ hours. Let it rest for at least 30 minutes before serving.

Oxtail
Oxtail gives you the most flavorful cooking liquid. I use oxtail when I want a sauce that's intensely beefy. Season the oxtail all over with Knorr bouillon powder and let it rest on a rack, uncovered, in the fridge for 24 hours. In a blender, blend garlic and yellow onions, along with roasted tomatillos, poblanos, and jalapeños; taste and season with salt as needed. Place a Dutch oven over medium-high heat and sear the oxtail on all sides until deeply golden brown. Remove and set aside. Add ground cumin, ground coriander, and dried oregano and toast briefly before adding the tomatillo mixture. Return the oxtail to the pot, bring the liquid to a simmer, then cover and transfer to a 350°F oven. Cook the oxtail until tender, 2 to 3 hours, then let it rest in the liquid for at least 30 minutes before serving with thinly shaved cabbage, cilantro, lime wedges, radish slices, pickled jalapeños, hot sauce, and tortillas.

Short Rib (from the plate)
Short rib is an interesting cut. I enjoy it seared hard, then braised in bone broth, covered, in a 325°F oven until tender (depending on the size, it can take 3½ to 4½ hours). I also enjoy it deboned, cleaned of sinew, and cut into steaks for searing or grilling. As a steak, it is best served medium-rare and has a more intense flavor than the fanciest steak. This is my favorite cut at any KBBQ spot.

Tongue
Since the tongue is such an active muscle, it needs to be cooked low and slow to become tender. Let the tongue sit in a 2 percent salt brine (2 grams of salt for every 100 grams of water) for 24 hours. Very gently simmer the tongue in water, seasoned with garlic, onion, celery, carrot, bay leaves, salt, and black peppercorns until tender. A skewerlike object should pierce all the way through without firm resistance. Be careful not to overcook; the meat should not become easy to shred; it should still have some bounce to it. Let the tongue sit in the liquid for at least 30 minutes before removing it and cutting the thin outer membrane off. Return it to the liquid and let it sit in the fridge until fully cool. Once cool, cut it into thick slices and sear in a cast-iron skillet until crisp. Serve with boiled potatoes, roasted beets, and a sauce made of loads of freshly shaved horseradish, finely chopped dill and parsley, freshly cracked black pepper, mustard, mayonnaise, and sour cream.

Tongue is also great quickly cooked
Cut off the outer membrane while raw, thinly slice the meat, then sear on a fiery grill or in a cast-iron skillet until deeply golden brown and crisp along the edges. Dip in a sauce of black vinegar, soy, and thinly sliced scallion, ginger, and garlic.

Top Round (from the round)
This is the best cut for roast beef. Rub it with lots of black pepper and Knorr bouillon powder, then let it rest on a rack, uncovered, for at least 24 hours. Rub it with oil and roast it in a 500°F oven until it forms a deep golden-brown crust. Lower the temperature to 325°F and roast until it registers 120°F in the center on an instant-read thermometer. Depending on the size of your roast, this can take a few hours. Let it rest for 30 minutes before slicing and serving. Or, after resting, let it cool completely in the fridge before slicing thinly as needed for sandwiches. It's exceptional served with any form of horseradish.

HOW TO CUT AGAINST THE GRAIN

Look at the direction the grains are running and cut at a 90-degree angle to shorten the fibers when slicing.

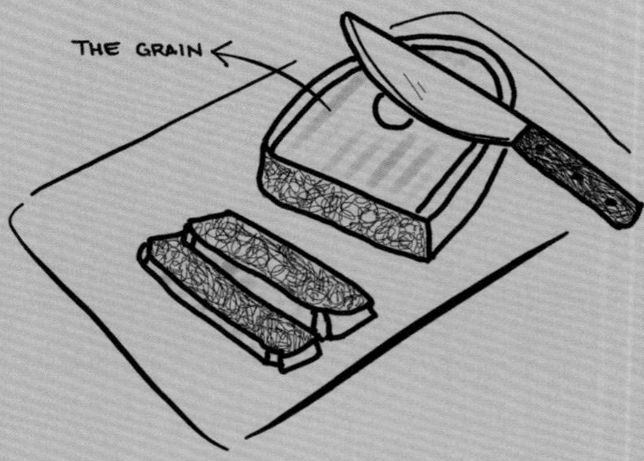

HOW TO SELECT AND STORE FISH

Fish can be intimidating to buy at grocery stores. Going to the frozen aisle is often a less scary option, but it is beneficial to be able to pick out quality fish at your fish counter. The texture and flavor of fresh fish is far superior to its frozen counterpart.

When selecting fish, look for fish that . . .
. . . never smell fishy.
. . . are not slimy.
. . . have eyes that are clear and glassy.
. . . have gills that are bright red.

The best way to store fish is to first pat it dry and then place, uncovered, on a rack in the coldest part of your fridge. If you have unlimited ice and a giant fridge, store your fish on ice but keep the ice in a resealable plastic bag so you don't wake up to the fish sitting in a puddle of water when the ice melts.

Visit Us: Pick Your Own
www.treeliciousorchards.com
KERY
POLO SPORT

Strip Steak, Baked Potato, and Wedge Salad

Classic for a reason

SERVES 2

Much like Ron Swanson, this is the dinner I make for myself every year for my birthday. No party. No outings. No "friends". Nothing but me, a perfectly cooked steak, and a movie. Learning how to cook a steak perfectly is an invaluable skill and only improves with experience. I cook any cut of steak with this same method, and it yields excellent results. Many will advocate for a butter baste at the end of the cook, but I feel like it gets in the way of what I'm here for: intensely beefy flavors.

INGREDIENTS:

For the Potatoes

- **2 large russet potatoes, scrubbed clean**
- **Neutral oil**
- **Kosher salt**

For the Salad

- **4 strips thick-cut bacon, sliced into ¼-inch strips**
- **6 ounces Bayley Hazen blue cheese**
- **½ cup buttermilk**
- **3 tablespoons red wine vinegar, plus more as needed**
- **2 tablespoons sour cream or labneh**
- **Kosher salt**
- **Freshly cracked black pepper**
- **½ cup cherry tomatoes, halved**
- **1 large head iceberg lettuce**
- **Handful of coarsely chopped parsley and finely minced chives**

For the Steak

- **1 New York strip (15 to 18 ounces and 1½ to 2½ inches thick)**
- **Kosher salt**
- **Freshly cracked black pepper**
- **Neutral oil**

For Serving

- **2 tablespoons unsalted butter**
- **¼ cup sour cream**
- **¼ cup finely sliced chives**
- **Flaky salt**
- **Freshly cracked black pepper**

1. Preheat the oven to 400°F.

2. ***To cook the potatoes:*** Poke the **potatoes** all over with a fork. Using your hands, rub a thin layer of **oil** on the potatoes and season all over with **kosher salt.** Place on a baking sheet and bake until the potatoes feel soft and tender when squeezed and a skewerlike object can be inserted into the center without much resistance, 45 to 60 minutes. Remove the pan from the oven and set aside while you are cooking the steak.

3. ***To prepare the salad:*** While the potatoes are baking, line a plate with paper towels.

4. In a medium skillet over medium heat, add the **bacon** and ¼ cup water and cook, stirring frequently, until the bacon has rendered its fat and is crisp, 8 to 10 minutes. Remove the bacon from the skillet with a slotted spoon and place on the prepared plate.

5. Crumble the **blue cheese,** reserving 2 tablespoons for garnish.

6. In a medium bowl, combine the blue cheese, **buttermilk, sour cream,** 1 tablespoon of the **vinegar,** a pinch of **kosher salt,** and a few cracks of **black pepper** and whisk until well incorporated. Taste and adjust the seasoning with more kosher salt, pepper, and vinegar as needed.

7. In a small bowl, toss the **tomatoes** with a pinch of salt and set them aside.

8. Smash the head of **iceberg,** core-side down, on a cutting board to loosen the core in the center. Hold onto the bottom of the core, give it a firm wiggle, then remove it. Trim ¼ inch off the top and bottom, so it resembles a disk that lies flat. Place the lettuce on a serving platter and drizzle the remaining 2 tablespoons vinegar on top. Season with more kosher salt and pepper as needed and set aside until ready to garnish.

9. ***To cook the steak:*** Turn down the oven temperature to 300°F.

10. Pat the **steak** dry with paper towels and season both sides aggressively with **kosher salt** and a few cranks of **black pepper.**

11. Place a medium cast-iron or ovenproof skillet over medium-high heat until lightly smoking. Add a splash of **oil** and swirl to coat the pan; it should shimmer immediately. Add the steak and press down firmly to maximize contact with the pan. Flip the steak every minute, until a deep crust forms on both sides, 6 to 8 minutes total. Using an instant-read thermometer, take the temperature of your steak. If it is not at your desired temperature (see chart on page 199), transfer the pan to the oven to finish cooking. Remove the pan from the oven, transfer the steak to a cutting board, and allow it to rest for at least 5 to 8 minutes before slicing and serving.

12. ***Serve:*** Top the iceberg with the blue cheese dressing, reserved blue cheese crumbles, bacon bits, cherry tomatoes, and herbs.

13. Finish the baked potatoes by making an incision across the top of each potato lengthwise, halfway through. Push the ends of the potato inward to force the potato open. Put a tablespoon of **butter** in each potato and use a fork to fluff up the insides. Top with **sour cream** and **chives.** Serve the potatoes with **flaky salt** and **black pepper** on the side, along with the sliced steak and salad.

STAUB

Chicken and Rice

With the flavors of machboos

SERVES 4

*Machboos, a fragrant rice dish like biryani that is found throughout the Arabian Gulf, was a special occasion dish as I was growing up. We used to have it at Qatari homes for iftars, Eid, and big gatherings, or at home for a 4.3 GPA report card day. It was how I celebrated my high school graduation, huddled on the floor around a large gleaming silver platter of meticulously spiced rice, topped with a golden roasted half of a lamb studded with nuts and raisins and shadowy orbs of black lime. Machboos is meant to be eaten with your hands; you tear off a hunk of meat and mix it with some of the rice directly in front of you (*never *cross into somebody else's rice territory). Lamb machboos is extremely labor intensive, and the chicken version is found more readily. This is not a recipe for chicken machboos; this one is much easier than that, although the seasoning evokes it. The sour-but-sweet-but-funky-but-bitter flavors all at the same time with notes of black lime are key to mimicking the traditional flavor of machboos. That said, this dish is just as delicious without the black lime; don't let that stop you from making it. The spicy ketchupy condiment known as daqus is a great complement to the rich, delicately spiced rice, but it is the buttery nut topping that makes this dish extra special.*

INGREDIENTS:

4 whole skin-on chicken legs
Kosher salt
2 cups basmati rice (preferably Sella)

For the Daqus

2 tablespoons extra-virgin olive oil
3 garlic cloves, finely minced
1 tablespoon tomato paste
½ cup tomato passata or freshly grated tomato
1 or 2 Thai red bird's-eye chilies, depending on your desired heat level

2 tablespoons unsalted butter
1 medium yellow onion, diced
2 garlic cloves, minced
1 tablespoon ground coriander
1 teaspoon freshly cracked black pepper
1 teaspoon Kashmiri chili powder or hot paprika
½ teaspoon ground cinnamon
½ teaspoon ground ginger
½ teaspoon ground cardamom
½ teaspoon ground turmeric
½ teaspoon ground black lime (optional)
¼ teaspoon ground cloves
2½ cups chicken bone broth
½ cup tomato passata

For the Topping

3 tablespoons butter
⅓ cup slivered almonds
⅓ cup whole, shelled raw pistachios
⅓ cup raisins

1. Set a wire rack on a baking sheet. Season the **chicken** with **salt** and put it on the rack, uncovered, and place it in the fridge for at least 6 hours and up to 48 hours.

2. Put the **rice** in a medium bowl and rinse under cold water until the water runs almost fully clear. Cover the rice with cold water and let it soak for 20 minutes. Drain well.

3. ***To make the daqus:*** In a small skillet over medium heat, combine the **oil** and **garlic.** Cook until the garlic is fragrant, softens, and turns a light brown, 3 to 4 minutes. Add the **tomato paste** and cook, stirring frequently, until it deepens in color, 3 to 5 minutes. Add the **passata** and **chilies** and simmer for 5 minutes. Taste and season with salt as needed. Transfer the daqus to a container and then to the fridge to cool.

4. In a large pot or braiser over medium-high heat, place the chicken skin-side down and cook until the chicken renders some fat and the skin turns golden-brown, 10 to 12 minutes. If some chicken pieces brown faster than others, remove those pieces first and allow the rest to catch up. Flip the chicken and cook until lightly browned on the other side as well, another 10 minutes. Transfer the chicken to a plate.

5. Add the **butter, onion,** and **garlic** to the pot with the rendered chicken fat. Turn down the heat to medium and cook, stirring frequently, until the onion softens and starts to brown, 3 to 5 minutes. Use the moisture from the onion to scrape up any bits stuck to the bottom of the pan. Add the **coriander, black pepper, chili powder, cinnamon, ginger, cardamom, turmeric, black lime** (if using), and **cloves** and cook until fragrant, about 1 minute. Add the drained rice and stir to coat in the fat.

6. Add the **broth** and **passata** and stir to incorporate. Increase the heat to medium-high. Once the mixture simmers, top with the chicken pieces, skin-sides up, and cover. Turn down the heat to low and cook until no moisture remains and the rice is fully cooked, about 15 minutes. Let rest, covered, for 10 to 15 minutes.

7. ***To make the topping:*** In a small skillet over medium heat, combine the **butter, almonds, pistachios,** and **raisins** and cook, stirring frequently, until the almonds are lightly golden, 4 to 6 minutes.

8. Top the rice with the nut mixture and serve with the daqus on the side as a condiment.

Kinda Shish Tawook Spread

My desert island meal

SERVES 4

Everybody loves shawarma, and I don't blame them; it's a perfect sandwich. But in the gifted Lebanese sandwich family, an overlooked sibling is just as brilliant: the shish tawook. Tender chunks of seasoned and grilled chicken breast are slathered in toum, a whipped garlic spread; cucumber pickles, french fries, and wrapped in a pita. I recreated that sandwich but made a significant and potentially controversial change. I opted for chicken thighs so they could broil long enough to get some char, which is essential to the flavor. Cooking breasts this way would leave you with chalky and dry pieces of meat, whereas the thighs render their fat and become unctuous and tender. I also swap out the traditional thin pita for a fluffy variation cooked on the stovetop. You can garnish your sandwiches with condiments and veggies, but know that the classic combo of toum, pickles, and fries is hard to beat.

INGREDIENTS:

For the Pita Dough

- **3¼ cups / 390g bread flour, plus more for dusting**
- **1 teaspoon / 5g Diamond Crystal kosher salt (see page 16)**
- **1 tablespoon / 12g instant yeast**
- **1 tablespoon / 14g sugar**
- **⅓ cup / 80g buttermilk**
- **1 cup / 240g warm water**
- **2 tablespoons / 30g olive oil, plus more for greasing**

For the Marinade

- **½ cup plain whole milk yogurt**
- **2 tablespoons tomato paste**
- **2 teaspoons ground coriander**
- **2 teaspoons kosher salt**
- **1 teaspoon ground cumin**
- **1 teaspoon hot paprika**
- **¼ teaspoon ground cinnamon**
- **¼ teaspoon ground cardamom**
- **¼ teaspoon ground allspice**

- **1½ pounds boneless, skinless chicken thighs**

For the Toum

- **10 garlic cloves**
- **¼ cup freshly squeezed lemon juice (about 1 large lemon)**
- **1 teaspoon Diamond Crystal kosher salt**
- **1½ cups neutral oil**

Extra-virgin olive oil, for drizzling

Cucumber pickles, pickled turnips, french fries, or whatever veggies you're into, for serving

1. ***To prepare the dough:*** In a medium bowl, combine the **flour, salt, yeast,** and **sugar** and whisk until combined, 1 minute. Make a well in the center of the flour. In the well, add the **buttermilk, water,** and **oil.** Using your hands, incorporate the flour into the water mixture. Once all the flour is wet, transfer to a clean surface lightly dusted with flour and knead until the dough is smooth and an indent does not stay when poked, about 10 minutes. Roll the dough into a taut ball, transfer to a medium bowl, and drizzle some oil on top. Roll the dough around so the ball is completely coated. Tightly cover the bowl in plastic wrap and transfer to your fridge for at least 12 hours and up to 36 hours.

2. ***To make the marinade:*** A few hours before the dough has finished proofing, prepare the marinade for the chicken. In a medium bowl, combine the **yogurt, tomato paste, coriander, salt, cumin, paprika, cinnamon, cardamom,** and **allspice** and whisk until well combined.

3. Add the **chicken thighs** to the bowl with the marinade and massage the marinade into the meat. Make sure all the chicken is well coated. Cover and transfer to the fridge to marinate for at least 3 hours and up to 12 hours.

Recipe continues →

Kinda Shish Tawook Spread

Continued

4. ***To make the pitas:*** Remove the dough from the fridge and, working on a clean surface dusted with flour, divide the dough into twelve even portions, about 2 ounces each. Roll the portions into balls. Cover with a kitchen towel and let sit for 5 to 10 minutes to warm up. Roll each portion into a 5- to 5½-inch-diameter circle, using a floured rolling pin. Place on a floured surface and cover with a kitchen towel; let the rolled-out pieces proof until they have risen very slightly and feel like what I imagine a cloud to feel like, 30 minutes to 1 hour.

5. Place a griddle or a large skillet over medium-high heat until very lightly smoking. Add a piece of dough to the hot pan and cook until the bottom is very lightly golden brown around the perimeter, 2 to 3 minutes. Flip and cook the other side until lightly golden brown, pressing down on the edges gently with a spatula to encourage it to puff up, 2 to 3 minutes more. Flip over to the first side again to get a little color in the center of the bread, 1 to 2 minutes. Transfer the hot bread to a kitchen towel and fold the towel over the bread to keep it covered and allow it to steam. Repeat until all the dough is cooked, adjusting the heat in case the skillet gets too hot and smoky.

6. ***To make the toum:*** In a tall, narrow container, add the **garlic, lemon juice, salt,** and 1 tablespoon water. Blend with an immersion blender until smooth. Let the mixture sit for at least 10 minutes to mellow out some of the raw garlic bite. Dump the oil on top, then lower the immersion blender to the bottom of the container. Turn the blender on high but don't move it yet. Once the mixture starts emulsifying and thickening, slowly tilt the blender to introduce more oil and very slowly pull the blender to the top of the mix. Plunge the blender up and down until the toum is fully emulsified and thick. If you do not have an immersion blender, add the garlic mixture to a food processor, turn it on, then very slowly stream in the oil until it is emulsified and thickened. Set aside.

7. ***To assemble the sandwiches:*** Turn your oven to the highest broil setting. Line a baking sheet with aluminum foil and place a wire rack on top.

8. Remove the chicken from the fridge and, using your hands, scrape off any excess marinade and place the chicken on the rack. Drizzle the top with the **oil** and place the pan in the oven. Cook until chicken thighs are lightly charred on one side, about 15 minutes. Flip the chicken over and cook until the other side is charred, another 10 to 15 minutes. Transfer the chicken to a cutting board and allow it to rest for at least 5 minutes before slicing.

9. Serve the chicken alongside the warm pitas, **pickles,** toum, or any other accoutrements your heart desires.

EUGENE
I'm Too SEXY
For My HAIR

A Roasted Chicken Dinner

That would make Ina proud

MAKES 2 TO 3 SERVINGS

This recipe mimics the rotisserie chickens you see in many grocery stores. The meat is tender and juicy, and the skin is fully rendered. The hardest part of roasting an entire chicken is getting the best out of the dark and white meat. I like the dark meat to hit at least 175°F on an instant-read thermometer, while the white meat is best right under 160°F. Roasting the chicken upside down over a moist environment ensures that the white meat doesn't overcook while the thighs can fully cook. Here, the greens and bone broth both turn into a gravy (and a silky side). Seasoning the chicken and letting it rest overnight is optional but will make a huge difference in the seasoning of the flesh and the texture of the skin. If you are skipping this step, you can omit the baking soda and just season the chicken liberally before roasting.

INGREDIENTS:

For the Chicken

- **1 whole chicken (3 to 4 pounds)**
- **3 to 4 tablespoons (1 tablespoon per pound of chicken) Diamond Crystal kosher salt (see page 16)**
- **1 teaspoon baking soda**
- **Neutral oil or ghee**

For the Greens

- **2 tablespoons neutral oil or ghee**
- **2 bunches of kale, leaves stripped and finely chopped**
- **1 head garlic**
- **30 ounces chicken bone broth**
- **2 shallots, roots trimmed and halved**
- **2 tablespoons unsalted butter**
- **Kosher salt**
- **Freshly cracked black pepper**

- **2 pounds baby gold potatoes**

1. ***To prepare the chicken:*** Using paper towels, pat the **chicken** dry all over. Place a wire rack on top of a sheet pan.

2. In a small bowl, mix the **salt** with the **baking soda** until evenly combined. Sprinkle evenly all over the chicken. Transfer the chicken, breast-side up, to the fridge, uncovered, and let it sit for 12 to 36 hours.

3. ***To roast the chicken:*** Preheat the oven to 450°F.

4. ***To cook the greens:*** Place a large skillet over medium-high heat and heat until lightly smoking. Add the **oil, kale,** and **garlic** and cook, stirring frequently, until the kale has wilted, about 5 minutes. Add the **broth** and **shallots** and bring to a simmer before killing the heat.

5. Rub the chicken all over with **oil.** Flip the chicken on the rack so it is breast-side down, then place the rack on top of the pan with the kale so the chicken is suspended above the kale. Transfer the pan to the oven and roast until the chicken is deeply golden brown and crisp and the thighs register at least 165°F on an instant-read thermometer, 40 to 50 minutes.

6. Carefully flip the chicken over and continue roasting until the breast is golden-brown and registers 155°F in the thickest part, about 30 more minutes. If the breast is at temperature but needs more color, turn the broiler on and broil until the skin is golden-brown. Transfer the pan to the stovetop and move the rack to a cutting board to allow the chicken to rest for 20 minutes before carving.

7. While the chicken is in the oven, simmer the **potatoes** in salted water until they are tender and can be easily pierced with a skewer, 35 to 45 minutes. Drain, cover, and set aside.

8. While the chicken rests, bring the kale to a simmer and swirl in the butter until it melts. Taste and adjust the seasoning with **salt** and **pepper** as needed before serving alongside chicken and potatoes.

Crispy Pork Belly

Crunchy skin that won't crack a tooth

SERVES 6 TO 8

My first bite of crispy pork skin was transcendental. It was a piece of suckling pig, served at my cousin's wedding in Santa Cruz, Bolivia. The tender, crisp skin shattered between my teeth without squeaking or fighting back. A thin layer of velvety fat hadn't been fully rendered yet, and a few strands of tender meat clung on to the fat. I could write wedding vows to that bite. This slab of pork belly checks all the same boxes. Sure, it takes a long time, but it's mostly inactive. Making more than you need isn't bad, either, because it keeps for a few days, and reheating leftover slabs in a 450°F oven will give you pork as good as the first day you made it. If you decide to make the yuca, check it by cutting a small notch in the skin. The flesh underneath should be pearly white, without any flecks or splotches of black. Boiled yuca is a great blank canvas starch for fatty meats or powerful sauces. It is also exceptional fried. To make the best fried yuca, boil it until fully tender, let it fully cool before breaking it into thick, English chiplike pieces, and fry in 350°F neutral oil until golden brown and crispy. The outside will crack like glass, and the inside will be fluffy and soft. It rivals the best fries.

INGREDIENTS:

- **1½ skin-on pork belly (4 to 4½ pounds)**
- **Kosher salt**
- **1 pint lager or other light beer**
- **10 garlic cloves**
- **2 pounds yuca, peeled, cut into 5-inch chunks, and cut in half lengthwise (optional)**
- **1 medium red onion, halved and very thinly sliced**
- **½ cup cilantro leaves and tender stems, coarsely chopped**
- **½ cup freshly squeezed lime juice (about 4 limes)**

1. Set a wire rack on a baking sheet.

2. Using a knife with a sharp tip, poke shallow incisions all over the skin of the **pork belly** (this will help the fat render). Don't become consumed by rage about your ever-rising rent and cut all the way down into the flesh. Don't go past the fat cap under the skin. Liberally cover the belly with salt on the top, bottom, and sides and place on the rack. Transfer the pan to the fridge and let it sit, uncovered, for at least 12 hours and up to 48 hours.

3. Preheat the oven to 325°F.

4. Add the **beer** and **garlic** to a roasting pan. Transfer the rack with the pork to the roasting rack (the pork should be sitting above the liquid). Wrap the pan tightly with a layer of plastic wrap, tucking the plastic into the lip of the pan, and then wrap with aluminum foil. Tuck the foil into the lip of the pan as well; there should be no plastic exposed. The foil acts as a shield, preventing the plastic from melting. Roast until the pork is tender and the flesh pulls apart when prodded with a fork, 3 to 3½ hours.

5. Remove the foil and plastic wrap. Turn the broiler on low and broil the pork until the top is crisp, 16 to 20 minutes. There will be popping; do not be alarmed. It's a good sign that the skin is crisping. Turn the pan if one side is crisping faster than the other. Once the skin is crisp, remove the pan from the oven, transfer the rack with the pork on it to a cutting board, and let it rest for at least 10 minutes before slicing. Reserve the roasted garlic and drippings.

6. If making the **yuca,** while the pork cooks, fill a medium pot with cold water, season with a couple of large pinches of salt, and add the yuca. Simmer over medium heat until the yuca is fully tender, about 45 minutes. It should smoosh when you poke it with a spoon. Drain the yuca and transfer it to a bowl. Pull out any tough strings that run through the center and set aside.

7. In a medium bowl, combine the **onion, cilantro, lime juice,** and a large pinch of **salt** and toss to combine. Add the reserved garlic that roasted under the pork. Stir to combine. Taste and adjust the seasoning with more salt if needed.

8. Transfer the drippings to a small bowl and, using a ladle or spoon, remove as much of the fat that has pooled on top as you can. It will look like a layer of oil. You can toss it or reserve as a cooking fat.

9. To slice, flip the pork so the skin is against the cutting board. Slice through the meat and firmly press to go through the crispy skin cleanly. Serve the slices with the yuca, onion salad, and drippings.

Pork Chops and Tomatillo Nam Pla Prik

Feat. a GOAT sauce. (Did I pull that off? Don't tell me if no.)

SERVES 3 OR 4

Thai nam pla prik is one of the world's greatest sauces. Preparing it presents the ultimate test of flavor balance: When the ratios are right, the sweetness is perfectly complemented by the funky salinity of fish sauce and brightened with lime. But when that harmony is out of whack, it tastes like it. And it pairs perfectly with pork chops (look for chops with a thick band of fat; it's the best part). Here, I blend nam pla prik with charred tomatillos to give the sauce more body and another layer of acidity. Skip the tomatillos and herbs for a more traditional nam pla prik that is just as delicious. When paired with thick juicy pork chops and raw, crisp vegetables, it really comes alive. The acidity brightens the fatty chops, and the herbaceous funk adds complexity to the bites of raw vegetables.

INGREDIENTS:

- **4 to 5 tomatillos (about 8 ounces)**
- **½ cup freshly squeezed lime juice (about 4 limes), plus more as needed**
- **½ cup fish sauce**
- **⅓ cup sugar, dissolved in 3 tablespoons hot water**
- **½ cup cilantro, tender leaves and stems, coarsely chopped**
- **½ cup (packed) mint leaves, roughly torn**
- **4 Thai red bird's-eye chilies, thinly sliced into rings (or fewer if you can't handle spice)**
- **4 garlic cloves, thinly sliced**
- **1 shallot, thinly sliced**
- **Kosher salt**
- **2 bone-in pork chops (each about 1½ inches thick; a total of 2¾ pounds)**
- **2 tablespoons neutral oil**

For Serving

- **4 Persian cucumbers, cut into spears**
- **2 heads Little Gem lettuce, leaves picked**
- **1 lime, cut into wedges**

1. Turn the oven to its highest broil setting. Line a sheet pan with aluminum foil.

2. Peel the **tomatillos** and rinse off the sticky residue. Place the tomatillos on the sheet pan and broil until they are charred and soft, about 15 minutes.

3. In a medium bowl, whisk together the **lime juice, fish sauce,** and **sugar syrup** until well combined. Add the **cilantro, mint, chilies, garlic,** and **shallot.** Taste and adjust the seasoning with salt or more lime juice as needed. If you want it spicier, add another chili, tough guy. Cover and transfer to the fridge until the pork is cooked and rested.

4. Turn down the oven to 300°F. Pat the **pork chops** dry with paper towels and aggressively season both sides with **salt.** Place a heavy, medium skillet over medium-low heat and heat until it's hot and slightly smoking.

5. Add the **oil** to the pan. Increase the heat to medium-high and add the chops. Press down firmly to ensure maximum contact with the pan. This is another good place to use one of those presses we discuss in the recipe for Tahini-Roasted Swordfish (page 241) if you have one. Flip the pork chops every minute until they are golden-brown on both sides, about 6 minutes total.

6. Check temperature, if not at desired temp, transfer to oven to finish cooking.

7. Transfer the pork chops to a cutting board and let rest for at least 6 minutes. Slice the pork chops against the grain and transfer to a serving platter. Spoon some of the sauce over the pork chops and serve the rest on the side. Serve the **cucumber spears, lettuce,** and **lime wedges** on another plate. Make lettuce wraps if you want. Live a little.

Pimpi's Chili con Carne

Star of the PTA

SERVES 6

This is the dish that reminds me the most of my mom, known to her closest friends as Pimpi. She would make this dish whenever I had friends over, and inevitably, as soon as they got home, she would get a call from their moms asking for the recipe. This chili is the ultimate crowd-pleaser, and it only gets better with time. Whenever Mom made it, I used to shadow her, learning all the little steps to its excellence: being sure the ground beef was browned enough, cooking out the tomato paste so the flavor deepened, making sure the spices got direct contact with the heat so they could come alive. And the best part about her making chili? The leftovers always became chili dogs.

INGREDIENTS:

- **2 tablespoons neutral oil**
- **2 pounds ground beef**
- **Kosher salt**
- **2 tablespoons tomato paste**
- **1 large yellow onion, diced**
- **6 garlic cloves, minced**
- **1 tablespoon ground cumin**
- **1 tablespoon hot paprika**
- **1 tablespoon chili powder (see Note)**
- **2 teaspoons ground coriander**
- **2 teaspoons dried oregano**
- **½ teaspoon ground cinnamon**
- **¼ teaspoon ground cloves**
- **1 bay leaf**
- **1 (28-ounce) can crushed tomatoes**
- **2 tablespoons (packed) dark brown sugar, plus more as needed**
- **2 (15-ounce) cans kidney beans, drained**

1. In a large heavy-bottomed pot over medium-high heat, add the **oil** and heat until it shimmers. Add the **ground beef** and a large pinch of **salt** and hit it with a whisk to break it up into smaller pieces. Cook, stirring occasionally, until the meat is browned and crisp, 16 to 20 minutes.

2. Add the **tomato paste,** stir to incorporate, and cook, stirring frequently, until it deepens in color and no longer smells metallic, 2 to 4 minutes.

3. Add the **onion, garlic,** and a large pinch of **salt** and cook, stirring occasionally, until the onion starts to soften, 5 to 6 minutes. Add the **cumin, paprika, chili powder, coriander, oregano, cinnamon, cloves,** and **bay leaf** and stir to coat. Cook until the spices are fragrant, about 1 minute.

4. Add the **tomatoes, brown sugar,** and a pinch of salt and stir to incorporate, scraping the bottom of the pot with a wooden spoon to remove the caramelized bits. Bring to a simmer, cover three-quarters of the way, then turn down the heat to medium-low. Gently simmer until the flavors meld and the sauce thickens, 16 to 20 minutes.

5. Stir in the **beans** and simmer for 5 more minutes. Taste the chili and adjust the seasoning with more brown sugar and salt as needed. Discard the bay leaf. Let the chili sit for 5 to 10 minutes before serving.

Note:
You can use any kind of chili powder—from chipotle for some smoky heat to cayenne for searing heat to more paprika—or a combination.

Brazilian Hot Dog Party

Step up your dawg game.

SERVES 4

Every Brazilian weeknight gathering had a giant pot of these hot dogs cooked in tomato sauce at its center. Countless options for toppings would surround the steamy cauldron of hot dogs: the standard ketchup, mayo, and mustard; thin shoestring potatoes; potato salad (double potato!); slices of avocado; sautéed corn; and what seemed like whatever random leftovers were in the fridge. We would grab a bun, pop a frank in there, and spoon on some onion and pepper sauce. Then, chaos would be thy master. I would try a different combo every time (with failed experiments like mashed potatoes, shoestring potatoes, apple slices, and olives still haunting my childhood memories). But I would always go back to my tried-and-true for a second dawg: mustard, mayo, shoestring potatoes, avocado, corn, and some mozz. Be sure to save any leftover sauce after eating all the hotdogs—and you will, sweet reader, eat all the hot dogs. The smoke permeates the sauce and gives it a deeper savory note that's great over pasta the next day. Traditionally, the sauce uses bell peppers, but I prefer Cubanelle peppers' bright vegetal tones.

INGREDIENTS:

- **¼ cup unsalted butter**
- **1 large yellow onion, halved and cut into ¼-inch slices**
- **6 Cubanelle peppers (or bell if you prefer), seeded and cut into ¼-inch strips**
- **8 garlic cloves, thinly sliced**
- **Kosher salt**
- **1 teaspoon dried oregano**
- **1 teaspoon chili flakes**
- **1 (24.5-ounce) jar tomato passata**
- **8 smoked hot dogs (make sure they're smoked!)**
- **8 hot dog buns**

For the Toppings

- **Finely grated Parmesan cheese**
- **Freshly grated mozzarella cheese**
- **Shredded carrots**
- **Steamed peas**
- **Sautéed corn**
- **Pickled chilies**
- **Coarsely chopped olives**
- **Mashed potatoes? Fuck it. Mashed potatoes**
- **Crunchy bits o' bacon**
- **Crunchy potato sticks (batata palha)**
- **Ketchup**
- **Mustard**
- **Mayo**
- **Whatever chaos grips you**

1. In a large pot over medium heat, add the **butter, onion, peppers, garlic,** and a large pinch of **salt** and cook, stirring occasionally, until the onion and peppers have softened, 12 to 15 minutes.

2. Add the **oregano, chili flakes,** and **passata** and bring to a simmer. Cover and simmer, stirring occasionally, until the flavors meld and the onion and peppers are fully softened, about 15 minutes. Add the **hot dogs** and cook until warmed through, about 10 minutes.

3. Serve with the **hot dog buns** and whatever toppings your heart desires.

Kofta Meatballs

Feat. Ritz panade panache

SERVES 4

These meatballs borrow the warming seasoning from the koftas you find grilling over charcoal throughout the Middle East. The addition of panade is what turns them from kofta into tender meat orbs. Panade is a dairy and bread paste mixed into ground meat to make it moister and more tender—loaves, balls, or patties. The starches absorb the dairy and form a gel that coats and lubricates the meat fibers. It's traditionally made from milk and stale bread or bread crumbs. But don't be limited to that; here, I use buttery Ritz crackers to add another layer of flavor. Any dried bread can be turned into panade; the key is that it be dry enough to absorb the dairy. You don't need to make a panade just from milk either. I like to use heavy cream to add much-needed fat to turkey meatballs and buttermilk to add a layer of tang to spicy pork patties. Depending on my mood, I like serving these meatballs in a pita, on spaghetti, or over rice.

INGREDIENTS:

For the Meatballs

- 1 **medium yellow onion, diced**
- 4 **garlic cloves, minced**
- **Kosher salt**
- 2 **tablespoons extra-virgin olive oil**
- 1½ **sleeves finely crushed Ritz crackers (about 1½ cups)**
- ¾ **cup whole milk**
- 2 **large eggs**
- 1 **pound ground lamb**
- 1 **pound ground beef**
- ½ **cup parsley leaves, coarsely chopped**
- 1 **tablespoon ground coriander**
- 1 **tablespoon hot paprika**
- 2 **teaspoons freshly cracked black pepper**
- 2 **teaspoons ground cumin**
- 1 **teaspoon ground allspice**
- 1 **teaspoon ground cardamom**
- 1 **teaspoon ground cinnamon**
- 1 **teaspoon baking powder**
- 8 **garlic cloves, thinly sliced**
- 2 **(28-ounce) cans crushed tomatoes**
- 2 **bay leaves**
- **Pita, pasta, rice, or your favorite hoagie roll, for serving**

1. ***To make the meatballs:*** In a medium skillet over medium heat, add the **onion, garlic,** a pinch of **salt,** and the **oil** and cook, stirring frequently, until the onion has softened, 8 to 10 minutes. If the onion starts to get color before it has softened, add a splash of water. Transfer to a plate to cool.

2. In a large bowl, add the **crackers** and **milk** and work with your hands until it is a moist paste. Add the **eggs, lamb,** and **beef** and knead with your hands until the crackers are evenly distributed. Add the onion mixture, **parsley, coriander, paprika,** 2 teaspoons **salt,** the **black pepper, cumin, allspice, cardamom, cinnamon,** and **baking powder** and knead again until the seasoning is evenly distributed. Wrap the bowl well with plastic wrap and put it in your fridge to rest for at least 3 hours and up to 48 hours.

3. Divide the meat into fourteen even portions (each around 100g) and roll into balls.

4. In a large pot over medium-high heat, add enough oil to coat the bottom and heat until it's shimmering. Add the meatballs and cook until the sides are a deep brown, 6 to 12 minutes. Transfer the seared meatballs to a plate.

5. Add the **garlic** to the pot and cook, stirring frequently, until lightly golden brown, 2 to 3 minutes. Add the **tomatoes,** a large pinch of salt, and the **bay leaves.** Bring to a simmer, then cover three-quarters of the way with a lid and turn down the heat to medium. Simmer until the sauce has thickened, reduced slightly, and deepened in flavor, 15 to 20 minutes. Nestle the meatballs in the sauce, cover, turn down the heat to medium-low, and cook until they are cooked through, 15 to 20 minutes. Let the meatballs rest for 10 minutes before serving.

PS:
This meatball mix also makes a great meatloaf: Form and bake it at 325°F until the center registers 155°F on an instant-read thermometer, then broil until the loaf is a deep golden-brown. Brush the loaf with ketchup and broil again until the ketchup is sticky and charred in spots.

Slow-Roasted Brisket

Aka keperi al horno

SERVES 6

My grandparents' Santa Cruz de la Sierra home was a few blocks from the local mercado where they did most of their shopping. My favorite summer activity used to be going to the Mercado Nuevo with my grandfather and his weathered tote bags. I loved walking through the giant concrete warehouse filled with makeshift stalls of bootleg DVDs, single-ply toilet paper, cell phone cases, fresh baguettes with paper-thin crackly crusts, the juiciest passion fruits, hanging chickens with golden fat, and full sides of pigs. We would go at least three times a day: first thing in the morning to get a fresh baguette for breakfast, then to get whatever we needed for lunch, and then right before teatime, to get some fresh baked goods. Some days we would explore the lunch stalls in the middle of the market. There, stalls made from gleaming white tile would house vendors selling arroz con queso, tender boiled yuca, keperi (aka beef brisket), luscious peanut soup, roast pork sandwiches, and spicy braised tongue, among countless other affordable, quick meals. I would always get some arroz con queso (Bolivian Cheesy Rice, page 164), tomato salad, and a thick slice of keperi (often, it was undercooked and tougher than a strip of leather wrapped in chewing gum). In my version, the sweetness from the Coca-Cola and the savoriness from the soy sauce make the brisket irresistible, and the cooking method ensures a tender brisket 100 percent of the time, so you don't have to haggle with a vendor (yourself) for a partial refund.

INGREDIENTS:

For the Brisket

- **1 brisket (about 4 pounds)**
- **Kosher salt**
- **3 tablespoons soy sauce**
- **2 tablespoons freshly cracked black pepper**
- **2 tablespoons neutral oil**
- **tablespoon ground cumin**
- **16 ounces Coca-Cola (do not use some weird new age version; use Coke Classic or Mexican Coke, please)**
- **1 cup sake or white wine**

For the Salad

- **3 large ripe tomatoes, cut into 1-inch chunks**
- **1 medium red onion, halved and thinly sliced**
- **3 tablespoons extra-virgin olive oil**
- **3 tablespoons red wine vinegar, plus more as needed**
- **Kosher salt**
- **Freshly cracked black pepper**

1. ***To cook the brisket:*** Set a wire rack on a baking sheet.

2. Season the **brisket** all over with **salt.** Be liberal with it and don't leave any surface unseasoned. Place it on the rack and put the pan in your fridge, uncovered, for at least 12 hours and up to 48 hours.

3. Preheat the oven to 325°F.

4. In a small bowl, add the **soy sauce, black pepper, oil,** and **cumin** and whisk until combined. Transfer the rack the brisket is on to a roasting pan with the brisket still on it. Slather the soy sauce mixture all over the brisket. Pour the **Coca-Cola** and **sake** into the pan. The liquid should not be touching the brisket. Cover the pan with plastic wrap and then aluminum foil. Tuck the foil into the roasting pan sides to make a seal as tight as possible. The foil will keep the plastic from melting in the oven as long as no plastic is exposed.

Recipe continues →

Slow-Roasted Brisket

Continued

5. Transfer the pan to the oven and cook until the brisket is jiggly and tender. It should pull apart easily when poked with a fork, 3½ to 4 hours.

6. Increase the heat to 450°F. Remove and discard the plastic wrap and foil. Carefully slide the brisket from the rack and into the cooking liquid. Using a spoon, baste the brisket and return the pan to the oven. Roast until the brisket is a deep golden brown, about 20 minutes.

7. Turn on the broiler to its highest setting and cook until the brisket is charred in places, about 5 minutes more. Remove the pan from the oven and let rest for at least 20 minutes. Transfer to a cutting board and slice it against the grain.

8. ***To make the salad:*** In a large bowl, toss the **tomatoes, onion, oil,** and **black pepper.** Season with a large pinch of salt and some cracks of black pepper. Taste and adjust the seasoning with more salt or vinegar as needed. Serve alongside the slices of brisket with the roasting juices.

VITO

Big Chunk of Kebab Halla

Pot roast, but make it Egyptian.

SERVES 6

The OG kebab halla is a thick stew of cubed beef and buttloads of gently cooked, thinly sliced onions. When we visited Egypt, beef was not as plentiful as poultry and rabbit, which my grandma reared on the roof of her house, so my Tante Hosna made this as a special last meal before we left. My favorite part of the dish are the silky onions saturated with the juices of slow-cooked (but often dry) beef. By swapping out the stew meat for a big chunk of chuck studded with garlic, I get the best of both worlds: the umami-laden soft onion and perfectly cooked, tender beef. The garlic in the meat softens as it slowly cooks, and its sweetness permeates and perfumes the meat. I can't think of a braised hunk of meat that wouldn't benefit from garlic implants. Gently warm any leftover slices of roast under a ladleful of onion gravy, melt cheese on top, and pop them on a roll for a sandwich that will please even the most potent jawn's Philly cheesesteak cravings.

INGREDIENTS:

- **1 chuck roast (about 4 pounds)**
- **Kosher salt**
- **8 garlic cloves, cut lengthwise into quarters**
- **1 tablespoon ground coriander**
- **1 tablespoon hot paprika**
- **2 teaspoons ground cumin**
- **½ teaspoon ground cinnamon**
- **½ teaspoon ground cardamom**
- **½ teaspoon ground allspice**
- **½ teaspoon freshly grated nutmeg**
- **2 tablespoons neutral oil**
- **4 medium yellow onions, thinly sliced**
- **3 cups beef or chicken bone broth**
- **½ cup parsley leaves, coarsely chopped**
- **Freshly cracked black pepper**

1. Set a wire rack on a sheet pan. Pat the **chuck** dry with paper towels and season it all over with **salt.** Place the chuck on the rack and let it sit in the fridge, uncovered, for at least 12 hours and up to 48 hours.

2. Using a knife with a sharp tip, channel your inner Jason Voorhees and stab 32-ish deep slits all over the chuck. Insert a **garlic** chunk into each slit and push it in. No garlic should be visible; at most, just the tips.

3. In a small bowl, combine the **coriander, paprika, cumin, cinnamon, cardamom, allspice, nutmeg,** and a large pinch of **salt.** Mix well to combine. Coat the chuck all over with the spice mix.

4. Place a large Dutch oven or oven-safe pot with a lid over medium-high heat until lightly smoking. Add the **oil;** it should shimmer immediately. Add the chuck and cook until it is light brown on one side, 2 to 3 minutes. Repeat on all sides. Remove the chuck and transfer it to a plate.

5. Add the **onion,** 1 cup water, and a large pinch of salt, cover, and cook, stirring occasionally and scraping the bottom of the pot to loosen any stuck-on bits, until the onion has fully softened, the water has evaporated, and the onion starts to get some color along the edges, 10 to 15 minutes.

6. Preheat the oven to 325°F. Return the chuck to the pot along with any collected plate juices. Add the **broth,** increase the heat to high, and bring to a boil. Season with a pinch of salt, give it a good stir, cover, and move the pot to the oven. Braise until the meat is fork tender, 2½ to 3 hours.

7. Transfer the pot to the burner, uncover, and simmer on medium-high heat, occasionally basting until the liquid is reduced by half, 20 to 25 minutes.

8. Turn off the heat, cover the roast with the lid, and let rest for at least 30 minutes before finishing with the **parsley** and **black pepper.** Taste the sauce and adjust the seasoning as needed.

9. Transfer the roast to a cutting board, then slice. Transfer to a serving platter, ladle the onion and sauce over the beef, and serve.

SHRIMP AND CELERY SALAD
p. 238

GINGER-GARLIC-
SCALLION
SHRIMP SCAMPI
p. 239

Shrimp and Celery Salad

A chance for celery to shine

SERVES 4

There's a traditional Italian seafood salad with octopus, squid, celery, and chickpeas that I order every time I see it on a menu. I developed this version with easier-to-use ingredients, like shrimp and clams, that pack just as much punch as the original. Seasoning with enough acid is key to this recipe. The dressing should have some pucker, almost like a ceviche, but if you feel like you have gone overboard with the acidity, use more olive oil to cut the sharpness. If you have celery leaves with your celery, be sure to chop them up and add them to the salad. Celery leaves are an underused herb that bring brightness and add a mild celery flavor.

INGREDIENTS:

- 1½ **pounds cockles or littleneck clams**
- **Kosher salt**
- ½ **cup sake or white wine**
- 1 **pound peeled, deveined shrimp, with tails removed (16 to 20 count)**
- 1 **(15.5-ounce) can chickpeas, drained and rinsed**
- 3 **stalks celery, cut into ¼-inch slices**
- 1 **small red onion, quartered and thinly sliced**
- ¼ **cup freshly squeezed lemon juice (about 1 large lemon), plus more as needed**
- ½ **cup coarsely chopped parsley leaves**
- ¼ **cup extra-virgin olive oil**

1. In a medium bowl, pop in the **cockles,** cover with cold water, and hit it with a tablespoon of **salt.** Swish it around with your hand and then let it sit for 15 minutes. Rinse the clams until the water runs fully clear and there are no pits of sand floating around. Drain well.

2. Place a medium pan with a lid over medium heat until hot (water splashed on the pan's surface should dance around as if it's at the club from *Save the Last Dance*), about 5 minutes. Add the clams and **sake,** increase the heat to high, and cover with the lid. Gently shake the pan while holding the lid down like you're making popcorn. Check every minute until all the clams have just opened, 3 to 4 minutes. Remove the clams with a slotted spoon and place in a medium bowl, discarding any that didn't open. Strain the leftover liquid through a fine-mesh strainer into a heatproof container. Clean the pot and then return the cooking liquid to the pot. Set aside.

3. Using a fork, remove the clam meat from the shells and add to a large bowl. Set aside and discard the shells.

4. Bring the clam liquid to a simmer over medium heat. Add the **shrimp,** stirring occasionally, and gently simmer until they start to curl up and look white instead of translucent, about 3 minutes. Kill the heat and, using a slotted spoon, add the shrimp to the bowl with the clams. Strain the remaining cooking liquid into the bowl.

5. Add the **chickpeas, celery, onion, lemon juice,** and **parsley.** Stir to combine. Taste some liquid and adjust the seasoning with more salt or lemon juice as needed; it should give you a slight pucker. Cover and transfer the bowl to the fridge until fully chilled. Before serving, taste again to see if it needs more seasoning and top with the **oil.**

Ginger-Garlic-Scallion Shrimp Scampi

A weird tribute to Rao's

SERVES 4

It took me fifteen years of New York City living to find my way into Rao's, the famously exclusive Italian restaurant with tables only for regulars. Even though it was my first (and probably only) time there, I have never felt more at home or as welcome at a restaurant. I was greeted with cheers and smiles. My glass was never empty. There was no menu, and everything was offered verbally. It felt like I was dining at a close friend's house in a dimly lit dining room with low ceilings. It was also the first time I saw the true potential of shrimp scampi. Usually, shrimp scampi contains rubbery crustacean bullets sitting in a slick of garlic butter. Not so here. The large butterflied shrimp were perfectly tender and a thin flour coating soaked up all the perfectly emulsified buttery garlic sauce. I took the scampi lessons I learned from Rao's and added a Chinese take-out vibe for an NYC mash-up that would make Girl Talk (am I… so old?) proud.

INGREDIENTS:

- **1 pound shrimp, peeled, deveined, with tails removed (13 to 15 count), butterflied**
- **½ cup all-purpose flour**
- **⅓ cup extra-virgin olive oil**
- **6 garlic cloves, minced**
- **1-inch piece of ginger, minced**
- **1 bunch of scallions, white and green parts separated and thinly sliced**
- **½ cup sake or white wine**
- **½ cup chicken bone broth**
- **1 tablespoon soy sauce**
- **Your noodles of choice or toasted pieces of bread (ideally garlic bread)**
- **2 tablespoons unsalted butter**
- **Juice of 1 freshly squeezed lemon**

1. Pat the **shrimp** dry with paper towels. In a medium bowl, toss the shrimp with the **flour.**

2. In a medium pot over medium heat, add the **oil** and heat it until it is very lightly smoking. Shake off the excess flour from the shrimp and add them to the pot in one layer (working in batches if needed). Cook until the shrimp are lightly golden brown on one side, 3 to 4 minutes, then flip and cook the other side for another 2 minutes. Remove the shrimp from the pot and transfer to a plate.

3. In the same pot, add the **garlic, ginger,** and **scallion** whites and cook until fragrant and softened, about 2 minutes. Add the **sake, broth,** and **soy sauce** and simmer until reduced by half and thickened, 3 to 4 minutes.

4. While the sauce simmers, prepare the **noodles** or bread. If using noodles, cook the noodles according to the instructions on the package. Drain the noodles, saving ¼ cup of the noodle liquid, then add the noodle water and noodles to the reduced sauce. If using bread, toast it using your machine of choice.

5. To the pot with the sauce, add the **butter, lemon juice,** scallion greens, and shrimp and stir until the butter has melted into the sauce. Serve immediately. (If using toast, spoon on top to serve.)

Tahini-Roasted Swordfish

Convert the fish hater in your life (there's always one).

SERVES 2

One of the few ways my fish-hating sister would eat the stuff was when my mom roasted fillets in a tahini sauce and topped them with fried pine nuts and parsley (a favorite Lebanese preparation). The tahini bakes into a rich, luxurious sauce that pairs especially well with meaty swordfish. But don't limit yourself to fish. Tahini roasting works great with everything from thick slices of eggplant and zucchini to skin-on chicken breasts and lamb meatballs. Just make sure to give everything a strong sear first; it won't get any additional color or crisp once you've slathered it in tahini.

INGREDIENTS:

- **2 skinless swordfish fillets (10 to 12 ounces)**
- **2 teaspoons Diamond Crystal kosher salt (see page 16)**
- **1 tablespoon neutral oil**

For the Tahini Sauce

- **½ cup tahini**
- **⅓ cup freshly squeezed lemon juice (about 2 lemons), plus more as needed**
- **2 tablespoons extra-virgin olive oil**
- **1½ teaspoons Diamond Crystal kosher salt, plus more as needed**
- **4 garlic cloves, finely grated**

For the Topping

- **2 tablespoons unsalted butter**
- **½ cup slivered almonds**
- **½ cup parsley leaves, coarsely chopped**

- **1 lemon, cut into wedges**
- **Rice and salad, for serving (optional)**

1. Set a wire rack on a baking sheet.

2. Pat the **swordfish** dry with paper towels and season all over with the **salt.** Put the swordfish on the rack and let the fish sit in the fridge, uncovered, for at least 3 hours or up to 12 hours.

3. ***To make the sauce:*** In a medium bowl, whisk together the **tahini,** 1 cup water, the **lemon juice, olive oil, salt,** and **garlic.** Taste and adjust the seasoning with more lemon juice or salt as needed. It should have the consistency of a melted milkshake. Add water a tablespoon at a time if it is too thick or a tablespoon at a time of tahini if it is too thin. (Taste and reseason if adjusting the consistency.) Set aside.

4. Preheat the oven to 350°F.

5. Place a large oven-safe pan over medium-high heat until lightly smoking. Add the **neutral oil,** swirl to coat, then add the swordfish. Press down firmly on the swordfish with a spatula to ensure maximum contact with the pan. If you have some kind of press, this would be your big moment to use it. Cook until the swordfish is golden-brown on one side, 3 to 4 minutes. Kill the heat, flip the swordfish over, and pour all the tahini sauce on the fish. The fish should be completely enveloped.

6. Transfer the pan to the oven and bake until the swordfish is cooked through; a skewerlike object should pierce the flesh without much resistance, and if you poke a fillet, it should no longer feel fleshy, 12 to 14 minutes.

7. ***While the fish roasts, make the topping:*** In a small saucepan over medium heat, combine the **butter** and **almonds** and cook, stirring frequently, until the almonds are lightly toasted, 3 to 5 minutes. Kill the heat and add the **parsley.** Stir to combine.

8. Transfer the fish and tahini sauce to a serving platter. Top with the almond mixture and serve with the **lemon** on the side. Serve with some white **rice** and a **salad** if desired.

Crispy Salmon and Bulgur Salad

I promised Lebanon I wouldn't call it tabbouleh.

SERVES 2

The honorable names of tabbouleh and hummus have been sullied over the years. Let's start with hummus. Hummus *is the Arabic word for "chickpea," so it should play a big part in the ingredient list. Black bean hummus is a scam, and chocolate hummus is an abomination. On to the tabbouleh rant. Tabbouleh has too often gone the way of the grain bowl. The bulgur used in tabbouleh is fine enough to fully soften in some moisture. A tablespoon (that's it!) is often tossed with the tomatoes to soak up excess moisture. The parsley is meticulously picked and then cut only once. Cutting the parsley multiple times will cause it to bruise and muddle its delicate, grassy flavor. The salad is then tossed in lemon juice and seasoned before tossing in a liberal glug of quality extra-virgin olive oil. The bulgur most readily available to me is… not that fine kind. So, in a plot twist you absolutely saw coming, I turn it into a grain bowl (sue me)—just make sure not to call it tabbouleh. Oh, and there's salmon, too.*

INGREDIENTS:

For the Salad

- **1 cup whole grain bulgur**
- **Kosher salt**
- **1 large ripe tomato, diced**
- **1 small yellow onion, diced**
- **¼ teaspoon ground cinnamon**
- **1 garlic clove, finely grated**
- **1 cup parsley leaves and tender stems, carefully chopped**
- **1 cup dill, carefully chopped**
- **½ cup scallions (white and green parts), thinly sliced**
- **½ cup mint leaves, roughly torn**
- **2 Persian cucumbers, diced**
- **Juice of 3 freshly squeezed lemons**
- **Freshly cracked black pepper**
- **¼ cup extra-virgin olive oil**

- **Neutral oil, for coating the pan**
- **2 skin-on salmon fillets (10 to 12 ounces)**

1. ***To make the salad:*** In a medium pot over medium heat, add the **bulgur** and a large pinch of **salt.** Toast, stirring frequently, until it smells nutty, 3 to 5 minutes. Add 2 cups water and increase the heat to medium-high. Bring to a simmer, then turn down the heat to low and cover. Cook for 12 minutes, turn off the heat, and let it rest for 5 minutes. Uncover and let cool.

2. Add the **tomato, onion, cinnamon, garlic,** and a large pinch of **salt** and toss to combine. Let it sit, uncovered, until fully cool, about 10 minutes.

3. Add the **parsley, dill, scallions, mint, cucumbers,** and **lemon juice** and toss until everything is coated. Taste and season with more salt and **black pepper** as needed. Add the **olive oil** and toss until everything is coated; taste again and season as needed with more salt and black pepper. Set aside.

4. Preheat the oven to 450°F.

5. Place an oven-safe medium skillet (preferably cast-iron) over medium heat and heat until very lightly smoking. Add enough **neutral oil** to coat the bottom of the pan when you swirl it. The oil should shimmer immediately. Add the **salmon,** skin-side down, to the pan; set it down away from you to protect yourself from any wayward hot oil splatter. Immediately press down firmly on the salmon with a spatula to flatten it. If you have a press, this is a good place for it. Let the salmon cook on the stove for 1 minute before transferring the pan to the oven. Bake until the salmon is opaque about halfway up and the skin is visibly crisp, 5 to 6 minutes. Remove the press if using and flip the salmon over. Continue baking until a thin skewer-type thing inserted into the middle of the fish doesn't feel like it's going through something fleshy, 1 to 3 more minutes.

6. Transfer the salmon, skin-side up, to a plate and let rest for at least 5 minutes before serving with a scoop of the bulgur salad.

Cod with Soy and Sake

Move over, miso cod.

SERVES 2

As a line cook, there were only a few things that I never got tired of tasting. This soy butter sauce is one of those things. We served it with a butter-basted Dover sole, and my heart fluttered every time I saw one on a ticket. It is the perfect balance of savory from the soy, briny from the capers and lemon, and smooth and rich from the butter. It elevates everything that it is poured on, including a tired line cook's fingertip. It's so quick and easy to put together that I find myself pouring it on top of everything from crispy-seared chicken thighs to steamed spring asparagus. This sauce is a punched-up version of a traditional beurre blanc, a classic French sauce where butter is emulsified into reduced wine. It is important that the butter is cold and cut into chunks; it helps it melt into the wine at the correct rate, ensuring that you get a stable emulsion as you swirl. If you are having trouble emulsifying the butter into the sauce, you can add a tablespoon of heavy cream to the reduced wine before adding the butter. It's a cheeky restaurant trick to ensure the beurre blanc stays emulsified. I won't tell.

INGREDIENTS:

2 skinless flaky white fish fillets (such as cod or hake), at least 1 inch thick and 8 to 10 ounces each
Kosher salt
Neutral oil, for coating the pan

For the Sauce

½ cup sake or white wine
2 tablespoons soy sauce
¼ cup cold unsalted butter, cut into tablespoon-sized chunks
Juice of 1 freshly squeezed lemon
Kosher salt
2 tablespoons coarsley chopped parsley leaves
2 tablespoons capers

1. Set a wire rack on a baking sheet.

2. Pat the **cod** dry with paper towels and season all over with **salt.** Place the cod on the rack and set it in the fridge for at least 20 minutes and up to 8 hours. Pat the cod dry again with paper towels.

3. Preheat the oven to 325°F.

4. Place a medium oven-safe skillet over medium-high heat and heat until slightly smoking. Add enough **oil** to lightly coat the bottom of the hot pan and swirl. Place the fish in the pan and press down firmly with a spatula until the fish stays flat. Cook until one side is golden-brown, 3 to 4 minutes. Flip the fish over and transfer the pan to the oven to finish cooking, 10 to 12 minutes. Check the fish by inserting a skewerlike object into the fattest part; it should go in without much resistance and not feel fleshy. Remove the pan from the oven and transfer the fish to a plate to rest.

5. ***To prepare the sauce:*** While the fish cooks, in a small saucepan over medium-high heat, add the **sake** and simmer until reduced to approximately 2 tablespoons, 10 to 12 minutes. Add the **soy sauce** and bring to a simmer again. Turn down the heat to low and add the **butter** all at once. Immediately start swirling the pan until the butter melts into the sauce. Season the sauce with **lemon juice** and **salt** as needed. Finish the sauce with the **parsley** and **capers** and pour on top of the fish. Serve immediately.

Crispy Fried Fish Tacos

A fish taco a day keeps the gloom away.

MAKES 8 TO 10 TACOS

I worked at Empellón, Alex Stupak's group of Mexican restaurants, for many years. I started on the cold station, frying tortilla chips, mixing fresh ceviche, and shucking oysters. I ended up running a few kitchens in his growing empire. No matter my position, one constant was the fried fish taco. I had one every single day. The subtly nutty corn tortilla, the creamy mayo and tangy tomatillo jalapeño salsa that turned into a pseudo tartar sauce, the cabbage, and the shatteringly crisp battered fish have all been seared in my brain. This recipe isn't the same as his, but it is an homage to that great taco.

INGREDIENTS:

For the Salsa

- **8 ounces tomatillos**
- **2 medium jalapeños, stemmed and cut in half lengthwise**
- **5 unpeeled garlic cloves**
- **¼ cup pickled jalapeños or pickled cherry peppers, liquid reserved (if needed)**
- **Kosher salt**

For the Fish

- **Neutral oil, for frying**
- **½ cup rice flour**
- **1 cup all-purpose flour, plus more as needed**
- **Kosher salt**
- **½ teaspoon baking powder**
- **3 tablespoons cold vodka**
- **¾ cup cold beer, plus more as needed**
- **1 pound skinless firm white fish fillets, cut into ½-inch strips**

For Assembling the Tacos

- **8 to 10 corn or flour tortillas, warmed**
- **Your favorite mayonnaise**
- **¼ head green cabbage, cut as thinly as possible**
- **5 radishes, thinly sliced**
- **1 cup cilantro, leaves and tender stems**
- **3 limes, cut into wedges**

1. ***To make the salsa:*** Arrange a rack 6 inches from the oven's heat source and turn on its highest broil setting. Line a baking sheet with foil.

2. Peel the **tomatillos** and rinse off. Place the tomatillos, **jalapeños** (cut-side down), and **garlic** on the baking sheet. Broil until the tomatillos are charred and burst, 13 to 15 minutes.

3. Remove the pan from the oven and peel the garlic cloves. Pop all the broiled vegetables into a blender. Add the pickled jalapeños and blend until everything is broken down but not fully smooth. Taste and adjust the seasoning with salt and a splash of pepper pickling liquid if it needs more brightness. Put the sauce in the fridge to cool.

4. ***To cook the fish:*** Heat ½ inch of **oil** in a medium heavy-bottomed pot over medium heat until the temperature is between 340° and 350°F.

5. In a medium bowl, combine the **rice flour,** ½ cup of the **all-purpose flour,** the **baking powder,** and a large pinch of **salt** and whisk for 1 minute to combine. Add the **vodka,** then slowly whisk in the **beer** until the batter is the consistency of a melted milkshake. Do not make the batter in advance.

6. In another medium bowl, add the remaining ½ cup all-purpose flour. Toss the fish strips in the flour and dust against your hand to knock off any excess flour. Using tongs or a fork, dip the fillets into the batter one at a time, letting the fillet hang above the bowl to drain some excess batter, then place in the oil. In batches, fry the fish until one side is golden-brown, about 3 minutes, then flip and cook the second side until golden-brown, another 2 to 3 minutes. Transfer the fillets to a wire rack and season with salt.

7. ***To assemble the tacos:*** Start with a warmed **tortilla** and top with a squirt of **mayonnaise**. Add a small handful of **cabbage,** a spoonful of **salsa,** then a piece of fish. Garnish with the **radishes, cilantro,** and a hearty squeeze of **lime juice.**

PS:
The key to this recipe is the batter. It needs to be as cold as possible—I keep my vodka in the freezer; you should too—and mixed right before using. This minimizes gluten development, which is what makes the batter bubbly and crisp rather than dense and chewy.

CHAPTER 6

Dess

FRITO GANACHE TART
p. 264

MOUSSE AU CHOCOLAT AU GRAPE-NUTS
p. 271

CARROT SHEET CAKE
p. 278

KINDA ICEBOX CAKE OF CANNED PEACHES
p. 277

LABNEH-CHERRY CHEESECAKE
p. 266

DATE FUDGE
p. 258

erts

The icing on the cake

SPICED APPLESAUCE BUNDT
p. 261

BASBOUSA BARS
p. 268

ROASTED RIPE PLANTAINS WITH MELTY CHEESE
p. 254

GLOSSY CHOCOLATE CHUNK COOKIES
p. 257

BEIJINHO SWISS ROLL
p. 272

GROWING UP in Doha, Ramadan was a special time. For most of the year, Doha was a sleepy town that simmered down when the sun fell: Traffic lightened, and everything went quiet in the early evening. But during Ramadan, the city came alive at night.

Most of the country fasts from sunrise to sunset. So, work schedules shift and businesses close during the fasting hours. Then, once the sun goes down and it's iftar time, Doha turns into a giant party. The streets are covered in lights, and the malls stay open late. The souks bustle with people until the sun comes up.

When I lived in Doha, Ramadan became a time of ultimate freedom. It felt like there were no rules. I would go out for shawarma and puffs of shisha with my friends at 4:00 a.m. because Ramadan made curfew obsolete for one glorious month.

Outside of Ramadan, dessert in our household was usually ripe fruit (though we would occasionally split a candy bar among the four of us, sliced evenly with a fork and knife like Mr. Pitt from *Seinfeld*).

But then would come Ramadan. My mom went all out for iftar dinners. She would plan meals a month out, scrutinizing newspaper clippings and random handwritten notes on recipes that she'd saved over the year, collecting everything that made the cut in her Madonna notebook. When I was researching for this cookbook, the first resource I reached for was this precious heirloom—a notebook held together with tape with a light blue cover where Madonna, in red lingerie, is singing into a microphone.

The pages of her notebook made me more nostalgic than any family photo album could have. I got to revisit my favorite loaves and puddings and to reminisce about the luscious sauces and comforting confections I grew up eating. It felt like standing beside my mom as she flipped through the thin pages of her notebook, a place where I learned so many basic techniques, like the proper ways to…

- fold a batter (gently and with a spatula).
- cream butter and sugar (room temperature butter and let it double in volume).
- set up a double boiler (only an inch of water at the bottom of a pot).
- roll up a roll cake (in a towel while it is still warm).
- grease and line a cake pan (with softened butter, wiped clean with a paper towel, then lined with parchment or flour that is shaken in the pan and then dumped out).

My mom would always label her greatest hits with a simple (good) to indicate that it was a recipe worth revisiting. Those are the recipes I cook out of her notebook these days. I cannot improve on them, and the soothing feeling of having them in their original form brings me so much comfort. Whenever I miss her, I still often flip through the book, instead of looking at photos. The kitchen is where she and I spent our best times, tasting cake batter together, learning that I hadn't creamed my sugar and butter enough, or walking me through the proper crimp of an empanada so the cheese wouldn't squeeze out.

THE MADONNA NOTEBOOK DEEP CUTS

My two favorites from my mom's notebook are the following recipes for banana nut bread and lemon loaf cake, transcribed as originally found.

Banana Nut Bread *(good)*

MAKES 1 LOAF

INGREDIENTS:

½ cup oil
1 cup sugar
2 eggs, beaten
3 ripe bananas, mashed
2 cups all-purpose flour
1 teaspoon baking soda
½ teaspoon baking powder
1 teaspoon salt
3 tablespoons milk
1 teaspoon vanilla extract
½ cup chopped nuts

1. Beat the **oil** and **sugar** together. Add **eggs** and **bananas,** beat well, and let sit for 30 minutes at room temperature. Add sifted **flour, dry ingredients, milk,** and **vanilla;** mix well and stir in **nuts.** Pour into a greased and floured loaf pan (9 × 5 × 3 inch). Bake in a preheated 350 degree oven for 1 hour. Cool well and store overnight before cutting.

HAM'S RETROACTIVE HEADNOTE

This banana nut bread recipe was one that became canon in our house. My mom would often buy bananas for a family that didn't like to eat them, so the fruit would turn mushy and brown. Perfect for this banana bread. She also enhanced the flavor by letting the bananas sit with the eggs. I loved warming a slice of this bread in the toaster oven for an afternoon snack, and on the rare occasion that we had some ice cream in the freezer, a scoop would make its way on top of the slice as well. When I make it these days, I like throwing in a handful of chopped chocolate for another layer of flavor. To make this, you can use a hand mixer, stand mixer, or a whisk, along with a strong will to live for banana bread.

Lemon Loaf Cake *(good)*

MAKES 1 LOAF

INGREDIENTS:

1 cup sugar
6 tablespoons butter, room temperature
2 eggs, beaten, room temperature
1½ cups all purpose flour
1 teaspoon baking soda
½ teaspoon kosher salt
½ cup milk, room temperature
2 lemons, juiced and zested
½ cup sugar

1. Cream together the **sugar** and **butter.** Add the beaten **eggs** and blend well. Sift together the **flour, baking powder** and **salt;** stir into the egg mixture alternatively with the **milk.** Stir in the lemon zest. Beat well. Pour into a greased (8 × 4 × 4 inch) loaf pan and bake in a 325 degree oven for 45 minutes.

2. Combine the **lemon juice** and **sugar;** pour over the loaf while still hot. Cool in the pan.

HAM'S RETROACTIVE HEADNOTE

I always ate this cake in the same way. A thick slice on a faded Teenage Mutant Ninja Turtles plate (the one with Donatello holding his staff in the middle). I would tear off pieces from the bottom, less the icing, until I was left with a handlebar mustache of icing clinging to a thin strip of cake. This was where the party started. Each bite from here on out was a puckery, sugary bite of bliss.

Roasted Ripe Plantains with Melty Cheese

And a cold glass of milk

MAKES 2 PLANTAINS

Papa Humberto, my Bolivian grandfather, had to have a roasted plantain with a glass of milk every day after lunch. The milk came in a thin, but indestructible, plastic bag. He would cut openings on both sides with giant tailoring scissors and place it in a bright orange holder. Even on days where we popped out to the restaurant on the corner for a sandwich de lomito (a grilled piece of meat on a fresh roll dressed with lettuce, tomato, and mayo), he would come home to have his slow-roasted ripe plantain with a tall glass of cold leche Pil, our local brand of milk. The key is making sure that the plantain is ripe enough: It should be completely black on the outside and softer than a ripe avocado when pressed. I always have plantains ripening in a cool, dark place so I'm never away from a perfectly ripe one.

INGREDIENTS:

- **2 ripe plantains (skin fully blackened)**
- **½ cup crumbled Akkawi cheese or shredded melting cheese (such as Muenster or mozzarella or a soft-rind cheese like Harbison or Camembert)**
- **2 tablespoons unsalted butter, room temperature**
- **Flaky salt**
- **Cold whole milk, for serving**

1. Preheat the oven to 400°F.

2. Rinse the **plantains** (skin on) and pat dry. With a sharp knife, cut along the curve of the plantains. Don't cut all the way through but slice enough so you can open up the plantains (like a baked potato). Fill the cavities with the **cheese,** spread a tablespoon of **butter** along the cut side of each plantain, and completely wrap in aluminum foil.

3. Place the wrapped plantains on a sheet pan and roast for 25 to 30 minutes, until they puff slightly.

4. Remove the pan from the oven and let the plantains rest for 2 minutes. Remove the foil and plate the plantains alongside two glasses of cold **milk.** Do not eat the skins.

Glossy Chocolate Chunk Cookies

Butterscotchy, crispy, and gooey all at once

MAKES 6 COOKIES

My mom didn't make chocolate chip cookies. She probably didn't even eat one until her late twenties. Luckily, I didn't have to wait that long. I would get them at school bake sales, which took place outside the cafeteria on a foldable plastic table lined with plastic tablecloths. The nerdiest (aka coolest) kid (aka me), along with the PTA mom du jour, was in charge of collecting the money. This meant that I had first pick of the baked goods. I always tried ones made by different parents; these were usually completely unique. Some were thin and fudgy; others were large and crackly. I learned early on that chocolate chip cookies are personal. I like mine with a lot of chocolate, a strong vanilla flavor, and buttery, butterscotch notes from the brown sugar. And there must be the sort of chocolatey puddles of different sizes that come from chopped, not chipped, chocolate. This version is that cookie. The best part is that it is a mix and bake—no overnight rest needed. I don't even need to bust out my scale.

INGREDIENTS:

- ½ **cup unsalted butter**
- ½ **cup (packed) dark brown sugar**
- 2 **tablespoons granulated sugar**
- ½ **teaspoon Diamond Crystal kosher salt (see page 16)**
- ½ **teaspoon imitation vanilla**
- ½ **teaspoon vanilla extract**
- ½ **teaspoon baking soda**
- 2 **large egg yolks**
- 1 **cup all-purpose flour**
- 1½ **cups chopped chocolate (any combination that you fancy: milk, dark, or even . . . white; the better the chocolate, the better the cookie)**

1. Preheat the oven to 375°F. Line a sheet pan with parchment paper.

2. In a medium pot over medium-low heat, add the **butter** and let it fully melt. Add the **sugars** and whisk until they dissolve, about 2 minutes. Transfer to a medium bowl and whisk gently until the butter and sugar combine into a homogeneous sauce with no pools of butter remaining. Keep whisking until the mixture starts to cool, another 5 minutes. (This takes some work, but it always makes me feel like I earned the right to eat all six cookies.)

3. Add the **salt, vanillas, baking soda,** and **egg yolks** and whisk until the yolks are fully incorporated. Add the **flour** and mix with a spatula until there are no patches of dry flour.

4. Add the **chocolate** and mix until it is well distributed. Divide the dough into six even pieces using your hands and roll each into a ball. Evenly space the dough on the prepared pan (use up the whole tray). Flatten each ball slightly with your hand. Bake until the cookies are crisp along the edges but still soft in the center, 11 to 13 minutes, depending on how you like your cookies. Transfer to a wire rack to cool before consuming.

PS:
Or eat them hot, right out of the oven, out of a bowl with a spoon with a scoop of vanilla bean ice cream.

PPS:
You can add up to ½ cup of any toasted, chopped (or whole) nut of your choice.

Date Fudge

That tastes like freakin' cookie dough, and that is not the legal THC talking.

MAKES 14 PIECES

This recipe has the biggest payoff in this entire book. If you are a fan of either fudge or of eating cookie dough, prepare to have your mind blown. (If you're not… lose my number?) The toasted flour not only brings notes of baked cookie, but it means you don't have to bother with cooking sugar to a specific temp. You're welcome. The dates and brown butter hit all those caramel-y roasty-toasty notes you want in your dough, without any added sugar. The key to this recipe is the brown butter. It should be nutty and deeply golden brown without entering coffee ground territory. Ensure everything is ready and measured so the butter doesn't burn. Nailing the brown butter rewards you with the perfect butterscotch flavor, and it is the CEO of chocolate chip cookie vibes. Other candidates need not apply.

INGREDIENTS:

- **½ cup / 70g whole wheat flour**
- **7 tablespoons / 100g unsalted butter**
- **2¼ cups / 350g pitted Medjool dates**
- **1 teaspoon imitation vanilla extract**
- **1 teaspoon / 5g Diamond Crystal kosher salt (see page 16)**
- **2 ounces high-quality milk chocolate, coarsely chopped (optional)**

1. Preheat the oven to 300°F. Line a sheet pan with parchment paper.

2. Evenly spread out the **flour** on the prepared pan and bake until it smells toasted, about 30 minutes (see Note).

3. In a medium pot over medium heat, melt the **butter** and keep cooking, whisking constantly until the solids separate from the fat, turn golden-brown, and smell nutty, 5 to 8 minutes.

4. Add the toasted flour and stir until well incorporated. Turn off the heat and add the **dates, vanilla,** and **salt.** Stir until everything seems evenly distributed and the dates start softening.

5. Transfer the mixture to a food processor and blend until no lump remains. Let the fudge cool at room temperature before mixing in the **chocolate** (if using).

6. Portion the fudge into two tablespoon-sized balls, roll into a log for slicing, or flatten out and cut portions. Transfer the fudge to the fridge to cool and firm up before serving.

PS:
The flour can be toasted in advance and in larger quantities. Keep it in a tight resealable plastic bag in the freezer for up to 6 months.

PPS:
Use this recipe as a template, with whatever mix-ins you like for added texture: coarsely chopped toasted nuts, Rice Krispies, or dried fruit.

ABC
2
1

Spiced Applesauce Bundt

It's like a fruitcake, but good.

MAKES 1 CAKE (SERVES 12)

When I found my mom's weathered Madonna notebook filled with her favorite recipes, this was the first recipe I searched for. It was the cake she made most often. She had convinced herself that the applesauce, dates, and nuts made it a healthy dessert. Our house billowed with the scent of warm spices and baking apples whenever she made this. It was what I imagined warm apple pie smelled like, even though I wouldn't know how that actually smelled until I moved to the States and made my own much later. But I was correct. This cake is impossibly moist. Let it fully cool before serving, or it will crumble in your hands. I like topping it simply, like my mom did, with just a flurry of confectioners' sugar, but you can top it with your favorite glaze if you must.

INGREDIENTS:

- **½ cup / 110g unsalted butter, room temperature, plus more for greasing the pan**
- **1 cup / 200g granulated sugar, plus more for the pan**
- **1 large egg, room temperature**
- **1½ cups / 365g unsweetened applesauce, room temperature**
- **1 teaspoon vanilla extract**
- **2 cups / 240g all-purpose flour**
- **1 cup / 155g Medjool dates, pitted and coarsely chopped**
- **1 cup / 100g raw walnuts, coarsely chopped**
- **2 teaspoons / 12g baking soda**
- **2 teaspoons ground cinnamon**
- **1 teaspoon / 5g Diamond Crystal kosher salt (see page 16)**
- **½ teaspoon ground allspice**
- **½ teaspoon freshly cracked black pepper**
- **½ teaspoon ground ginger**
- **½ teaspoon ground nutmeg**
- **¼ cup / 30g confectioners' sugar, for topping**

1. Preheat the oven to 350°F. Using a pastry brush, grease the inside of a 12- to 15-cup Bundt pan, making sure to get all the corners. Ensure there is a thin, even layer of **butter** or else the cake will stick when you try to unmold it. Roll a handful of **granulated sugar** around the interior of the pan; it should stick to the butter. Tap to remove any excess sugar over the sink (or back into your sugar container if you are nasty like me).

2. In the bowl of a stand mixer fitted with the paddle attachment, combine the butter and granulated sugar and cream on medium-high speed until fluffy and white, stopping to fully scrape down the bowl and paddle every 3 minutes, about 12 minutes total.

3. Add the **egg** and beat on medium-high until fully incorporated, fluffy, and looking like frosting, 4 to 5 minutes.

4. Add the **applesauce** and **vanilla** and beat on medium until dispersed into the batter, about 2 minutes. Scrape down the bowl. The mixture will look broken; don't worry.

5. In a large bowl, combine the **flour, dates, walnuts, baking soda, cinnamon, salt, allspice, black pepper, ginger,** and **nutmeg** until evenly distributed. Add to the butter mixture and, using a spatula, fold together until no dry pockets of flour remain. Make sure to go down to the bottom of the bowl to incorporate all the butter into the flour.

6. Transfer the mixture to the prepared pan and spread so the batter is even. Firmly tap the pan against the counter five times to help the batter settle and to knock out any air pockets. Bake until the cake is dark brown and puffed up and a toothpick inserted into the center comes out with a few moist crumbs stuck to it, 40 to 50 minutes.

7. Remove the pan from the oven and let the cake sit in the pan for 10 minutes before carefully flipping it onto a wire rack. Let the cake fully cool before dusting it with the **confectioners' sugar,** then slice and serve.

Frito Ganache Tart

For the BFFs Alex and Jordan.

MAKES 1 TART (SERVES 8)

While I was working at Alex Stupak's Empellón Cocina, during Jordan Kahn's guest chef dinner, he taught us how to make "chocolate in the Japanese method" (aka namelaka). Namelaka *means "extremely smooth" in Japanese, and it is the perfect expression of ganache. It is* silky *smooth, and the chocolate melts the instant you put it in your mouth. We put a version of it on the menu, and it quickly became a core component of my favorite on-the-line snack. I would grab a fresh shard of masa crisp, our lard-laden version of a tortilla chip, slather it with "chocolate in the Japanese method," and top it with flaky salt. It tasted salty, sweet, impossibly creamy, and deeply crunchy. This tart is inspired by that snack. The Frito crust has a similarly pleasing grittiness as masa. While this ganache is much easier to make for home use and may not be "chocolate in the Japanese method," the honey in the ganache makes the humble chocolate chips taste much bougier than usual.*

INGREDIENTS:

For the Crust

- **1 (9.25-ounce) bag Fritos**
- **½ cup sugar**
- **1 teaspoon Diamond Crystal kosher salt** **(see page 16)**
- **½ cup unsalted butter, melted, plus more for greasing the pan**

For the Filling

- **1 cup heavy cream**
- **1 tablespoon honey**
- **¼ teaspoon Diamond Crystal kosher salt**
- **1 (12-ounce) bag semisweet chocolate chips (or 50/50 milk and dark chocolate, chopped)**
- **1 teaspoon vanilla extract**

1. ***To make the crust:*** Preheat the oven to 350°F. Using a pastry brush, grease a 9-inch tart pan or a standard 9-inch pie plate with melted butter.

2. In a food processor, add the **Fritos** and blend until finely ground. Add the **sugar** and **salt** and process until evenly distributed. Add the melted **butter** and pulse until fully combined.

3. Dump the mixture into the prepared pan. Using your hands, press the crust along the sides and bottom, then use the bottom of a measuring cup to tightly pack and smooth it. Bake until set and lightly toasted, 25 to 30 minutes. Set the pan aside on a wire rack to cool fully.

4. ***To make the filling:*** In a small pot over medium heat, add the **cream, honey,** and **salt** and bring to a simmer.

5. In a medium bowl, add the **chocolate chips,** then pour the hot cream mixture over the chocolate and let sit for 1 to 2 minutes. Add the **vanilla.** Start to stir the chocolate in the center in small circles, gradually widening the circles as the mixture comes together and stirring until the ganache is shiny, smooth, and glossy. (If the chocolate doesn't fully melt, place the bowl over a medium pot with an inch of barely simmering water or in the microwave for 15 to 20 seconds and gently stir until smooth.)

6. Pour the ganache into the crust, swirl the top with a spoon, and let it rest at room temperature for 1 hour before wrapping in plastic wrap and transferring the pan to the fridge to fully set, another 2 hours. Then slice and serve.

PS: If you want to attempt the OG Jordan Kahn Namelaka for yourself, here is the recipe.

Namelaka

MAKES ABOUT 1½ QUARTS

INGREDIENTS:

- **2 sheets silver gelatin**
- **240g whole milk**
- **12g glucose syrup (or corn syrup)**
- **4g Diamond Crystal kosher salt**
- **450g Valrhona milk chocolate fèves**
- **480g heavy cream**

1. Soak the gelatin sheets in ice water until soft and pliable.

2. Bring the whole milk, glucose syrup, and salt to a boil. Place the chocolate in a medium bowl, then pour the hot milk mixture over. Stir immediately to distribute the heat. Remove the gelatin sheets from the ice water and squeeze all excess water out of them, then add to the chocolate mixture and stir until fully dissolved. Let it sit for a couple of minutes and then stir with a spatula until the chocolate is fully melted.

3. Add the cream to the chocolate mixture and blend using an immersion blender until fully incorporated. Spoon into small serving bowls to eat as pudding, or cool and use as a ganache to garnish cakes or just eat it with tortilla chips. Live your life.

Labneh-Cherry Cheesecake

A classic with some tang

MAKES 1 CHEESECAKE (SERVES 10)

I love a dense, New York–style cheesecake. It is how I ended my first experience eating at an American steakhouse, when I visited as a kid (see page 198), and how I like to end a steak dinner as an adult. It was the first dessert I learned how to make. Luckily, Philadelphia cream cheese was easy to come by, even while growing up so far away from Philly. No other cream cheese makes as good a cheesecake. This recipe sports a similar density to the New York classic, but the labneh brings a little more tang to the party and plays well with the cherries. Nigella seeds are a traditional pairing with some cheeses throughout the Middle East, and they add another dimension to the cheesecake.

INGREDIENTS:

For the Crust

- **12 / 180g graham crackers**
- **¼ cup / 50g sugar**
- **1 teaspoon / 5g Diamond Crystal kosher salt (see page 16)**
- **6 tablespoons / 90g unsalted butter, melted, plus more for greasing the pan**

For the Cheesecake

- **2 (8-ounce) packages / 450g Philadelphia cream cheese, room temperature**
- **2 cups / 455g labneh**
- **1 cup / 200g sugar**
- **1 teaspoon / 5g vanilla extract**
- **¼ teaspoon Diamond Crystal kosher salt**
- **3 large eggs, room temperature, well beaten**
- **1 tablespoon nigella seeds (optional)**

For the Cherry Compote

- **1 pound / 450g frozen cherries**
- **¼ cup / 50g sugar**
- **2 tablespoons freshly squeezed lemon juice**
- **1 teaspoon tapioca starch**

1. ***To make the crust:*** Arrange a rack in the center of the oven. Preheat the oven to 350°F. Grease a 9-inch springform pan.

2. In a food processor, combine the **graham crackers, sugar,** and **salt** and process until finely ground. Drizzle in the melted **butter** and pulse to combine.

3. Dump the graham mixture into the prepared pan and, using the bottom of a measuring cup, press the mixture evenly along the bottom.

4. Place the pan in the oven and bake until browned and dry, 13 to 16 minutes. Remove the pan from the oven and place on a wire rack to cool completely, at least 30 minutes.

5. ***To make the cheesecake:*** In a food processor, puree the **cream cheese** until smooth. Add the **labneh, sugar, vanilla,** and **salt.** Process until evenly combined, stopping to scrape down the sides of the processor and under the blade with a silicone spatula. Add the **eggs** and process until evenly combined. (Do not overmix.) Add the **nigella seeds** (if using) and pulse to combine.

6. Pour the cheese mixture into the baked and cooled crust. Set the pan in a water bath (see Note) and bake until the edges are set but the center is still wobbly, 55 to 70 minutes. (An instant-read thermometer inserted 1 inch from the edge should register between 170° and 175°F.) Turn off the oven and prop open the door with a wooden spoon. Let the cheesecake sit in the hot oven for 1 hour.

7. Remove the pan from the oven and water bath, cover, and cool fully in the fridge for at least 4 hours, and preferably overnight, before serving.

8. ***To make the compote:*** In a medium pot, combine the **cherries, sugar, lemon juice,** 1 tablespoon water, and the **tapioca starch** and stir until all the ingredients are fully combined. Turn the heat to medium and cook, stirring occasionally, until the sauce has simmered for 2 full minutes and

PS:
To make a water bath, tightly wrap some aluminum foil around the bottom edge of your springform pan to prevent water from seeping into the pan and ruining your crust. Place the wrapped springform pan into a roasting pan. Then fill the roasting pan with boiling water until it goes halfway up the sides of the springform pan.

has thickened. Pour the cherries into a bowl and transfer to the fridge to cool completely.

9. When ready to serve, remove the springform, then use a paper towel to blot (*gently!*) any condensation on top of the cheesecake before serving. Slice the cheesecake using a knife dipped in hot water; wipe the knife dry between each cut. Top the slices with the cherry compote.

10. Tightly wrapped, the crust will keep at room temperature for 1 week or in the freezer for up to 1 month. Store the baked cheesecake, tightly wrapped, in the fridge for up to 5 days or in the freezer for up to 1 month.

Basbousa Bars

A lighter way to 'bousa

MAKES 16 BARS

Basbousa is a delightfully dense and chewy semolina-based cake that is soaked in orange blossom syrup. It is found on the tables of every Egyptian household during Ramadan and Eid. It was one of my favorite desserts, but the syrup makes it too treacly to have as regularly as I would like. These bars have the flavors of a basbousa, but in an undrenched, cakier form. I like serving them alongside a potent mug of unsweetened PG Tips tea.

INGREDIENTS:

- ½ **cup / 110g unsalted butter, plus more for greasing the pan**
- 1½ **cups / 300g (packed) light brown sugar**
- ½ **cup / 112g labneh**
- 2 **tablespoons orange blossom water**
- 1 **teaspoon vanilla extract**
- ¾ **teaspoon / 4g Diamond Crystal kosher salt** **(see page 16)**
- ½ **teaspoon baking powder**
- 2 **large eggs**
- ¾ **cup / 90g all-purpose flour**
- ½ **cup / 80g coarse-ground semolina**
- 16 **whole blanched almonds, for garnish**

1. Preheat the oven to 350°F. Grease and line an 8 × 8-inch pan with parchment paper, leaving a 2-inch overhang on two sides.

2. In a medium pot over medium heat, add the **butter** and melt. Whisk the butter until the milk solids turn a light golden brown and it smells like roasting hazelnuts, about 4 minutes.

3. Transfer the butter to a medium bowl. Whisk in the **brown sugar, labneh, orange blossom water, vanilla, salt,** and **baking powder.** Crack in the **eggs** and whisk vigorously until there are no errant streaks.

4. Add the **flour** and **semolina.** With a spatula, gently stir the dry ingredients into the wet until there are no patches of dry flour. (The batter will be slightly lumpy.)

5. Pour the batter into the prepared pan and tap against the counter to settle. Place an **almond** approximately every 2 inches, in rows that are roughly every 2 inches apart. The end result should look like a 4 × 4 grid, punctuated by almonds. Bake until set and golden-brown, 30 to 35 minutes.

6. Remove the pan from the oven and set on a wire rack to fully cool before slicing into bars, each with an almond in the center.

BAKE SALE

Mousse au Chocolat au Grape-Nuts

For only the fanciest of dinner guests or visiting children

SERVES 2 TO 4

This is my all-star utility dessert. I make it for myself when I'm up way too late in a haze watching the Harley Quinn *animated series and desperately need a crunchy, salty, sweet snack. I also make it as a fun tableside dessert for guests. It's perfect for when you're feeling lazy—it's ridiculously quick and easy to make—but impressive enough to astound even the poshest company or their cereal-loving toddlers. The Grape-Nuts bring a hearty crunch to the light mousse and, more importantly, a maltiness that adds another dimension to the chocolate. I also like throwing other crisp snacks I have lying around for different layers of crunch (see Note). And the topping situation may be versatile, but you can also top it with…nothing and eat it directly out of the bowl you mix it in, which is how Harley watches me eat it as the sun starts to appear. This is a great place to use that precious stash of Valrhona milk chocolate because the better the chocolate, the better the mousse. But honestly, any milk chocolate makes something good enough to keep me awake for another episode.*

INGREDIENTS:

For the Mousse

- **1 cup coarsely chopped milk chocolate**
- **1 cup heavy cream**
- **¼ cup mascarpone**
- **2 tablespoons maple syrup or honey**
- **1 teaspoon vanilla extract or vanilla paste**
- **Kosher salt**
- **1 cup Grape-Nuts**
- **1 cup mix-ins (such as crushed Fritos, pretzels, or toasted hazelnuts or pecans; optional)**

Toppings of Your Choice

- **Freeze-dried fruit (I like cherry or strawberry)**
- **Diced ripe mango**
- **Toasted nuts**
- **Toasted coconut chips**
- **Ice cream**

1. ***To make the mousse:*** Fill a medium pot with 1 inch of water and set over medium heat until it comes to a simmer. Place a medium heatproof bowl on top, ensuring it sits on the pot without letting steam out or touching the simmering water. Put the **chocolate** in the bowl and melt, stirring occasionally so it does so evenly, 4 to 8 minutes. Remove the pot from the heat and allow to cool slightly. (You can also melt the chocolate in the microwave by blasting in 15-second bursts, stirring in between each blast.)

2. While the chocolate cools, in a medium bowl, combine the **cream, mascarpone, maple syrup, vanilla,** and a pinch of **salt.** Whisk vigorously until the cream turns into the texture of shaving cream and, when you lift the whisk, the cream stays in the cage without falling, about 5 minutes. Do not overwhisk; it should still be silky smooth.

3. Add the chocolate and fold with a spatula until evenly incorporated. Add the **Grape-Nuts** and any **mix-ins** (if using) and stir until evenly combined. Taste and adjust the seasoning with more salt as needed.

4. Divide the mousse among serving bowls and top with your desired toppings. Serve immediately (do not refrigerate; it ruins the velvety texture).

PS:
My favorite combo is hand-crushed Rold Gold pretzels and coarsely chopped toasted peanuts, folded in with the Grape-Nuts and topped with a handful of lightly crushed freeze-dried strawberries.

Beijinho Swiss Roll

Celebrate like a Brazilian.

SERVES 8

No Brazilian celebration is complete without a table full of brigadeiros and beijinhos. Brigadeiros, chocolate truffles made with condensed milk and rolled in chocolate sprinkles, have had their moment to shine. Their lesser known, and in my opinion superior, sibling has not. Beijinhos, *or "little kisses" in Portuguese, are little balls of condensed milk fudge, rolled in coconut and studded with a clove. In this recipe, I give them the platform they deserve, turning them into a roll cake. Tasting this cake is a surreal experience, as it gives me the exact flavor of biting into a beijinho. It is trippy.*

INGREDIENTS:

For the Cake

- **1½ cups / 180g all-purpose flour**
- **1¾ teaspoons baking powder**
- **6½ tablespoons / 85g, plus ½ cup / 100g sugar**
- **⅓ cup / 80g neutral oil**
- **6 large eggs, separated**
- **1½ teaspoons / 6g Diamond Crystal kosher salt (see page 16)**
- **1½ teaspoons / 8g vanilla extract**
- **1 teaspoon cream of tartar**

For the Filling

- **1 cup / 225g heavy cream**
- **½ cup / 120g mascarpone**
- **2 tablespoons sugar**
- **1 teaspoon vanilla extract**
- **Kosher salt**
- **½ cup / 45g shredded unsweetened coconut, plus another 1 cup / 90g for rolling**

For the Glaze

- **1 (14-ounce) can sweetened condensed milk**
- **¼ cup / 58g heavy cream**
- **¼ teaspoon Diamond Crystal kosher salt**
- **1 tablespoon unsalted butter**
- **½ teaspoon vanilla extract**

1. Arrange a rack in the center of the oven. Preheat the oven to 375°F. Line a 13 × 18-inch half sheet pan with parchment paper.

2. ***To make the cake:*** In a medium bowl, whisk together the flour and baking powder.

3. In a large bowl, add 6½ tablespoons / 85g of the **sugar,** the **oil,** ½ cup / 120ml water, the **egg yolks, salt,** and **vanilla** and whisk until well combined. In three additions, sift in the flour mixture, gently whisking between each addition until it's a smooth batter.

4. In the bowl of a stand mixer fitted with the whisk attachment (or a large bowl if using a hand mixer), combine the egg whites and **cream of tartar** and whisk on medium-low until soft peaks form (the whites will hold their shape but will fall off the whisk), 1 to 2 minutes. While whipping on medium, gradually sprinkle in the remaining ½ cup / 100g sugar until a meringue with medium peaks forms (the whites will hold their shape and stay on the whisk but will droop at the top), about 2 minutes.

5. Fold the meringue into the batter in three additions.

6. Spread the batter evenly in the prepared pan. Tap firmly against the counter. Bake until golden and the cake springs back when gently pressed, 18 to 20 minutes.

7. Remove the pan from the oven and drop it onto the counter, then loosen the edges with a metal spatula or knife. Lay a kitchen towel over the cake and then quickly flip it onto the counter. Peel off the parchment. Starting with a short end, roll the cake in the towel, to maximize the spiral. Let the

Recipe continues →

cake fully cool, seam-side down, in the towel at room temperature before unrolling, about 1 hour.

8. ***To make the filling:*** In the bowl of a stand mixer fitted with the whisk attachment, combine the **cream, mascarpone, sugar, vanilla,** and a pinch of **salt** on medium and whisk until stiff (starting on low speed to minimize splashing), about 2 minutes. Be careful not to overwhip. Delicately fold in the **coconut** with a spatula until evenly distributed. Transfer the bowl to the fridge until the cake is fully cooled.

9. Unroll the cake and spread on an even layer of the filling. Carefully roll the cake back up, leaving the towel behind, and transfer to a serving platter seam-side down.

10. ***To make the glaze:*** In a medium pot over medium-low heat, combine the **condensed milk, cream, salt, butter,** and **vanilla** and cook, stirring constantly, until the glaze thickens, 10 to 14 minutes. When you scrape the bottom of the pot, a line should remain.

11. Pour the warm glaze over the rolled cake, spreading it along the top and sides. Sprinkle coconut all over the top and sides of the cake and have any remaining coconut surround the cake. Let the glaze cool before slicing and serving.

Nestlé Carnation
Sweetened Condensed Milk
Nestlé Carnation
Sweetened Condensed Milk
Nestlé Carnation
Sweetened Condensed Milk
Borden
EAGLE BRAND
AMERICA'S MOST TRUSTED
Sweetened Condensed Milk
JUST MILK & SUGAR
Essential Everyday
SWEETENED CONDENSED MILK
Borden
EAGLE BRAND
AMERICA'S MOST TRUSTED
Sweetened Condensed Milk
NO ARTIFICIAL INGREDIENTS
JUST MILK & SUGAR

Kinda Icebox Cake of Canned Peaches

Aka pavê de pêssego

SERVES 8

Pavê is a Brazilian dessert of ladyfingers or cookies layered with a pudding made from condensed milk and left to soften overnight. It comes in as many flavors as the ice cream at Baskin-Robbins. Chocolate, passion fruit, and peach are my three all-time favorites. Whenever my mom would crack open a can of canned peaches, I knew exactly what was about to go down. I would always be on ladyfinger dipping duty, and it was a job I treasured because it meant that I got to shoot any leftover syrup at the end of the process like a bad boy on spring break. Be sure to let the cake sit in the fridge overnight; this dessert will be dry and crumbly if the ladyfingers don't fully soften. You can substitute any other canned fruit or leave it out altogether, and for a chocolate variation, you can add melted chocolate to the pudding and top with cocoa powder.

INGREDIENTS:

- 1 **(14-ounce) can condensed milk**
- 2 **cups whole milk**
- 2 **egg yolks**
- 1 **teaspoon vanilla extract**
- 1 **tablespoon cornstarch**
- ½ **teaspoon Diamond Crystal kosher salt (see page 16)**
- 1 **(32-ounce) can peaches in syrup**
- 7 **ounces ladyfingers (about 20 biscuits)**
- 1¼ **ounces freeze-dried peaches (or another freeze-dried fruit like mango, strawberry, or raspberry)**

1. In a large saucepan over medium heat, combine the **condensed milk, whole milk, egg yolks, vanilla, cornstarch,** and **salt** and whisk constantly until the mixture thickens into a custard, 8 to 10 minutes. Ensure the mixture simmers for 1 full minute before transferring to a heatproof bowl to fully hydrate the cornstarch. Place a piece of plastic wrap directly on the surface of the custard to prevent a skin from forming and transfer the bowl to the fridge to cool.

2. Drain the **peaches,** reserving the syrup. Cut the peaches into ¼-inch pieces, then fold them into the custard. Return the bowl to the fridge to continue cooling. Keep all that delicious peach syrup; you'll need it for the ladyfingers . . . and for whatever else you decide to do with any surplus (party at mine!).

3. Assemble the cake in a 2-quart casserole dish. Transfer the peach syrup to the smallest bowl that can fit a ladyfinger. Dip the **ladyfingers** in the peach syrup, fully submerging them for at least 5 seconds. Make a layer of soaked ladyfingers in the bottom of the casserole. Top with half the custard. Repeat with another layer of soaked lady fingers, then the rest of the custard. Let sit in the fridge for at least 12 hours so the ladyfingers fully soften.

4. Before serving, hand-crush the **freeze-dried peaches** and sprinkle over the top of the cake.

Carrot Sheet Cake

Parabéns

SERVES 12 TO 24,
When I was a kid, Brazilian carrot cake was my favorite birthday cake. It's fluffy and moist like it came out of a box (a cake's highest honor), and I was always intrigued that it came together in a blender instead of a mixer. I would ask for it every year. It is traditionally baked in a Bundt pan and topped with a sticky, chocolatey brigadeiro glaze. This sheet cake folds my favorite parts of an American birthday cake into the one I grew up eating. I turned it into a slab cake for easy portioning and serving and topped it with a fluffy chocolate frosting to bring some classic Americana to it. It's the cake I hope my daughter grows up appreciating, since it is the perfect combination of my past and my present.

INGREDIENTS:

For the Cake

- 1 **pound / 450g carrots, cut into 1-inch chunks**
- 1½ **cups / 300g granulated sugar**
- 1 **tablespoon / 12g baking powder**
- ¾ **teaspoon / 4g Diamond Crystal kosher salt (see page 16)**
- 4 **large eggs**
- 1 **cup / 226g neutral oil, plus more for greasing the pan**
- 2½ **cups / 300g all-purpose flour**

For the Frosting

- 1 **(12-ounce) bag semisweet or dark chocolate chips**
- ½ **cup / 120ml water or coffee or milk**
- ½ **cup / 110g unsalted butter, room temperature**
- 8 **ounces / 225g cream cheese, room temperature**
- 1 **teaspoon vanilla extract**
- 1 **teaspoon kosher salt**
- 3 **cups / 360g confectioners' sugar**
- ½ **cup / 45g unsweetened cocoa powder**

For Decorating and Serving

- **Sprinkles of your choice (optional)**
- **A candle if it is for a birthday (not optional)**
- **Perhaps a hat (never optional to not at least consider it)**

1. ***To make the cake:*** Grease a 9 × 13-inch pan and line with parchment paper. Preheat the oven to 350°F.

2. In a blender, add the **carrots** and pulse until finely minced. Add the **granulated sugar, baking powder,** and **salt** and pulse until well combined: The mixture should look wet and jammy. Add the **eggs** and **oil.** Blend to combine.

3. Pour the mixture into a large bowl, then sift in the **flour.** Gently fold with a silicone spatula to combine. Pour into the prepared pan and bake until fully set in the middle, about 30 minutes. Remove the pan from the oven and set on a wire rack to fully cool at room temperature before frosting.

4. ***To make the frosting:*** Using a double boiler or in a bowl with short bursts in a microwave, melt and combine the **chocolate** and the **water;** set aside to cool.

5. In the bowl of a stand mixer fitted with the paddle attachment, combine the **butter, cream cheese, vanilla,** and **salt** and beat on medium until light and fluffy, 4 to 5 minutes. Sift in the **confectioners' sugar** and **cocoa,** stir with a spatula to combine, and continue beating on medium until as poofy as a cloud, another 4 to 5 minutes. Add the chocolate mixture and whip for another 1 to 2 minutes on medium until light and fluffy.

6. Invert the cooled cake onto a serving tray and tap the pan to release. Peel off the parchment. Frost the cake using a spatula, top with sprinkles (if using), place a candle (if using), put on your hat (if using; c'mon, live a little), and sing your favorite rendition of "Happy Birthday."

MY BIRTHDAY

IT'S MY BIRTHDAY

Acknowledgments

Sohla, thank you, my partner in everything. This cookbook would not exist without you. There is nobody I would rather have by my side as we go through this wild life.

The Child. You're a good one, and I can't wait to see the person you become.

Mom. I miss you. Thanks for all the great meals and sorry I didn't tell you that enough.

Dad. Thank you for all the constant support.

Tamara. Thanks for being the younger big sister.

Salma, Muzibur, and Mila. Thank you for always making me feel welcome and well fed.

Mama Carmela y la tropa de cambas. Gracias por su amor y cariño. Los extraño muchísimo.

Tante Hosna and everybody in Egypt. ألف شكر على كرمك، وآسف إني مش بجي كتير

People who worked on the book. It takes a lot of people to make a book happen: Kitty, Francis, Laura, Ella, Chris, Tara, Lisa, Marysarah, Darian, Jess, Serena, Dolores, and Sophia.

Anoop, Michael, Geri, and the Strange Delight team. Thank you for bringing me back into the restaurant world.

To the people who took the time to teach me in kitchens. Alex, JJ, Cliff, Puiz, Wylie, Jackie, Isabel, Matt, Frank, and all the chefs, sous, cooks, and porters that I worked side by side with.

Anybody who took the time to feed me, you are all somewhere in this book.

Index

C

D

E

F

G

H

I

J

K

L

M

N

P

Q

R

S

CLARKSON POTTER/PUBLISHERS
An imprint of the Crown Publishing Group
A division of Penguin Random House LLC
1745 Broadway New York, NY 10019
clarksonpotter.com
penguinrandomhouse.com

Library of Congress Control Number: 2025009658

ISBN 978-0-593-79657-3
Ebook ISBN 978-0-593-79658-0

Editor: Francis Lam
Assistant editor: Darian Keels
Creative Director and Designer: Chris Cristiano
Art director: Marysarah Quinn
Production designer: Christina Self
Production editor: Serena Wang
Production: Jessica Heim
Compositors: Merri Ann Morrell and Nick Patton
Contributing editor: Ella Quittner
Food stylists: Sohla and Ham El-Waylly
Prop stylist: Ham El-Waylly
Recipe developer: Ham El-Waylly
Illustrator: Sohla El-Waylly
Copyeditor: Dolores York | Proofreaders: Heather Rodino, Rita Madrigal, Hope Clarke | Indexer: Stephen Callahan
Publicist: Jina Stanfill | Marketer: Joey Lozada

Manufactured in China

10 9 8 7 6 5 4 3 2 1

First Edition

The authorized representative in the EU for product safety and compliance is Penguin Random House Ireland, Morrison Chambers, 32 Nassau Street, Dublin D02 YH68, Ireland, https://eu-contact.penguin.ie.

Ham El-Waylly is a chef, recipe developer, and video creator based in New York City. You may know him from the NYT Cooking channel, where he shares ingenious tips and whips up opulent feasts from niche ingredients alongside his wife, Sohla.

Clarkson Potter/Publishers
New York
clarksonpotter.com

Cover design: Chris Cristiano
Cover photography: Laura Murray